EMPERORS IN THE JUNGLE

AMERICAN ENCOUNTERS / GLOBAL INTERACTIONS

A Series Edited by Gilbert M. Joseph and Emily S. Rosenberg

This series aims to stimulate critical perspectives and fresh interpretive frameworks for scholarship on the history of the imposing global presence of the United States. Its primary concerns include the deployment and contestation of power, the construction and deconstruction of cultural and political borders, the fluid meanings of intercultural encounters, and the complex interplay between the global and the local. American Encounters seeks to strengthen dialogue and collaboration between historians of U.S. international relations and area studies specialists.

The series encourages scholarship based on multiarchival historical research. At the same time, it supports a recognition of the representational character of all stories about the past and promotes critical inquiry into issues of subjectivity and narrative. In the process, American Encounters strives to understand the context in which meanings related to nations, cultures, and political economy are continually produced, challenged, and reshaped.

JOHN LINDSAY-POLAND

EMPERORS IN THE JUNGLE

THE HIDDEN HISTORY OF THE U.S. IN PANAMA

Duke University Press Durham and London 2003

© 2003 Duke University Press

All right reserved   Printed in the United

States of America on acid-free paper ∞

Designed by C. H. Westmoreland

Typeset in Sabon with Gill Sans display

by Keystone Typesetting, Inc.

Library of Congress Cataloging-in-

Publication Data appear on the last

printed page of this book

To those who seek the truth.

May their curiosity and vision be strong.

CONTENTS

ACKNOWLEDGMENTS

This book is borne on the contributions of many individuals whom I can never adequately thank. More than that, it would not have been possible without the dedication of many people to social movements that seek the truth about the past and justice in the future. In that respect, I am grateful to the many organizations in Panama with whom I had the fortune to collaborate, and to the Fellowship of Reconciliation, which gave me the opportunity to work on Panama for more than a decade.

For teaching me about Panama, I thank Orlando Acosta, Jesús Alemancia, Mariela Arce, Olier Avila, Ramiro Castrejon, Marco Gandásegui, Jaime Espinoza González, Arturo Griffiths, Sayda de Grimaldo, Tomás Guardia, Raúl Leis, Fernando Manfredo Jr., Gonzalo Menéndez, Juan Méndez, Rodrigo Noriega, Conrado Sanjur, Walter Smith, Nicolasa Terreros, and Lamoin Werlein-Jaén. I am thankful to the many people who spoke with me about the U.S. military and Panama, many of whom are cited in this book, and some of whom preferred to withhold their names.

Researchers rely profoundly on reference librarians. I am indebted to the staff of the San Francisco Public Library, U.S. Army History Institute, and Jimmy Carter Presidential Library, and to Martin Gordon of the Army Corps of Engineers Archives, Richard Boylan of the National Archives, Steve Wofford of the Livermore Laboratory archives, and Bryan Stoneburner of the Naval Postgraduate School Library.

For help in obtaining important documents and articles, I am grateful to Fernando Eleta Casanova, Henry Heitman, Eric Jackson, Betty Brannan Jaén, Rafael Pérez Jaramillo, Nick Morgan, Henry Raymont, Craig Reinarman, Juan Antonio Samudio, Nathan and Joy Schnurman, Lenny Siegel, and Rick Stauber. Rick and I formed an unusual alliance — an explosives expert and a pacifist — in the quest for U.S. accountability for ordnance left behind in Panama. Neil Popovic gave legal assistance with Freedom of Information Act (FOIA) requests that yielded significant new information. On the receiving end of FOIA requests, Teresa Shinton of the Judge Advocate's Office at Dugway Proving Ground in Utah was very helpful.

For their gracious hospitality when I visited Panama and Washington, I give warm thanks to Jesús Alemancia and Maria Angelica Arribau; Cristina Espinel and Charlie Roberts; Debra and Greg Riklan-Veckstein; Kurt Dillon and Beatrice Stern; the Episcopal Church in Ancon, Panama; Olier Avila and Rosaura de Avila; and Assisi House.

For general encouragement and advice, I am grateful to my family, friends, and colleagues, especially my coworkers Phil McManus, Andrés Mares Muro, and Sarah Town. For reading and commenting on drafts of the manuscript, I thank Charlotte Elton, Barbara Hirshkowitz, Mary MacArthur, Caroline Pincus, Becky Rees, Paul Sutter, Stephanie Troyan, and Lisa Zamarin. Guillermo Castro, David Page, Gloria Rudolf, and Pete Stanga were an author's dream: they read the whole draft and gave me indispensable insights. Valerie Millholland at Duke University Press has been supportive and gracious with an author from outside academia. Any errors and misinterpretations remain my responsibility.

Finally, I could not have written this book without the rock of my soul, James Groleau. Between the quixotic quests for understanding, you are the home I return to.

EMPERORS IN THE JUNGLE

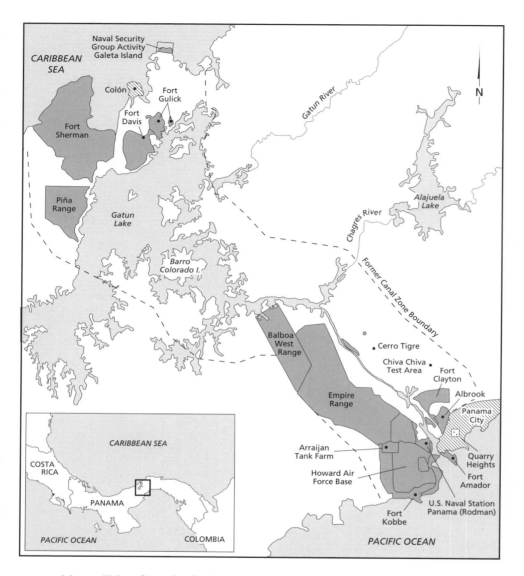

Map 1. U.S. military land in Panama, 1995. (Department of Defense, *Rapid Ecological Assessment of the Lands in Panama Managed by the U.S. Department of Defense.* Redrawn by Mark Ingles.)

INTRODUCTION

When the United States invaded Panama in December 1989, I felt personally involved, although I lived in California. The previous month, human rights coworkers of mine had been arrested and expelled from El Salvador during a violent spasm that brought the killing of six Jesuit priests and the bombing of neighborhoods in San Salvador by armed forces trained and supplied by the United States. Two of my colleagues ended up with the Central American Human Rights Commission in Costa Rica, where they typed accounts that arrived on blurry fax paper of the names of bombed neighborhoods in Panama City and of the simultaneous combat, chaos, and indiscriminate bloodshed.

The midnight invasion was the largest U.S. military operation at that time since the Vietnam War, and it led to the killing of at least hundreds of Panamanian civilians, the loss of homes for fifteen thousand, and economic losses estimated in the billions of dollars. The invading forces dismantled Panama's government and armed forces and arranged for a new president to be sworn in at a U.S. air base. In twenty-one years of military rule, Panamanians had never seen anything like it.

President George Bush justified the invasion of Panama partly on the grounds that an American woman had been threatened sexually by Panamanian soldiers. But the very next day, another human rights coworker in Guatemala City, a twenty-seven-year-old woman from Virginia, was stabbed in an attack that the president of Guatemala later said had been carried out on military orders. My friend's stabbing wounds did not invoke Washington's rage. During the 1980s, the United States gave considerable support to the same militaries of Guatemala and El Salvador that were attacking international humanitarian workers — not to mention civilians from those countries. To me, President Bush's rationale for the invasion rang false.

Aware before the invasion of the growing tensions between the governments in Washington and Panama, my organization, the Fellowship of Reconciliation, had invited a Panamanian human rights leader, Nicolasa Terreros, to do a two-month speaking tour of the United

States. As U.S. troops continued operations in Panamanian communities in the spring of 1990, Terreros told visceral stories and asked some pointed questions. Having walked in El Chorillo neighborhood in the days after its destruction, she said, "I will never forget the smell of burnt bodies." She spoke of the never resolved debate over how many civilians had been killed during the invasion, and asked, "How many victims must there have been, how many thousands or how many hundreds must there have been, in order to condemn this kind of action in whatever country?"

These stories and questions were soft-pedaled by a U.S. mass media that, as we will see, often identified itself with the military forces that carried out the attack. The invasion occurred during the euphoria generated by the fall of the Berlin Wall and a collective, racially charged panic over crack cocaine. In this atmosphere, the stories that Terreros and others told had an almost secret quality. It was difficult for most listeners to reconcile the perspective of those whose homes were hit — from the air, at night, shortly before Christmas — with the triumphal tone of the networks and the White House. Panamanian accounts of the invasion were later available to U.S. audiences, but by then they were not "news" and never compelled the sustained and front-seat attention that the invasion had. The U.S. invasion of Panama dominated TV screens and newspapers for two or three weeks and was gone. As I accompanied Terreros and worked with community groups that were organizing speaking events for her, I realized the gap that existed in popular knowledge about Panama and the U.S. military's role there. Even among Central America activists, for example, few knew that the invasion represented the twentieth U.S. military intervention in Panama since 1856.

My sense of this hidden history deepened during the 1990s as I investigated the environmental effects of the U.S. military's presence in Panama. As I experienced military officers' resistance to disclosing key environmental documents about the fourteen U.S. bases in Panama, I began to see that the U.S. military harbored many secrets about its history on the isthmus. Then, with the help of a whistle-blower who had been under contract to the Pentagon, I found evidence that the U.S. Army had tested depleted uranium and tested and disposed of chemical weapons in Panama. The deployment and testing of chemical weapons had spanned nearly five decades, beginning in 1923, in most cases with no Panamanian knowledge of the weapons' presence on the isthmus. The departure in 1999 of U.S. soldiers and transfer of bases next to the canal under the terms of the 1977 Panama Canal Treaties made this hidden history especially relevant. Panamanians would be responsible for properties with little information about their history of use, but unified in the desire that the United States should clean up the lands to a condition that would make Panamanian sovereignty over them meaningful. As Panama considered extending the U.S. military's stay, disclosure of the hidden history might itself affect history by publicly establishing some of the costs of the military presence.

Throughout this process, I heard and read U.S. expressions of both fascination and repulsion for the tropical environment and its inhabitants. I also noted that the stories U.S. officials and media told about Panama usually portrayed themselves and the military men who led the country in Panama as rational and scientific, unlike the torrid, uncontrolled life of the tropics. This was the dominant story the United States told about itself that helped justify continued control of the isthmus and a virtual apartheid system.

The Panama Canal Zone was a strip of land and water fifty miles long and ten miles wide that was established by the 1903 Canal Treaty as a virtual U.S. colony in the heart of Panama. The United States introduced a racial caste system into the Canal Zone that strictly segregated White and Black workers and assigned the West Indian majority worse conditions and lower pay. These Jim Crow laws, a reflection of ideas about white supremacy, have been widely documented and analyzed.[1] But the U.S. military's impact on the environment and how notions of U.S. entitlement or racial superiority were employed to support environmentally and socially destructive practices were largely undocumented.

This book describes how, in pursuit of its strategic aims in Panama, the United States sacrificed regard for Panama's people, its tropical environment, and, often, the empire's own soldiers. It is not a comprehensive military or diplomatic history of U.S.–Panama relations. Nor do I focus on the multiple prejudices and errors of Panama's own leadership. Instead, the book examines the manner in which Panama served as an instrument for grander U.S. aims and the role of ideas about race and the tropics by recounting several key episodes in the history of U.S. military experimentation and intervention in Panama.

The United States' construction of the canal in Panama responded to strategic imperatives in the rise of American imperial power. Prevailing U.S. attitudes toward the tropical environment, civilization, and race served to rationalize the ways in which the United States pursued its objectives. Tropical ecology was seen as an enemy or obstacle to civilization and its military, while people of color were understood to be less deserving than Whites, a threat to efficient civilization, or simply unimportant. Although the form and articulation of these attitudes shifted over the course of the twentieth century, they persisted throughout the life of the U.S. presence on the isthmus.[2]

The paradigm for U.S. rule and preservation of order in Panama was established early in the century. A key element was the establishment of a racial hierarchy that was consonant with the scientific racism then current in the United States. Political actors across the political spectrum, including many in the anti-imperialist movement then near its peak, pictured Panamanians, Colombians, West Indians, and others from the region as incapable of democratic habits and incompatible with White society.

During construction of the canal from 1904 to 1914, Blacks made up at least three out of every four workers, and they continued to be a majority after the canal began operating.[3] The Jim Crow system, however, required that neither Panamanians nor West Indians would have any meaningful role in the canal's administration or protection. White U.S. citizens, skilled and unskilled, were paid on a Gold Roll (so called because payment was in gold coins), while unskilled Europeans and Black West Indians were paid in Panamanian currency on what came to be known as the Silver Roll. In addition to a discriminatory pay system, the Silver and Gold Rolls established segregation and unequal conditions in the Canal Zone's housing, hospitals, recreational facilities, train coaches, and eating places—a system so complete that White and Black workers often had no contact with each other outside the workplace.

U.S. leaders and observers consistently identified Panamanians, Blacks, and indigenous people with the tropical ecology itself, so that perceptions of one were often conflated with the other. West Indians and "natives" (an ambiguous term that referred sometimes to indigenous people and at other times to any Panamanian) were pictured as exotic in both appearance and culture—different from civilized Whites. The idea that Panamanian and West Indian workers, who were needed to build and run the canal, were immune from tropical diseases made them more like the landscape against which White men had to be on guard.

For many White observers, Panama's riotous vegetation and wildlife were associated with human corruption in the country's political and social life. "In all the world," James Anthony Froude wrote about Panama in 1885, "there is not perhaps now concentrated in any single spot so much swindling and villainy, so much foul disease, such a hideous dung heap of physical and moral abomination."[4] When the Colombian Senate unanimously rejected the Hay–Herrán Treaty in August 1903, Theodore Roosevelt's apoplexy led him to call the Colombians "contemptible little creatures" and "jackrabbits," a "corrupt pithecoid community" undeserving of the rights and privileges enjoyed by Europeans.[5] After the canal works began, a U.S. congressman called Indian and West Indian communities in jungle areas "of no more use than mosquitoes and buzzards. They ought all to be exterminated together."[6] U.S. leaders used charges of Panamanian corruption to justify the military invasion of 1989 and "clean out" Panama's army, which was no longer "of use." No one then spoke of extermination, but the U.S. actions had the effect of partly carrying out the congressman's recommendation.

Newspaper cartoonists at the time of Panama's separation from Colombia in 1903 supported the view that the people in both countries were either thieves or subhuman creatures. A commentator in the *Philadelphia Inquirer* showed Colombia as a bulldog; attached to his tail by a string was Panama, a smaller dog wrapped in a mantle titled STUPIDITY, with its tongue hanging out. Another cartoonist portrayed Roosevelt's critics—whose nationality is ambiguous—as hysterical witches labeled MALICE, VENOM, SPLEEN, and HATE, with Roosevelt sitting calmly in a wicker chair reading the newspaper, a picture of civilized calm. Many other cartoonists showed Panama and other Latin American countries as children, especially picaninnies, and always diminutive. Uncle Sam, for his part, was pictured as sensible and shrewd, if occasionally unscrupulous.[7]

Each of these depictions implied that the United States acted with scientific tools at its disposal. To reach the conclusion that Latin Americans could not be trusted as partners in the canal enterprise, and that the United States was justified in using force to ensure a favorable canal treaty, a civilized self-image was as necessary as an image of the Other as savage or childlike. According to the conventional telling of the Panama Canal story, the United States provided rational engineers who carved a miraculous waterway out of a wild rain forest while the "natives" — be they Panamanians, indigenous, or West Indian immigrants — were un-self-controlled, subject to intoxication, and identified with a hostile natural environment. Popular and juvenile biographies of Roosevelt; of the chief canal engineer, Colonel George Goethals; and of other key figures in the canal enterprise reiterated and celebrated the story of civilization's triumph over nature in the tropics, thus extending the ideas to new generations.

U.S. policymakers in the 1990s were wont to say that times had changed, that gunboat diplomacy was a relic of history, and that Panamanian sovereignty was the basis for Washington's dealings with the isthmus. But earlier U.S. leaders' attitudes toward Panamanians and the jungle environment continued to serve as a template for U.S. conduct toward Panama. The White military men who led the U.S. canal project and the social and organizational structure established for building the canal in Panama put an imprint on the enterprise that pervaded the project, with variations, to the end of the twentieth century. The canal treaties of 1903 and 1977 provided the legal framework for this unequal and troublesome relationship.

In the construction and operation of the Panama Railroad, the canal, and the military bases on the canal's banks, Panama itself was never the central object of U.S. aims and concerns. It was an instrument — for gaining access to the markets and resources of Asia, for example, and extending the reach of U.S. military control. As some of the United States' most secure tropical possessions, the Canal Zone and other sites in Panama became centers for testing ideas and technology that had applications elsewhere. This included examining racial differences in resistance to disease and testing technology that ranged from lethal chemical agents and nuclear-excavation techniques to electronic monitoring of the illicit drug trade and of regional insurgencies.

The U.S. garrison in Panama during the twentieth century was a small-scale player in the scheme of things, peaking at sixty-three thousand troops in 1942 in a U.S. Army of four million men. It played a supporting role during the Vietnam War and in interventions in Latin

America. Relative to the military–industrial society of which it was part, the garrison was small. The U.S. military in the Canal Zone was like a little child in the imperial family, requiring attention from time to time; it was a psychological fixture in the American self-image but not one of the adults that generated the major actions, as in Europe or East Asia.

In the context of the tiny strip of Panama, however, the U.S. military had the reputation and lack of accountability of royalty. The establishment of a significant military garrison, combined with the Army's responsibility for canal engineering and administration and for sanitation in the canal area, made the military the dominant U.S. actor in bilateral relations from the beginning of the canal project. This dominance was given initial impetus by Roosevelt's decision to place the canal project in the hands of the Army. "Colonel Goethals here is to be chairman," he told fellow members of the Isthmian Canal Commission on their appointment. "If at any time you do not agree with his policies, do not bother to tell me about it — your disagreement with him will constitute your resignation."[8] Jack Vaughan, the U.S. ambassador to Panama in 1964–65, said that he never won one battle against the Pentagon.[9]

To Panamanians, the U.S. military's power was even more daunting. It was the guarantor of Panama's separation from Colombia and of Panamanians' dream of an interoceanic waterway. The wielder of overwhelming force, the military was looked on as untouchable. Only poachers and servants of that royalty dared approach the Canal Zone. The U.S. military in Panama, responding to the dictates of its larger family, was indeed a little prince. That is why this book's title invokes royalty.

Chapter 1 offers a snapshot of Panama when U.S. involvement on the isthmus began in the 1850s, then recounts the military interventions from 1856 to 1925 that occurred as a consequence of U.S. interests in the region. These interventions reflect both Washington's strategic aims and the ways in which racial stereotypes were employed to strengthen the interventionist impulse. It also gives an account of tropical medicine's achievements against yellow fever and malaria in Panama, which made the canal possible, as well as the ideas of the Canal Zone's Army doctors about race and the tropics. Although their medical breakthroughs have had benefits for all people, their emphasis on preventing diseases believed to strike Whites more than Blacks and ideas about White destiny leave no doubt about whom the Army's sanitation program was meant to benefit.

Chapter 2 follows the history of chemical-weapons testing, in which Panama became a laboratory for quasi-scientific military tests, first for canal defense, and later as preparation for combat in tropical environments. The tests were part of a growing interest by the U.S. military in tropical warfare and reflected the military's view that the tropics were a potential obstacle. Panama again became a means to overcoming those obstacles when they were encountered elsewhere.

The plan to build a sea-level canal using nuclear explosions, part of what was known as Project Plowshare, is the subject of chapter 3. This chapter explores the contest between the military's imperial prerogatives on the isthmus and environmental awareness and Panamanians' ambitions for complete sovereignty, a conflict that became more acute as the 1960s wore on.

Chapter 4 examines the intimate military relationship between the United States and Panama and the evolution of the drug war, then looks at events surrounding the 1989 invasion of Panama. Although General Manuel Noriega's history of drug trafficking provided the public rationale for the invasion, U.S. interests stemming from the military's relationship with Noriega, the Panamanian military, and the canal offer more convincing explanations of Washington's motives. The premises of drug policy continue to frame U.S. attitudes toward Panama and the region, as illustrated by the failed negotiations for a "multinational counter-drug center" on U.S. bases in Panama after 1999.

Chapter 5 describes the U.S. military's attempts to reframe environmental issues in Panama in ways that favored its self-image as "good stewards" of the canal area, rather than addressing the environmental legacy of its own experiments and operations. The military's policy toward base cleanup in Panama conformed to a pattern evident within the United States: people without sufficient resources or effective political representation in Washington — especially communities of color — do not receive the attention that communities with political clout get when it comes to dealing with explosives or chemicals left by the military's activities.

Chapter 6 reviews the plans for redevelopment of the canal area with the departure of the U.S. military under the terms of the 1977 treaties. These plans illustrate how Panama, in the redevelopment of bases, has incorporated some of the same attitudes toward the tropics that the United States held, and some objectives of its own. The U.S. Right's reactions to Panama's privatization of its ports and to its contract with a Hong Kong-based port developer show how U.S. imperialist attitudes linger even after the military's departure. The chapter also includes a brief profile of the country's society and environment as the U.S. military departs.

The final chapter examines continuity and evolution in the U.S. military's views of the meaning of Panama. It also distinguishes seven distinct missions during its presence there: policing, engineering, sanitation, canal defense, training soldiers for jungle combat, weapons and equipment tests, and intelligence gathering.

As representatives of the United States' imperial interests in Panama, U.S. soldiers and officials acted with privilege and impunity, even when their individual motives were unrelated to Washington's aims. But such imperial impunity faced relentless resistance from Panama's inhabitants. People inevitably will struggle to reveal the empire's secrets and seek compensation for its wrongs. This book traces the tensions between these forces.

1 ☆ A PLATFORM FOR CONTROL

INTERVENTIONS AND ARMY DOCTORS, 1856–1925

> The Colombians are a mixture of Spanish, Indians, and negroes, and have the negro crimp of hair. They have negro blood enough to make them lazy, and Spanish blood sufficient to make them mean.
> — *Harper's Weekly*, 1902

> Our work in Cuba and Panama will be looked upon as the earliest demonstration that the white man could flourish in the tropics and as the starting-point of the effective settlement of these regions by the Caucasian. — Colonel William C. Gorgas, 1909

To understand U.S. attitudes toward Panama, it is crucial to examine the historical roots of the U.S. military presence on the isthmus.[1] Those roots were planted fifty years before the United States began working on the Panama Canal, on the eve of the U.S. Civil War, and were later deepened through a U.S. Army regime of environmental control to stem diseases that affected Whites.

Two events drove early U.S. military intervention and presence in Panama: the California Gold Rush, which brought thousands of North American travelers across the isthmus, and the construction of the trans-isthmian railroad using New York capital and West Indian labor. The relationships established during this period, as racial tensions in the antebellum United States mingled with local conflicts in Panama, shaped the intervention that followed. Popular images portrayed local governments and populations either as undisciplined savages who posed a hostile threat to U.S. interests and hegemony or as children who needed guidance (for example, to supervise elections). Private enterprise, local elites, and officials within the military itself also called on racial tropes to justify using force on the isthmus and establishing a more permanent U.S. presence, effectively preventing Panama from developing its lands and economy independently.[2]

Apart from the 1899–1902 civil war in Colombia known as the Thousand Days War, the most memorable conflicts in Panama occurred when the conclusion of transit-construction projects generated widespread unemployment among Caribbean workers—as in 1856 and 1925—and when the canal's construction was generating disease and highlighting inequities between Black workers and foreign capital, as in 1885. This period also traces the rise of the new U.S. Navy and the development of gunboat diplomacy in the region.

PANAMA BEFORE THE TRANSIT BONANZA

Panama did not spring whole from Theodore Roosevelt's machinations as if from the loins of Zeus. Over the course of the nineteenth century, isthmian political leaders developed a growing ambition for independence. When Panama separated from Spain in 1821, its leaders decided to incorporate the isthmus into the Gran Colombia federation. Panama subsequently declared its independence from Colombia in 1830, 1831, and 1840, but each time the separation was quickly aborted.[3] Panama's separatist impulses were strengthened by the absence of roads connecting the isthmus to Colombia and by the fact that Panama's trade was carried out not with the Colombian capital, Bogotá, but with Caribbean and South American ports.[4] Ultimately, however, cementing Panama's separation from Colombia would require the crystallization of the canal ambitions of both the isthmus's elite and the Colossus of the North.

Panama's population in 1900 consisted of five principal groups: White residents of the capital; Mestizo peasants from the savannas on the Pacific slope; a merchant class in the provinces; and poor Blacks or Mulattos, mostly concentrated in Panama City, in Colón, and on the United Fruit Company plantations in Chiriquí Province. Indigenous people made up a fifth group, uncounted in nineteenth-century censuses. The Blacks were primarily the descendants of slaves who had experienced emancipation in 1852, or West Indians brought to Panama during the eras of railroad and French canal construction. Panamanian Whites in the capital dominated the economy because of their command of external relations and their ability to supply the railroad and canal enterprises with goods that ranged from beef to cement. They also controlled urban real estate, which allowed capital elites to tax foreign interests and local Blacks, and to revive after periodic defeats.[5]

The rural economy during the nineteenth century was based primarily on cattle ranching. Although peasant families lived widely dispersed from one another on subsistence farms, land tenancy was largely communal in nature, without fences between plots. Transportation of cattle to markets in Panama City was difficult, so peasants developed cottage industries such as production of silk, dried meats, and leather items.[6]

Another social group, albeit a transient one, was Colombian soldiers stationed on the isthmus, who constituted the principal public expenditure in Panama from the late 1700s until the railroad was built in Panama in 1855. The foreign troops' presence accentuated the province's externally oriented trade structure.[7] The isthmus as a whole had fewer than 123,000 inhabitants in 1843, and fewer than 20,000 lived in Panama Province, which includes Panama City. Colón, which became the Caribbean port city, was a town of only 3,200 people.[8]

IN THE WAKE OF GOLD

Facing competition from British interest in constructing a trans-isthmian canal or railroad, the United States signed the Bidlack Treaty with Colombia in December 1846. The treaty, concluded during the expansionist war with Mexico, made the United States the guarantor of Colombian control over Panama in exchange for free access to any future canal. The agreement also ratified Panamanians' status as pawns of foreign powers, which was reinforced in 1850 when the United States and England signed the Clayton–Bulwer Treaty guaranteeing U.S.–British cooperation in any future canal without reference to Colombia or Panama.

The discovery of gold in California in 1849 led thousands of foreigners eager for wealth — U.S. citizens prominent among them — to trek across Panama, the shortest land route between the Atlantic and Pacific coasts. The boom in the years that followed packed Panama City and Colón with travelers, yielding windfalls for local Whites who owned or built housing. The United States' successful annexation of a third of Mexico, including California, prompted many Americans to swagger like arrogant victors and to talk in the U.S. press about annexing the isthmus.

Just before news of gold reached the East Coast, the New York investors of the Pacific Mail Steamship Company obtained a concession to build a railroad. The company imported workers from China, Ireland, and elsewhere for the job, but most workers were Blacks from Jamaica and Cartagena. The imported workers gave rise in 1853 and 1855 to epidemics of yellow fever, which previously had been rare.[9] Exploited, sick, and full of despair, hundreds of Chinese workers and their families killed themselves en masse in 1854. More than six thousand laborers — perhaps twice that many — died in the railroad's construction.[10]

Completed in 1855, the railroad allowed passengers to cross the isthmus and leave Panama more quickly — in three hours, instead of the three days required by mule and boat. Charging $25 in gold per passenger and with forty thousand passages annually, the railroad was a cash cow for its New York owners. It netted more than $7 million in its first six years of operation.[11] It was also the largest U.S. investment in Latin America at the time. Gold mined from California's soil would pass across Panama, $29 million worth in 1855 alone.[12]

Panama was a free-for-all, a dangerous place in the 1850s. Millions of dollars in gold treasure led inevitably to temptation and robberies, and many ordinary people armed themselves with guns and knives. Thousands of Black laborers who had worked on the railroad were left without jobs when the line was completed. Moreover, Panama lost up to $150,000 in monthly income previously generated by those who paid for non-rail transportation of passengers, freight, and merchandise, and an economic depression settled on the isthmus. Tension and resentment were made more intense, especially among Blacks, by a rumor that mercenaries from the U.S. adventurer William Walker's band were present in Panama City. Walker's army had recently taken over Nicaragua and declared it an annexed slave state.[13]

This was the setting for the clash between Americans and Panamanians on April 19, 1856 known as the Watermelon Riot. The events unfolded outside the railroad station, where a crowd of travelers waited to board a steamer anchored in the bay and the train to Colón. A drunken man bound for California, John Oliver, wanted a piece of watermelon from a fruit stand run by José Manuel Luna. After taking a bite, Oliver walked away; Luna chased him. Oliver drew a gun; Luna, a knife. When another man grabbed Oliver's gun, a shot went off, and foreigners chased the man away. Word of what had happened spread, and local residents formed a mob and flooded toward the rail station, attacking men and women and looting. In the end, sixteen passengers were killed and another sixteen were injured. One or two local people were killed.[14] The United States did not land troops during the riot, but it did demand reparations for the loss of human life.

William Mervine, commander of the U.S. Pacific Squadron, had an opportunity to demonstrate U.S. force five months later. When internal struggles in Panama's Legislative Assembly led the opposition party, known as the Blacks, to threaten to take up arms, Mervine ordered troops landed to protect U.S. citizens from the conflict.[15]

Four years later, as the U.S. prepared for civil war, a conflict broke out on the outskirts of Panama City, again pitting Blacks against the governing power. On September 27, 1860, railway agent William Nelson wrote to the U.S. consul: "The niggers are at the railroad bridge and I fear if they get out of ammunition, they may come here to take our arms." Nelson asked for a contingent of marines to protect the railroad station. Colombian authorities declared martial law and requested a landing of U.S. troops, who stayed for ten days (see table 1).[16]

The pressure generated by the U.S. Civil War and the need to address slavery definitively prompted Abraham Lincoln to propose another kind of intervention — specifically, to establish a colony of emancipated and deported Blacks in the western province of Chiriquí. In 1855, the Chiriquí Improvement Company, founded in Philadelphia by Ambrose Thompson, obtained a concession from Colombia for one hundred seventy thousand acres in Chiriquí, and in 1861 it tendered a proposal to the U.S. Navy to sell it coal at half the price it was then paying. Lincoln, who believed that Whites and Blacks could not coexist harmoniously, sought a place to which emancipated slaves could be shipped and put to work. Coal mines, he told a roomful of free Blacks in August 1862, "will afford an opportunity to the inhabitants for immediate employment till they get ready to settle permanently in their homes." Colombia, however, saw the plan as a kind of subtle invasion. Central American countries were also opposed, and many freed Blacks in the United States greeted Lincoln's proposal with hostility. It was scrapped.[17]

In 1880, after the interlude of Reconstruction, President Rutherford Hayes declared, "The policy of this country is a canal under American control." Hayes warned Europeans that, if a canal on the isthmus were under their control, they could not expect to send their navies to protect European investments on the isthmus without America's invoking the Monroe Doctrine and military opposition. In the days before

Table 1. U.S. military interventions in Panama

Date	Rationale
September 19–22, 1856	"To protect American interests during an insurrection"[a]
September 27–October 7, 1860	Local disturbance; with British participation
1861	Political disturbance
March 9–10, 1865	"To protect the lives and property of American residents during a revolution"
April 1868	"To protect passengers and treasure in transit during the absence of local police or troops"
May 7–22 and September 23–October 9, 1873	"To protect American interests during hostilities over possession of the government of the state of Panama"
March and April 1885	"To re-establish free transit during revolutionary activity"
March 8–9, 1895	"To protect American interests during an attack on the town of Bocas del Toro by a bandit chieftain"
November 20–December 4, 1901	"To protect American property on the isthmus and to keep transit lines open during serious revolutionary disturbances"; with French participation
April 16–22, 1902	Bocas del Toro occupied at request of United Fruit Company
September 17–November 18, 1902	"To place armed guards in all trains crossing the isthmus"
November 1903	Colombian military prevented from putting down independence

(Table 1 continued)

Date	Rationale
November 17–24, 1904	"To protect American lives and property at Ancón at the time of a threatened insurrection"
1908, 1910, 1912	U.S. troops supervised elections outside the Canal Zone.
1918–1920	"For police duty, according to treaty stipulations, at Chiriquí during electoral disturbances and subsequent unrest"
April 1921	U.S. naval squadrons held maneuvers on both sides of the isthmus during a border dispute between Panama and Costa Rica
October 12–23, 1925	Panama City: "Strikes and rent riots led to the landing of about six hundred American troops to keep order and protect American interests"
January 9, 1964	Panama City, Colón: To stop Panamanian students who sought to raise the Panamanian flag in the Canal Zone, U.S. soldiers killed twenty-one and wounded more than five hundred
December 20, 1989	U.S. invades with twenty-five thousand troops to protect U.S. lives and the canal, stop drug trafficking, and restore democracy
December 5, 1990	Panama City: U.S. troops intervene to put down a protest by police who call for higher wages and political reforms

[a]Quotes from testimony by Secretary of State Dean Rusk in 1962 to justify possible direct intervention in Cuba. (Senate Committee on Foreign Relations, *Situation in Cuba;* Michael Conniff, *Panama and the United States: The Forced Alliance.*)

Hayes's statement, U.S. Navy ships anchored in Almirante Bay on the Atlantic coast and Golfo Dulce on the Pacific coast to conduct explorations without notifying the Colombian authorities. The ships' commanders had orders to fire at their discretion on any who might attempt to dislodge them and to await replacements before leaving the isthmus. Colombia's representative in Washington, Justo Arosemena, protested the incursion, writing: "When governments attempt to acquire land in foreign countries for construction or enterprises such as that under discussion, they normally begin by obtaining the consent of the sovereign of the country in which the land is located."[18]

Congress subsequently recommended constructing naval coaling stations along the isthmus, and in January 1881, Secretary of the Navy Nathan A. Goff Jr. requested and obtained $200,000 for naval coaling stations, asserting that coal in Panama would save the Navy money. This interest in coaling stations would be an important factor in the U.S. Navy's role on the isthmus in 1885.[19]

THE PRESTAN REBELLION

By that time, Colombia was in the grip of a civil war between the government in Bogotá, controlled by the Conservative Party, and an insurgent Liberal army. In mid-March, railroad transit ceased as a result of the fighting between the federal and Liberal factions. In Panama, the Liberals in arms were led by Rafael Aizpuru, former president of the state of Panama, and Pedro Prestan, a Mulatto lawyer and onetime representative of Colón in the Panama state assembly. New York representatives of the Pacific Mail Steamship Company and United Magdalena Steam Navigation Company clamored for U.S. Navy intervention.

The atmosphere in Colón had turned ugly by mid-March. "The ominous word of 'Lynch,' . . . is become of hourly use," wrote the U.S.-owned *Panama Star and Herald* in a note reprinted by the *New York Times*. "Should that judge unfortunately find himself compelled to act, it is probable his decisions would lead to a quieter feeling prevailing, while his judgments would be confirmed by every one of repute in the community."[20]

Meanwhile, Prestan ordered that a load of weapons should be sent from New York to Colón on a ship owned by Pacific Mail. The weapons were crucial to the rebels, who were outgunned (if not outmanned) by the government forces. Colombian Minister Ricardo Becerra had strenuously objected to such shipments of arms to the insurgents as violations of U.S. neutrality law. Secretary of State Thomas Bayard told Becerra that the United States had to maintain the "right of its citizens to carry on . . . the ordinary traffic in arms with rebellious or other parts" of Colombia.[21]

But when the weapons arrived at port on March 30, the U.S. agent refused to release the cargo. Prestan took six U.S. hostages, who escaped without harm, and Prestan's men retreated to the city, where fighting continued.[22] U.S. marines guarded the railroad office, the U.S. consulate, and the Pacific Mail wharf, but some people apparently used the chaos to loot properties owned by the French canal company. The company formed a guard that included U.S. marines, who caught dozens of the looters. "All caught red handed were immediately tried and on the following day shot," the New York Times reported. "Fifty-eight persons, among whom, it is believed, were several innocent people, were thus summarily despatched."[23] Defeated by government troops, Prestan fled by boat to Cartagena.

The worst calamity during this period was the destruction by fire of virtually the entire city of Colón on March 31, as the rebels retreated. The fire left thousands of West Indians and Panamanians homeless and killed hundreds of residents and wounded soldiers who were caught in the blaze. The material damage was heavy. All of the docks except Pacific Mail's were destroyed.[24]

The events in Colón catalyzed Navy Secretary William C. Whitney into action. He ordered three warships, a steamer chartered from Pacific Mail, and six hundred marines and sailors to Colón to open the transit line, which was achieved on April 11. Three days later, the Colombian government in Bogotá formally requested U.S. intervention, now a fait accompli.[25] Foreigners and Colombian government authorities accused Prestan of igniting the city. The Navy sent a ship in pursuit to Cartagena, where Prestan was arrested by Colombian forces, returned to Colón, and tried there by a military court. Four foreign witnesses testified that he had been heard to threaten to burn Colón if his forces lost, while he asserted that he was being tried because he had laid hands on Whites representing the U.S. government. His claims of innocence and the context leave room for doubt about whether Prestan was responsible.[26]

In any case, the military intervention was undertaken too late to save

Colón. Navy correspondence shows that its purposes were to promote an active role for the Navy overseas and to protect the railroad and U.S. property, not to give succor to Colón's refugees. Before Commander Bowman McCalla departed New York, he received a secret order from Commodore John G. Walker, a powerful figure in the Navy, to report extensively and covertly. His information was to "be given out to the press," so that "we should keep the country with us in the matter" and "the people kept in accord with the Department." In addition to carrying out this public-relations function, McCalla was ordered to investigate the Bay of Panama thoroughly to find sites for naval bases. Despite the Cleveland administration's lack of interest in permanent intervention, Walker and McCalla exploited the opportunity for eventually establishing a long-term U.S. naval presence on the isthmus.[27]

McCalla took with him from New York two journalists whose reportage offers graphic examples of how the lens of race and civilization shaped the ways that U.S. intervention was conceived as necessary and promoted for public consumption. In these news accounts, the Colombian army came across as a group of ignorant clowns, a "mongrel garrison penned up in the cuartel." They "are almost all negroes or Indians," the New York Herald reported. "Their ideas of drill and discipline seem to be confined to having a gigantic negro appear in front of the barracks every hour or so and blow a complicated call on a demoralized fish horn. But these fellows will fight like devils let loose."[28]

The civilian population was portrayed as hapless, animal-like: "The vast majority of the inhabitants of the Isthmus have never emerged from a half-savage condition, or else have relapsed into that state," the Herald continued. "But . . . no one can afford to underestimate the prowess of savages when they are mustered in swarms, as they can be here from the miserable morass and the jungle-clothed mountains."[29] "The Isthmians are, to all intents and purposes, savages," wrote Irving King of the New York Tribune "[The isthmian Indians] are expert in a kind of savage warfare and are always aided by a mob of negroes."[30]

What might drive natives to fight so fiercely was indicated only indirectly. "Life is the cheapest thing on the Isthmus," King declared, noting that killing a Negro brought only two weeks in jail. " 'Bushwhacking' [robbery] is now indulged in by the natives all over the isthmus. Almost every night the American pickets shoot a few of the outlaws."[31]

Some of the most emotional writing was reserved for Prestan—his "reckless character" and his Negro followers "lurking in the bush."[32] The U.S. soldiers who had landed in Panama, by contrast, "captured the place as if by magic. . . . Their neat and clean appearance and quick and precise movements elicited the admiration and respect of men of all nations, even that of those who were most opposed to the proceeding."[33] The encounter between such different species of humans necessarily illustrated the rational control of one and the outrageous emotionalism of the other. King described General Aizpuru as "hysterical" when arrested by McCalla's forces.[34] Yet when U.S. troops lost their cool, it was different matter. On the night of the general's arrest, trouble broke out in a crowd near where Aizpuru was being held. When shots were fired, a U.S. gunner let loose with a Gatling gun and did not cease until an officer frantically waved him to stop. "Everyone of them would have been killed had not the range of the Gatling been over their heads," a journalist observed.[35]

Three weeks after the intervention began, U.S. troops were returned to their ships.[36] Despite a reluctant U.S. administration, the case had been made for unilateral occupation of the isthmus when the conditions became ripe.

FROM COAL TO A CANAL

Those conditions were accelerated by the growth of U.S. territorial, commercial, and military ambitions, which fed Washington's interest in a canal. The economic depressions in 1873–78 and 1882–85 resulted in surplus U.S. production and led U.S. commercial sectors to turn their attention to Latin America as a gateway to the Pacific and as a market in its own right. The French attempt to build a canal in Panama from 1879 to 1889 was viewed with great apprehension as a European foothold in controlling access to such markets.[37]

Another nonmilitary strategic aim for a U.S.-controlled isthmian canal, articulated most forcefully by the naval strategist Alfred Thayer Mahan, embodied the drive to "people" the U.S. West Coast with Europeans.[38] Mahan, who strongly influenced the young Theodore Roosevelt, believed that control of the sea determined the world's struggles for power and had done so throughout history. Mahan's strategic thinking about the Panama Canal also had a racial dimen-

1. Uncle Sam's Museum of Curios.
"I wonder if I ought to put it in my collection."
(*Literary Digest*, 1903.).

sion. A canal would allow Europeans to reach Oregon and California without even stepping off the boat en route, thus avoiding contact with "savages" in the Western Plains or along the Panama Railroad. "The greatest factor of sea power in any region is the distribution and numbers of the populations, and their characteristics," Mahan wrote in an essay about the canal two years before its completion. "The foremost question of the Pacific, as affecting sea power, is the filling-up of the now partly vacant regions, our own Pacific coast . . . by a population of European derivation. It is most desirable that such immigration should be from northern Europe."[39]

Asian immigration threatened political efficiency, in Mahan's view, because the different ethnic peoples' ideas "do not allow intermingling, and consequently, if admitted, are ominous of national weakness through flaws in homogeneity."[40] Roosevelt shared Mahan's thesis. "No greater calamity could now befall the United States than to have the Pacific slope fill up with a Mongolian population," he wrote.[41]

By the turn of the century, the United States' reach and self-confidence were unprecedented. The Spanish–American War had served to demonstrate how useful a maritime shortcut through Central America would be for a power that had new colonial holdings in the Philippines, Guam, and Hawai'i, as well as trade ambitions in China and elsewhere in the Far East. With the commencement of combat in Cuba in 1898, the warship *Oregon* began a widely broadcast journey from San Francisco around the southern tip of South America to the Caribbean. The trip took sixty-seven days and became a national drama as the same presses that had agitated for war in Cuba narrated the ship's arrival in ports along South America's eastern coasts. With the victory of the United States, a two-ocean Navy would be critical to maintaining and extending U.S. military control of its conquests.

WAR OF A THOUSAND DAYS

During the Colombian civil war between Liberals and Conservatives from 1899 to 1902, most Whites in Panama City attempted to remain apart from the conflict. In the rural interior, however, the Liberals found widespread support among peasants. The war in Panama, at a remove from the ideological and power conflicts in Colombia, became a struggle of the masses against Colombia's Conservative central government, which was seen as arrogant and neglectful of the isthmus's needs and contributions. Major battles were fought on the isthmus in 1900, 1901, and 1902.

As Liberal troops gained total control of the isthmian interior in 1902, the U.S. Navy increasingly exerted force that decided the war's outcome, at least in Panama. The Bidlack Treaty of 1846 gave Washington the right to use military force to protect the Panama Railroad's right-of-way if Colombia proved unable to defend its transit. In November 1901, faced with the Liberals' imminent takeover of Colón, the government in Bogotá sought U.S. protection of the transit route, and Captain Thomas Perry of the gunboat *Iowa* informed Liberal officers that marines would be landed if any interruption of railroad operations occurred. Unable to complete their victory, the Liberals signed a peace agreement in the presence of U.S. Navy officers.

The Liberals renewed fighting the following month, however, again gaining control of all of Panama except Colón and Panama City. Again, Colombia requested U.S. intervention, and marines barred the Liberals' entry into Panama City and Colón. By mid-September, Rear Admiral Silas Casey had placed U.S. troops aboard railroad cars and informed the Liberal commander in Panama, General Benjamin Herrera, not only that combatants would be barred from interfering with transit, but that "*no other troops* but those of the United States *may occupy or use the line*." This went considerably beyond the Bidlack Treaty, which permitted U.S. intervention only to ensure continued operation of the railroad.[42] Barred from military victory by the United States, the Liberals came to terms with the Conservative government and signed a final peace treaty aboard the U.S. naval ship *Wisconsin* on November 19, 1902.

More than 60 percent of Panama's cattle were destroyed during the war.[43] The armies reportedly committed atrocities, leading thousands of civilians to flee into the mountains.[44] The historian Humberto Ricord summarized the conditions: "The ultimate consequence was the total disappearance of most of the cattle ranches on the Pacific slope; the extermination of agriculture; and general impoverishment from, among other causes, war taxes and depopulation of towns, because those men who were not part of one of the contending armies, fled from their homes and hid in the bush."[45] The war not only destroyed the economy; it also did away with some of rural Panama's most respected and experienced leaders—most notably, Victoriano Lorenzo, who eventually became a martyr to the nationalist cause.

In contrast, the transit area's infrastructure and economic capacity were relatively unaffected by the war. The combination of physical destruction and peasant defeat in the countryside and the Liberals' frustration at the hands of the U.S. Navy established the Conservative elites of Panama City as the isthmus's main negotiators with Washington, D.C., for orchestrating the separation of Panama from Colombia and the subsequent canal treaty.

This was the landscape in June 1902, when Congress authorized President Theodore Roosevelt to negotiate a concession from the French company for a canal in Panama. If Roosevelt could not reach "reasonable" terms with the French company and the Colombian government, he was authorized to turn to the Nicaragua route, which was favored by some powerful Senators.[46]

When the Colombian war ended in November, Washington expected Bogotá to agree on a canal treaty. The French company, eager to extricate itself from financial difficulties, was amenable. Roosevelt sought a definitive answer from Bogotá, and Tomas Herrán, the Colombian chargé, believed that Roosevelt might seize Panama unless a

2. "Guilty!" (*Literary Digest*, 1914.)

treaty was signed. The fated Hay–Herrán Treaty was signed on January 22, 1903, and ratified by Washington in March.[47] The Colombian Senate viewed the treaty as an assault on Colombia's sovereignty and its initial payment of $10 million inadequate, however, and it unanimously rejected the treaty on August 12.[48]

Seeing their chance at a canal slipping away, Philippe Bunau-Varilla, a shareholder in the French canal company, and Roosevelt met twice in October. Circumstantial evidence suggests that Roosevelt ordered the Navy to prevent Colombia from landing troops against an uprising. When Manuel Amador's Panamanian forces declared independence on November 3, U.S. officials kept Colombian troops from reaching the uprising in Panama City via the railroad, and U.S. warships kept the Colombian Navy at bay. Instead of guaranteeing Colombian sovereignty and free transit on the isthmus, as the Bidlack Treaty required, the United States did the reverse.[49]

Roosevelt lost no time in recognizing the new country and authorizing the negotiation of another canal treaty. Panama's new leaders, browbeaten by Bunau-Varilla, reluctantly permitted him to negotiate an initial agreement and steamed toward Washington posthaste, only to find that Bunau-Varilla had already concluded the treaty. Infamously known as the treaty that no Panamanian signed, it was ratified

3. "They Would Like to Get In." (*Cleveland Leader*, 1904.)

by Panama's new legislature after Washington threatened to with-draw the warships that still prevented Colombia from re-asserting its authority.[50]

Hay acknowledged that the new treaty gave the United States more than it could have hoped. It granted to the United States control over a ten-mile-wide zone in perpetuity; transferred both the French canal works and equipment and rights to the railroad; authorized the expro-priation of lands in the rest of Panama if the United States believed them necessary for the maintenance, defense, or sanitation of the canal area; exempted the zone from Panama's judicial jurisdiction; and empowered the United States to police Panama City and Colón and build military garrisons (see table 2).

In his message to Congress in January, Roosevelt framed all events, from the United States' various treaty obligations to Panama's independence, in terms of the urgency of constructing an isthmian canal. Impatience became reason; lawlessness became civilization. "Reasons of convenience have been superseded by reasons of vital necessity, which do not admit of indefinite delays," he said. "If ever a government could be said to have received a mandate from civilization . . . the United States holds that position with regard to the interoceanic canal" (see figure 2).[51]

When the United States formally began work on the canal in Panama in May 1904, it found a country wracked by Colombia's War of a Thousand Days, haunted by the failure of the French to complete a sea-level canal, and beholden to the United States. The lopsided arrangement between Washington and the new republic was made possible by the devastation of war and the interventionist role played by the Navy in the war.

The constitution adopted by Panama codified the power of U.S. intervention and made Panama, like Cuba, a protectorate of the United States. Despite the State Department's desire not to be bound to a mandate for intervention outside the Canal Zone, Minister William Buchanan advised the Conservative Party majority in Panama's constituent assembly to take measures against internal disturbances. The result, Article 136, permitted the United States to intervene militarily "in any part of the Republic of Panama to reestablish public peace and constitutional order in the event of their being disturbed."[52] The U.S. Army in Panama was also responsible for a different kind of intervention that was not strictly military: the transformation of the Canal Zone to make it biologically safe for White men.

SANITATION AND THE WHITE MAN

The canal enterprise undertaken by the U.S. Army became the largest single human alteration of a tropical environment in history. Men operating U.S–built machines removed nearly one hundred million cubic yards of soil and deposited the soil in dumps in the canal watershed between one and twenty-three miles away, including the creation

Table 2. United States' expropriations of land in Panama, 1908–31

Date	Location	Purpose	Comments
June 1908	Portobelo	quarry for canal construction	
December 1908	Punta de Chame	sand extraction from beach for construction	
May 1912	Lake Gatun	flooding for canal	167 square miles
July 1914	Rights-of-way: Empire–Chorrera; Balboa–Chorrera; Juan Diaz–mouth of Juan Diaz River	for construction of roads for canal defense	
June 1915	Lands at mouth of Chagres River	for canal defense	
December 1915	Village of Chagres, same area	for canal defense	
May 1918	Punta Paitilla	for military post	123 acres; Panamanian fishermen driven off by U.S. soldiers at gunpoint
July 1918	Land between Chagres River, Majagual River, Atlantic and Canal Zone		3,168 acres
August 1918	Stations along Atlantic and Pacific coasts	for coaling stations	
September 1919	Largo Remo, Las Minas Bay	for canal defense	544 acres on Droque Island and two other islands

(Table 2 continued)

Date	Location	Purpose	Comments
June 1920	Taboga Island	for canal defense	Initial U.S. demand (November 1918) was for 1,160 acres of total 1,410 acres; eventually reduced to 37 acres
December 1920	Cerro de Doscientos Pies, Las Minas Bay		309 acres of land was taken by force by U.S. but abandoned July 1921
October 1923	Land on Chagres River	for water reservoir	22 square miles
February 1924	Alhajuela territory		
July 1926	New Cristóbal, Manzanillo Island		part of 1926 treaty
August 1927	Taboga and Taboguilla Islands	for canal defense	five areas of 82 acres
September 1928	Cerro de Doscientos Pies	for canal defense	8 acres
July 1930	Jicarita Island; Punta de Morro de Puercos	construction of lighthouses for canal navigation	62 acres and 148 acres, respectively
April 1931	Alhajuela	expansion of Madden Dam	

(William D. McCain, *The United States and the Republic of Panama.*)

of a 676-acre landfill that became the town of Balboa.[53] Whole towns sprang up to house the fifty thousand workers imported from dozens of countries to make up the construction labor force. The flooding of 423 square kilometers from 1910 to 1914 to create Gatun Lake displaced thousands of Panamanians from their homes and lands without ceremony. Others were displaced to make way for military forts.[54]

This transformation — especially the importation of non-immune workers and the creation of landfills of organic matter — generated new vectors for disease. These, in turn, led to large-scale attempts to control conditions in which mosquitoes could breed, from cutting vegetation to layering water surfaces with oil.

From 1879 to 1889, the period of French canal construction in Panama, about 16,600 laborers died in an average annual work force of just over 10,000.[55] Yellow fever's dramatic speed of mortality, once it struck, provoked panic and exodus among the workers who had come to the isthmus for the undertaking. Those who left Panama in fear of contracting yellow fever conveyed their fear to others, who were effectively inoculated against any desire to work on the canal. As some saw it, the tasks for anyone wishing to complete the canal were not only to address the conditions that had created such disaster for the French, but also to rehabilitate Panama's image and make it attractive or at least survivable to the prospective workers who were to be imported for the job. Building the canal, then, would require a war on the vectors of disease. This war not only had to be waged against mosquitoes and through treatment of those who were ill. It also meant fundamentally altering the habitat of both human and insect, an adaptation of non-human ecologies to fit social objectives.

The leaders of this war saw it as largely defensive but requiring military action nevertheless. "If aggression is to be alleged," wrote Hugh Gordon Miller, assistant attorney general during Roosevelt's tenure, in an essay responding to anti-imperialist criticism, "it was wholly on the side of the Caribbean, and its weapons were malaria and yellow fever, the deadliest invaders imaginable, which respect neither treaty nor any sovereignty save death."[56]

The leader of the offensive was William Gorgas, by all accounts a cheerful man of determined optimism whose very presence served to animate sick patients. He was born in Alabama in 1854 to Josiah Gorgas, an explosives expert who became the chief of ordnance for the Confederacy during the Civil War. William became an enthusiast for all things military, as a boy even reading the Bible not for its religious content but for the accounts of battles. As a youth, his longing to enroll at West Point frustrated, Gorgas went to Bellevue Medical School, then joined the Army, serving on several frontiers of the expanding United States: in South Dakota, where the wars with Indians were still simmering; in Texas; and in Cuba in the wake of the U.S. takeover of the island in early 1899.[57]

Before the Spanish–American War, most medical thinking assumed that yellow fever was transmitted by filth, a theory that Gorgas and his associates first applied in Puerto Rico and Havana by scouring and disinfecting the streets of towns and cities. When yellow fever appeared in Siboney, Cuba, Gorgas recommended that the town be burned to destroy the disease germs, which was then done. But within weeks, yellow fever struck with force at U.S. troops occupying the islands. Another method of fighting the disease was urgently needed.[58]

Gorgas's novel contribution was to apply in Cuba the finding that yellow fever was carried from human to human by the *Stegomiya*, today known as *Aedes aegypti*. The *Stegomiya* required fresh standing water to propagate its young, and it could not fly far. If its larvae could be eradicated within a hundred yards of where people lived and worked, the *Stegomiya* would have access neither to the yellow fever virus in human victims nor to fresh material among nonimmune humans. Gorgas's campaign required all Havana residents to cover cisterns on pain of a ten-dollar fine and eliminated other standing bodies of fresh water. It would later be the precedent for the regimen of grass cutting and mown lawns in the Canal Zone. The campaign worked. Within eight months, yellow fever had been eradicated from Havana, and Gorgas was recruited to lead the fight against disease on the isthmus in 1904. In both Havana and Panama, military control lent itself to the effectiveness of Gorgas's measures. In Panama, the canal treaty granted U.S. rights to undertake sanitation not only of the Canal Zone and the terminal cities, but of lands and waters outside the zone that the United States might decide to use.

Most accounts of Gorgas's regimen emphasize the elimination of man-made bodies of standing water, such as the water receptacles that had been maintained by the French at the base of bed legs to keep ants at bay. The inspectors also entered every home in Panama City and Colón on a regular basis to enforce regulations against open cisterns and barrels of water. But much of the Sanitary Department's efforts focused on the nonhuman world by cutting down and poisoning the environment in which insects and rodents lived. Puddles of fresh water that formed without human aid made excellent breeding places for mosquitoes. One of the methods employed to eliminate such breeding places was simply to do away with the jungle. "Many square miles of jungle" in the Canal Zone were cut or burned during the construction period, wrote the chief sanitary inspector in 1916, which increased evaporation from sunlight, shortened the mosquito season, and enabled the sanitary soldiers to locate hidden water. It also facilitated sanitary social control. "Clearing made it impossible for the negroes to throw containers into the tall grass or brush near their houses without detection," he added.[59]

Another important tactic was to spread oil and other larvacides on all standing water, which killed mosquito larvae by depriving them of oxygen. The Sanitary Department devised myriad ways to distribute the oil, from sprinkling cans to horse-drawn oil barrels. At the peak of this method, the sanitation men distributed 65,000 gallons of crude oil a month on the isthmus's waters.[60]

Moreover, canal construction itself generated conditions for the spread of tropical disease. As Gorgas and others pointed out, the importation of a large number of foreigners who were not immune to yellow fever favored propagation of the disease, as the nonimmunes became carriers of the fever once it was introduced through even a single case. The physical construction also radically disrupted the environment, leading in some cases to malarial mosquito incubators of the kind that Gorgas's Sanitation Department was imposing fines on Panamanians to eliminate. "The canal work itself was constantly creating the most desirable places for the same great biological purpose," wrote Gorgas's widow. "Every time a steam shovel made a deep hole, water would almost immediately collect, and the *Anopheles* [malarial mosquitoes] would at once seek such a depression as a breeding ground."[61] In 1912, for example, suction dredgers employed to deepen the canal ditch in Gatun pumped enormous quantities of saltwater and silt into the jungle, killing the trees and vegetation. The resulting mass of dead matter generated a swamp that attracted swarms of *Anopheles* mosquitoes.[62] As a result, the death rate from malaria in 1906 was higher than it was for workers in the French canal effort from 1888 to 1903.[63]

"CERTAIN RACIAL FEATURES"

Racial constructs deeply infused the Army's medical and labor objectives on the isthmus. To set up possessions in the tropics controlled from Washington, U.S. leaders were obliged to take cues from those

European colonizers with comparable experience, particularly the British and French. European literature defined disease in the tropics as that which affected White people. Diseases that hit other populations disproportionately and that occurred in temperate climates, such as pneumonia, were generally neglected as less significant to the project of establishing settlements.

More than any other set of causes, however, it was pneumonia and tuberculosis that killed West Indians who made up the majority of canal workers. From July 1906 through June 1907, pneumonia killed 466 canal employees, more than 90 percent of them classified as "colored." Pneumonia in that year accounted for more than twice as many deaths as malaria did for employees of all races and would continue to be the leading killer in the Canal Zone through the construction era. These diseases did not strike White Gold Roll workers as severely, however, and were neglected in public-health literature on Panama. The Canal Commission recorded 4,513 deaths from disease among its workers from 1906 through 1914; 85 percent were "colored," who died at nearly three times the rate of Whites. Because many employees did not die in the Zone or under Canal Commission care, the actual number of deaths is probably much greater[64] (see figure 4).

The causes of the West Indians' respiratory disease were not hard to find. Especially before 1907, they lived in cramped conditions and often worked whole days half-submerged in rain water at the Canal Commission's insistence. Their mostly unscreened quarters were barracks or converted boxcars housing six dozen men each, often far from outhouses, in contrast to the comfortable furnished apartments provided to White employees. After 1907 these workers were free to live in the cities or in their own shacks, away from the Canal Commission's strictures. Although the conditions were also poor there, they marked an improvement on the quarters and meals provide by the United States.[65]

Army doctors commonly believed that Negroes and "natives" were immune to yellow fever. In fact, Whites consistently contracted malaria at higher rates than did West Indians.[66] Doctors did not yet comprehend that yellow fever is like the measles: Mild cases during childhood produce individual — not racial or collective — immunity. But the notion was part of a much larger set of ideas about the tropics and White people that had circulated during the rise of European colonialism during the nineteenth century. According to those ideas, the coun-

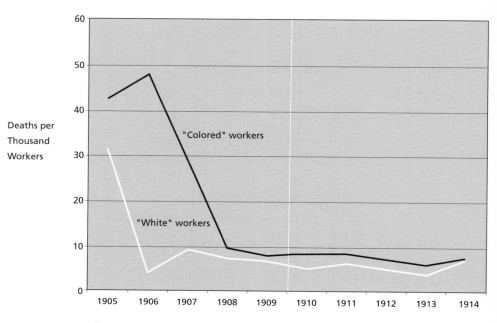

4. Mortality Rate of Canal Workers by Race, 1905–14.

terpart to Negroes' immunity to tropical diseases was White vulnerability not only to yellow fever and malaria, but also to tropical heat and sun.

The idea of Whites' vulnerability in the tropics had broad ramifications for the U.S. presence in Panama. One tenet of this vulnerability was that Whites could not stay for years in the tropics without "degeneration," a term used to refer to physical and psychological health but also, over the longer term, to tendencies to mix and interbreed with allegedly inferior populations. Tropical physicians believed that the tropics reduced Whites' reproductive abilities and stunted children's growth. Some believed that the long-term effects of tropical heat on Whites would be seen only in the children or grandchildren of the canal builders. "The third generation would be pretty weedy," noted Dr. Herbert Clark.[67] Physicians were uncertain, however, about the extent to which overall White degeneration was caused by the climate and how much by "association with natives, which is apt to have a detrimental effect upon [children's] moral and mental outlook" in the words of Navy Surgeon General E. R. Stitt.[68]

Racial and physical vigor required periodic rejuvenation in the North's healthy climates and thus rationalized White benefits such as extended annual vacations for the canal's Gold Roll employees and for maintaining other racially unequal privileges. In 1914, an outgoing president of the Canal Zone Medical Association laid out for his colleagues some of the challenges that lay ahead, stressing particularly questions of tropical deterioration in White people. "Will efficiency be maintained by leave of absence and, if so, for how long?" he asked. "Or will it be necessary every ten years or so to renew the population here?"[69] Some observers also interpreted the thesis of vulnerability to mean that hard manual labor in the tropics should be restricted to colored workers.[70]

The Army's tropical doctors were obsessed with racial classification. Gorgas's annual reports, published by the Isthmian Canal Commission, listed the names of each White U.S. employee who had died in the preceding year, but the many more West Indians who had perished were not named in the record.[71] Instead, they were anonymous to history, reaffirming the notion that White U.S. workers built the canal.

Canal Zone doctors frequently reported on their studies of pathology in "colored" populations, and Sanitary Department statistics rigidly classified health and disease according to skin color and nationality, not working conditions, housing, or other environmental factors. Reading the language of medical researchers, one would think that these doctors were talking about horses. Indeed, their practical mission centered on getting sick employees back on the line, and their thinking was strikingly similar to that of military medicine. "In the building of this Canal," noted one doctor, "the stress of work has usually necessitated a rapid diagnosis and an intensive treatment, so as to return the laborer to his work as soon as possible."[72]

Beginning in 1910, doctors gathered autopsy data on canal workers to answer questions "concerning certain racial features." The data included brain weight, skull thickness, cephalic index (skull shape), and homicidal or altercation tendencies, broken down into categories according to race. Clark's discussion of the data reached some tautological conclusions—for example, that the large number of violent accidents befalling West Indians indicated "a striking lack of appreciation for a dangerous environment [in] the negro's mental processes." When the largest number of skull shapes of West Indians belonged to a type thought to be more characteristic of Whites and Chinese, Clark wrote that these were "no doubt the results of intergradation from race mixtures."[73]

Similar ideas colored labor policy in the Canal Zone. "Don't let another Jamaican touch another tool," Colonel George Goethals, the chief canal engineer, reportedly said when he heard a complaint that a shop was assigning skilled labor to Silver Roll West Indians instead of to White union workers.[74] The Isthmian Canal Commission went on record claiming that West Indians were not only "disqualified [from such work] by lack of actual vitality, but their disposition to labor seems to be as frail as their bodily strength." Although the writer Frederic Haskin acknowledged in 1913 that "the West Indian negro laborer . . . was pretty certain always to make a fair return to the United States on the money it paid him in wages," he was nevertheless "shiftless always, inconstant frequently, and exasperating as a rule."[75]

"Colonel Goethals once said that if the West Indian negro were paid twice as much he would work only half as long," recalled Ira Bennett, author of an early history of the canal, "for a full pocketbook was too heavy for him to carry around."[76] The historian Velma Newton points out that, if West Indian workers showed less energy than others, the reason may have been poor nutrition, the effects of malaria, long work hours — ten hours a day, six days a week — or the resentment caused by the abuses of White foremen. They worked measurably harder when assigned to West Indian foremen. Moreover, the productivity of European workers that was so noted by White observers tended to flag after a couple years on the job.[77]

THE WHITES' RETURN

In Gorgas's understanding of the origins of humans, the species started out in a tropical climate; although this environment was adapted to infectious germs, people were unable to migrate to temperate regions because of cold. "As the infections spread through the tropics," he wrote, "the environment in those regions became unfavorable to man, to such an extent that he ceased to be able to improve in his mental and physical characteristics." The discovery of fire and development of clothing, however, enabled people to move away from the tropics. "When we first begin to learn anything about him historically, the most vigorous and healthy races, mentally and physically, were to be found in the temperate zones."[78] The Spaniards, Gorgas said, had made the mistake of establishing colonies in the tropics, with the result that those nations did not prosper. But the only thing preventing Europeans from settling in the tropics was disease.

The significance of the Canal Zone, then, went far beyond the engineering triumph of the canal, the uniting of the oceans, and the consequent growth in trade and social contact. Concerns about overpopulation in the United States found a response in the prospect of Whites' settling tropical countries to the south. The conquest of tropical disease would "enable man to return from the temperate regions to which he was forced to migrate long ages ago, and again live and develop in his natural home, the tropics," Gorgas wrote.[79] An implicit premise was that those already living in the tropics were not "men."

Given this transformation of tropical conditions, a new cause of White illness and death in the tropics had to be found. This cause was no longer perceived simply in the climate but also in individual failings, often moral failings, which were targets of moral crusades of the times. "By far the larger part of the moribundity and mortality formerly attributed to tropical climates was due not to climate per se," wrote one of Gorgas's successors, Colonel Weston Chamberlain, "but to isolation, tedium, nostalgia, venereal disease, alcoholic excess, poor municipal conditions, and, most important of all, to infection with specific parasites, whose invasion is now wholly preventable."[80]

What was needed, according to Dalferes Curry, a Canal Zone health officer in the 1920s, was a "sanitary conscience," a set of internalized rules that both individuals and nations could follow.[81] But while Whites might be perceived as reliably civilized and obedient to sanitary regulations, West Indians were seen as disturbingly negligent. "As elsewhere in the world, the enforcement of sanitation among the negroes is a gigantic task," wrote William Deeks, director of the Medical Service during the construction era. "As long as he has a roof over his head and a yam or two to eat he is content, and his ideal of personal hygiene is on a par with his conception of marital fidelity."[82] In these circumstances, only physical segregation would protect Whites from Black carriers of disease, which could establish reservoirs in infected West Indians living in the bush. A policy of segregation that had begun as a measure for social control was institutionalized in the 1920s on the grounds of protecting Whites' collective health.

After Gorgas died in London in 1920, his peers organized the Gorgas Memorial Laboratory in 1928 in Panama on the idea that, as one of its directors said, "if [White men] are ever to conquer the Tropics, it will be by establishing a great many outposts of intelligence and information so that they may attack their problems."[83] The laboratory named as its director Herbert Clark, the pathologist who had measured West Indians' skulls during the construction era. He remained in the position for twenty-six years and continued to propagate racial ideas in U.S. studies of tropical disease.[84]

The Gorgas lab also conducted research on protection against malaria and other diseases and experimented in the 1940s with a new insecticide known as DDT in villages along the Chagres River. The lab sprayed up to fifty thousand houses in Panama a year, and regular DDT spraying would be expanded to the Canal Zone's residential areas. Initially, the decreasing effectiveness of the chemical led Clark to research how mosquitoes find their human prey. "In the present study a group of native male subjects, without clothing other than an athletic supporter, were exposed during the evening mosquito flight," Clark wrote about the experiment in 1949. Some of the men were lying down. "The subjects had their bodies marked, by use of an odorless dye, into 12 areas — head, neck, chest to level of nipples, shoulders to level of nipples, trunk between nipples and umbilicus (including buttocks), thighs, hands, legs, feet. Numbers from 1 to 12 were assigned to these areas."

After an hour, Clark wrote, the men were "suspended in an inverted position for 10 minutes each. The hands and forearms were in contact with the substratum to help support the body which was suspended by ropes from the ankles." In this way, the scientists discovered that mosquitoes alight most often within three feet of the ground, whatever the man's position.[85]

While the technicians mapped out the native body in Panama, Clark wrote a paper based on his experiences in the tradition of General Gorgas, titled "The Tropics and the White Man," and published by the *American Journal of Tropical Medicine*.[86] His concern was whether White men could adapt permanently to tropical conditions, to "ultimately permit the permanent colonization of certain parts of the tropics." Clark did not consider Spaniards to be White and cited a summary of the debate on the question, which had been published in 1920 by Andrew Balfour, a lieutenant colonel in the British Royal Army. "There are those who believe that it is very doubtful," Balfour wrote, "if the white man can accomplish manual work out-of-doors under true tropical conditions . . . and that if he tries to do so he will assuredly degenerate." Balfour added that "the settlers should drive machines rather than do work with their own muscles."[87]

Clark belonged to the second school: those who, like Gorgas, believed that Whites could live in the tropics, given proper sanitation, but required segregation to "keep their blood pure." He offered as a model the success of Dutch soldiers abandoned on a tropical island who survived and reproduced for 250 years. "They are still fertile," he wrote, "indeed prolific, and still keep their Northern European characteristics."

"I find it hard to believe that the time will ever come when it will be necessary for the northern white race in vast numbers to colonize the tropics," Clark wrote. "The northern white sojourner with the assistance of native tropical labor and artisans will produce and transport the necessary food products and other necessities without colonization of the tropics by that race."

POST-INDEPENDENCE INTERVENTIONS

Periodic military and unarmed interventions by the United States managed to keep the "northern white sojourner" in the ascendant on the isthmus, while such force successfully held the fledgling republic in a subordinate, sometimes servile, position. The unarmed interventions included electoral supervision and interference; the disbanding of Panama's army and subsequent supervision of its police force; and an economic protectorate whereby U.S. officials often vetoed Panamanian expenditures.

One of the consequences of the treaty's land concession to the United States was the establishment of what became permanent military bases in Panama. Until 1904, all U.S. military activity on the isthmus, except some early canal surveys, was conducted from the sea and exclusively by the Navy. At first, the bases were no more than camps with tents for the soldiers. In 1904, a battalion of U.S. marines established Camp Elliott, at a distance from a settlement of Black canal workers. In July 1908, the Marine Corps force was increased to 1,350 men.[88] Eventually the garrison would expand to fourteen military bases along the banks of the canal, with an average of 7,400 troops between the world wars.[89] As a result of the bureaucratic struggle to determine Canal Zone administration after construction was completed, substantive control of relations with Panama fell to the Canal Zone's governor (an Army major general), except during wartime, when it was wielded by the garrison commander.

For U.S. officials, the usefulness of a visible if small military presence became plain. "The masses of people are schooled and experienced in all kinds of uprisings, agitations," U.S. minister John Barrett wrote, "and great harm might be done on some occasion if there were not a force, like a company of marines, convenient at Ancón, the effect of whose moral presence, even if they did not participate in preserving order, would maintain quiet or protect property."[90]

The marines did not have to wait long for action that would shape Panamanian politics. The small army established by the new republic was a band of 250 men led by General Esteban Huertas, a former Colombian officer and hero of the independence movement. When Huertas threatened revolt in October 1904, U.S. Chargé J. W. J. Lee and Barrett shepherded President Amador through the crisis by advising him to dismiss Huertas and disband the army. Three warships were anchored near Panama City, and a company of marines moved into Ancón, from which they could quickly move into any part of the city. Huertas and his men succumbed without a fight, and Panama lost its army for the next fifty years.

When President José Domingo de Obaldía died in office in 1910, he left Vice President Carlos Mendoza as the incumbent in a contest for succession. Mendoza, a Liberal Party member who had drafted Panama's declaration of independence, was also a Mulatto; his wife was Black. Race disqualified him as presidential material in the eyes of U.S. Chief of Mission Richard Marsh. Marsh reported to Washington that "there is a large population of negroes in Panama, who idolize Mendoza because of his Negro blood. These negroes are mostly ignorant, and irresponsible, unable to meet the serious obligations of citizenship in a republic."[91] Marsh publicly threatened a military occupation, and even the annexation of Panama by the United States, if Mendoza were elected. Mendoza withdrew. Goethals and President Taft publicly repudiated Marsh's threats, but they allowed the coerced outcome of the contest to stand.

Another president died suddenly in office on June 4, 1918, and when Panama announced an indefinite postponement of elections, U.S. troops occupied Panama City and Colón. By this time, the United States was on a war footing, and the political decisions about intervention had shifted to General Richard Blatchford, the Army's garrison commander. Blatchford had other purposes in mind besides orderly succession. He went on a crusade in the terminal cities to eliminate prostitution — legal in Panama then as now — and to close saloons as corrupting influences on U.S. troops. "The United States has rid them [the Panamanians] of the evils of yellow fever, and why should it not rid them of the greater curse?" Blatchford asked Washington. "If there is any real cleanup, it must start with the property owners," whom he identified as the denizens of vice.[92]

Because the intervention was justified nominally to ensure clean elections, soldiers were withdrawn from the terminal cities on July 9. But Blatchford continued his campaign by forbidding soldiers to enter Panama City and Colón until Panama had done away with liquor and opium sales to servicemen. This prohibition remained in effect until Armistice Day in November, when hundreds of soldiers broke away from the bases on the Atlantic after months of enforced abstinence and stormed Colón as a mob. That night Blatchford mounted a podium in Balboa Stadium to condemn the occurrence. But instead of acknowledging the soldiers' carnal behavior, he condemned Panama City and Colón, suggesting they be renamed Sodom and Gomorrah. He wrote afterward to Washington, "If Sodom and Gomorrah were in existence today, they would probably sue me for slander."[93]

Blatchford's tenure in Panama ended the following April. But a further legacy of his intervention continued in Chiriquí, where after the July 7 election an existing U.S. troop presence received reinforcement, despite Panama's diplomatic protests. The occupation there would continue for more than two years in an attempt to protect the interests of U.S. landowners in the province. In time, friction mounted between the soldiers and local *chiricanos* over a host of incidents, ranging from drunken verbal abuse to petty theft by soldiers and the burning of Indians' huts on property claimed by a powerful U.S. landowner. After Panamanian courts convicted and sentenced two men seen by U.S. officials as litmus cases, the occupation was withdrawn in August 1920.[94]

Army troops were called into Panama City again in October 1925, this time at the request of President Rodolfo Chiari, to put down a massive renters' strike. There were twenty thousand unemployed Blacks in Panama in 1924, most of them formerly employed on the canal, and many of whom were evicted from the Zone the same year at the request of Panamanian landlords.[95] Conditions for tenants in Panama City and Colón were horrendous, a result of exploitation by Panamanian landowners and a restricted housing stock because of the Panama Railroad Company's possession of large tracts in both cities.[96] When owners announced large rent increases in June, labor unions formed the Renters League and announced a rent boycott.[97]

Despite the peacefulness of demonstrations by the league, Panamanian police opened fire on an open-air meeting on October 10, killing two demonstrators. The crowd responded angrily and the following day effectively shut the city down. Chiari appealed to U.S. authorities for help, who responded with a battalion of six hundred troops marching into the city with fixed bayonets. A large crowd that had gathered dispersed, but a direct confrontation between U.S. troops and protesters followed the burial of one of the protesters that evening. Three Panamanians were killed in the chase by soldiers with bayonets, and dozens were arrested.[98]

The U.S. media portrayed the intervention as a necessary measure against unreasonable radicals, whose deaths were invisible. The *New York Times* quoted the captain and a passenger of a cruise ship that happened to be docked at Panama City on October 10, who asserted that the "nucleus of a revolution is a bottle of rum, two halfbreeds and a negro armed with rifles and machetes."[99] The intervention clearly assisted Panamanian elites under duress from a movement by the urban poor, although the boycott brought about a reduction in rents. The chief of the Army's Panama Canal Department, General William Lassiter, wanted to go further and remain in Panama City to oversee mass evictions of tenants, but the State Department in Washington overruled him.[100]

Panama objected to another aspect of the U.S. protectorate throughout the 1903–25 period: land takeovers that were ostensibly needed to operate or defend the canal. After the original land grant was delineated in 1904, the United States expropriated land nineteen times between 1908 and 1931 in different parts of the republic (see table 2). Although authorized by the 1903 treaty, the expropriations were often carried out by the military, with Panama notified after the fact, or not at all. Panamanian officials sought compensation from the United States, but none was forthcoming.

REGIONAL INTERVENTIONS FROM PANAMA

As a center for U.S. military forces in the region, the bases in Panama served as a launching pad for troop deployments outside the isthmus. In 1910, the marines camped at Empire and led by Major Smedley Butler were called twice to sail to Nicaragua to put down political conflicts. In May 1910, the marines interceded to support a revolution when Butler saw that "it was plain that Washington would like to see the revolutionists come out on top."[101] Butler's Panama battalion returned to Nicaragua in August 1911 for an extended stay and battles against the country's Liberal army, which lasted until November 1912.[102] The battalion was deployed from Panama once more in January 1914 — to Tampico, Mexico, from which it sailed in April as part of the Wilson administration's occupation of Veracruz.[103]

When civil war again wracked Nicaragua in May 1926, the United States immediately deployed marines from Panama, who landed in Bluefields and became the vanguard force for what would turn into a full-fledged war against Liberal leader Augusto Sandino that lasted six years.[104] The marines' war against Sandino in Nicaragua provoked widespread indignation both in Latin America and the United States and became the fulcrum for a renunciation of intervention in Latin America by the United States. With the advent of the Good Neighbor Policy, the United States established or supported local military forces to accomplish its policy aims. After the 1920s, the use of U.S. troops or installations in Panama to put down local and regional uprisings declined, with some exceptions.[105]

But the interventions' impact had been sown in U.S–Panama relations. Meanwhile, Panama acquired a new and secret role for the U.S. military: as a testing ground for the use of toxic gas in the tropics.

2 ☆ "TEST TUBE ISLAND"

The four-seater plane lifts off imperceptibly from the airstrip in Panama City, then climbs to three thousand feet on its way to the Pearl Islands. After cruising above the sparkling bay and a large uninhabited island, we bounce onto the grass strip of San Jose Island, where military planes once landed daily. A teenage boy with machete in hand greets us. He and a dozen other laborers live incommunicado on the island, clearing plants from roads and building what will be fifteen cabins for tourists. Otto Probst is one of the island's owners. He comes every other week and stays in a trailer to help with the work; the others live in tents.

Probst drives over the dirt roads laid on top of the military roads used during World War II. In the island's far southern corner, he stops the truck, and we walk. Off to the side, we see dozens of cylindrical metal containers, well rusted and scattered down a ravine. He has seen these all over the island, he says. When he recleared the roads in the 1980s, he bulldozed the containers off to the side of the roadbed. He knows quite well that the United States used the island as a chemical weapons proving ground from 1944 to 1948. At the other end of the island, on what is known as Bald Hill, he shows me the remains of a five-hundred–pound bomb.

I show Probst a map of the island produced by the Army, which outlines "artillery squares," or impact areas for the weapons tests. "I've seen fragments of bombs and the big holes they made all over the island," Probst tells me. "The papers that say they only dropped in certain places. I don't believe them. They dropped everywhere." Probst, who grew up in Germany during World War II, saw the destruction of air-dropped bombs as a boy, and he became a refugee after the war. To overcome the island's stigma as a chemical weapons proving ground, he and other owners have met with U.S. Ambassador William Hughes to press for certification that the island is safe or a cleanup of remaining hazards.[1]

The United States' entry into World War II increased the military's sensitivity to the Panama Canal's vulnerability to attack and brought with it whole new areas of responsibility and control. For the first time, Alfred Thayer Mahan's vision of a canal extending the capabilities of the navy into two oceans was put into practice. In addition, the rise of military air power opened the canal to the kind of attack that would devastate Pearl Harbor and made the Army anxious to establish installations farther from the canal to intercept potential enemy airplanes. After Hitler signaled Germany's expansionist aims in August 1939, the War Department authorized new construction of housing and antiaircraft stations and the deployment of thousands of troops to the Canal Zone. Between early 1939 and June 1940, the number of soldiers on the isthmus nearly doubled, to 22,375.[2] The Army planned to build up its air wing in Panama to some five hundred aircraft, crowding into Howard and Albrook airfields on the Pacific and France Field on the Caribbean side.

But only a month before the outbreak of the European war, the Senate had ratified a new treaty with Panama, signed in 1936, that ended the country's protectorate status. The treaty specifically dissolved the United States' right, contained in the 1903 treaty, to occupy without the government's consent any site in the interior of Panama. Despite objections by the Army and Navy, being a good neighbor from now on meant that the United States would have to obtain agreement from Panama before occupying lands outside the Canal Zone. With the onset of war, the United States' effort to obtain military sites in the republic went into high gear.

In March 1941, after the Army put Panamanian businesses out of bounds to U.S. troops and civilian employees, an oft-used strong-arm tactic, President Arnulfo Arias consented to the military's occupation of nine airfields and two radar sites in Panama's interior provinces, followed in May 1942 by a formal agreement with Panama to occupy 134 sites throughout Panama. The agreement was to terminate "one year after the date on which the definitive treaty of peace which brings about the end of the present war shall have entered into effect."[3]

The buildup in Panama reached its zenith in late 1942 and early 1943, when nearly 63,000 U.S. troops were stationed there, concentrated in the Canal Zone. In rural David alone, in Chiriquí province, some one thousand soldiers manned a local air base. In the region fanning out from the Panama Canal, including Puerto Rico and Trinidad, fifty thousand more soldiers belonged to the Caribbean Defense Command.[4]

The increased strategic importance of the canal and its garrison, and the influx of so many young Yankees into Panama, intensified discussions in the United States of the exotic jungle that the isthmus represented in the American imagination. This was especially true in popular descriptions of the firebrand Panamanian President Arnulfo Arias, who presided in Panama from 1940 until 1942, when he was deposed in a U.S.-supported coup. "Uncle Sam's life hangs by a slender blue thread — the Panama Canal," blared a headline in *American Magazine* in late 1941. "Enemies, domestic and foreign, lurk in near-by towns and jungles, plotting to slash that life line." Arias was portrayed as a flamboyant and anti-U.S. Latin, "a man of many moods." Although its subject was purportedly the canal's military vulnerability to Axis powers, the article repeatedly emphasized jungle, danger, and the wild.[5]

Yet as most of the United States emerged from its long season of isolationism, forays into the tropics were also marked by unmistakable excitement. "The jungle night takes over . . . a big cat prowls around looking for something to kill," wrote a military engineer tasked to retrieve a fallen bomber in the Amazon headwaters in 1942. Danger here is mixed with desire: "Presently she materializes out of the night. Instead of reaching for the coffee cup she presents to me, I take her hand — dawn would reveal a rather bulging hammock with a hastily dropped coffee cup under it." Then the engineer is bitten by a poisonous snake and must shoot off his finger "to avoid dying." Calculations for the clearance of an airstrip mingle with musings about "the prowling male" versus "man the domesticated animal."[6]

A serialized novel in *Woman's Home Companion* in 1941 was titled simply "Panama Threat," although virtually no Panamanians appear as characters in the story. An anonymous Panamanian, a "paid agent" whom the heroine sees in the dark, has a "dark and ruthless face." Panama is seen as a steamy bed of German spies and U.S. military and romantic intrigue.[7]

Along with the intrigue on the isthmus that was portrayed in both diplomatic and popular dispatches, the United States had secrets of its own. Foremost among them were the presence and testing of chemical weapons.

Chemical weapons were a component of U.S. canal-defense tactics from the canal's early years, and the United States had an active chemical weapons program in Panama from at least 1923 until 1968. From 1923 to 1946, the program focused on defending the canal. From 1943 until 1968, the program aimed to test chemical munitions under uniquely tropical conditions.

The canal was completed in August 1914, only days before the outbreak of World War I, the war in which mustard gas was used for the first time in battle. Public awareness of chemical weapons began with horrific images of troops gassed by the German military in the fields of France. One hundred twenty-five thousand British soldiers were casualties of mustard gas — three of every four British casualties during the whole war.[8]

General William Sibert, the Army engineer who had designed the Gatun locks in Panama, commanded the first division of U.S. troops to go overseas in the war, sailing for France in June 1917. Without gas masks of its own, and with chemical-warfare activities fragmented in four departments, the United States was not well prepared to face massive gas attacks. Within a year, Sibert was made director of a newly consolidated Chemical Warfare Service. He brought the agency's disparate activities together, so that by the end of the war the United States was producing more lethal gas than all of the other belligerents combined.

After the war, Sibert became a vocal proponent of the continued development of chemical weapons. "When the armies were provided with masks and other defensive appliances, something less than four percent of the gas casualties were fatal," Sibert ruminated. "These figures, I think, meet one of the chief objections brought against the use of gas — that of humanity. So far from being inhumane, it has been proved that it is one of the most humane instruments of warfare, if we can apply the word humane to the killing and wounding of human beings." Sibert cited even a national organization of former Army doctors as favoring gas because it was more humane.[9]

To the military, gas was scientific, and as such it potentially conferred greater legitimacy on the military's institutions, as hundreds of chemists and chemical engineers were made to serve the military. Chemistry was a budding and successful branch of science in the

1920s, with a novelty that appealed to the military, akin to how computers affected people in the 1990s.

Sibert contrasted the irrationality of civilians with soldiers by recounting a story about an accident during the first months of operations at Edgewood Arsenal in Maryland. When a chemist spilled some chlorine, a nearby "workman" (not a scientist or "technician") yelled, "The gas is loose!" The news spread quickly and caused a panicked stampede of thousands, even symptoms of gas poisoning. "They all saw gas, smelled gas, and were affected by gas, but there was no gas to see, to smell, or to affect. Imagination did the whole thing."

"Fear sometimes does queer things to a man," Sibert wrote, without noting that the fear it provoked was one of gas's military virtues. But the civilians' fear made it "impracticable to employ them in this plant," and the Army brought in soldiers to do the work at Edgewood.[10]

In 1921, the Chemical Warfare Service, like the Army's seven other supply arms and services, was told to draw up plans for defense of the Canal Zone and other outlying U.S. possessions.[11] The first chemical defense plans were thus drawn up in 1923 and would be updated every year through at least 1946. "As unusually favorable conditions exist in Panama for the employment of chemical agents in defense of the canal, maximum use of chemical and anti-gas equipment is anticipated," according to the doctrine. The plan involved bombing with mustard gas the trails and routes that led inland from landing beaches on both the Atlantic and Pacific coasts, spraying the beaches, and firing chemical mortars at military targets.[12]

Those who inherited Gorgas's sanitation regime extended gas weapons to the eradication of nonhuman life considered to be a threat, leading to heavy-handed methods for controlling tropical vermin. One of the most novel was the use of a variant of gas warfare against rats and insects on ships passing through the Panama Canal. In 1923, the canal's Quarantine Division took to fumigating ship holds with cyanogen chlorid, which chemically is closely related to lethal CK gas, and found it very effective. The fumigation crew was equipped with gas masks and made sure that no sailors or stowaways were aboard when they released the cyanide gas. "Rats in cages placed at a considerable distance from the generator and covered with several layers of sacking were killed in twenty minutes after the gas was liberated," noted W. C. Rucker, the canal's chief quarantine officer.[13]

Another true believer in chemical weapons, Major-General Preston

Brown, came to the helm in Panama in 1930. At this time, the military kept a supply of thirty tons of persistent gas, maintained by a chemical company of two officers and seventy-seven men. "I have long been of the opinion that the hot, damp, breathless tropical jungle offers ideal conditions for the use of persistent gas," Brown wrote to Washington in March 1931. Brown believed that, in the case of a land invasion, troops could use gas defensively as they retreated through the jungle. This had been demonstrated by a two-week set of maneuvers by the First Chemical Company in La Chorrera, twenty-two miles west of the canal, in February 1931.[14]

By 1940, the United States had eighty-four tons of mustard gas; ten tons of phosgene; thousands of mustard-charged mortar rounds; and hundreds of assorted chemical projectors, shells, and cylinders on hand in the Canal Zone.[15] From July of that year to the following May, the Chemical Warfare Service (CWS) acquired expanded space in Panama — code-named "Mercury" — and received shipments of gas masks.[16] The space included chemical munitions magazines in eight bases along the canal, as well as in Rio Hato to the east.[17]

Most of the chemical munitions were stored at Cerro Tigre, a wooded area on the canal's east side between Panama City and Gamboa, where a monorail hoist had been installed for moving munitions. Some of the munitions were kept outdoors in apparently vulnerable conditions. "At the upper end of the row of sheds, a set of mustard gas drums are placed in a niche in the side of the hill," wrote Lieutenant-Colonel Homer Saint-Guadens in spring 1941. But Cerro Tigre was subject to earth slides, including one that had destroyed a magazine in 1935, prompting the selection of a new site when conventional ammunition-storage areas were expanded in 1938.[18]

"WE WERE USED AS GUINEA PIGS"

Jack Cadenhead had enlisted in the Army in Greenville, South Carolina, in 1940 to escape the Depression and an oppressive job in the local cotton mill. Sent to the Canal Zone, he and others in the 33d Infantry Regiment were brought to a long narrow building on Fort Clayton one day in July 1941. There they were given gas masks, exposed to a form of tear gas, and told to lift their masks and sniff it. Then the officers running the experiment asked for ten volunteers. "They said they wanted some men who didn't smoke," Cadenhead recalled. He raised his hand. "It's hot, close to a hundred degrees in Panama, with no air conditioning, especially in those chambers. They would drop stuff in a container, and it would fog up."

The operators had gas masks on, Cadenhead told me, but "they didn't tell us a thing, they just run us through there pretty fast." The building was long—so long that the men were forced to breathe in the mustard as they ran. The men quickly developed problems breathing and were rushed to nearby Gorgas Hospital. "The guy with me, Bill Hansard, almost choked to death when we got to Gorgas," Cadenhead recalled. "I was in ahead of him. He was blue around his mouth. They said, 'We need to get him in here.' It was one of the medical aides, I think, and he asked the doctor, 'What's wrong with them?' And the doctor said, 'It's that damn mustard gas!'"

"Mustard gas loves wet, low places; that's where it hangs out. It's the same on your body, where you sweat or it's humid," said Cadenhead, who has had health problems ever since. The gas affected his speech; blisters as big as a half-dollar came up on his feet; and the end of his penis turned white. "I thought I had leprosy for a while," Cadenhead said. More than fifty years later, he still had problems breathing. When he wrote to the Veterans Administration, the VA wrote back to say that his records from Gorgas Hospital had been destroyed. "We were all just kids, we didn't know what was going on," Cadenhead said. "After I got older and wiser, I felt we were used as guinea pigs."[19] Cadenhead's experience may have reflected the decision of one or two field commanders, because widespread use of human subjects for chemical tests did not begin until 1943. Soon enough, it would become a matter of policy.

In early 1944, the Navy conducted a four-day gas exercise with what one officer described as a "rugged group" of marines. The ordeal was so grueling that some of the marines tried to maim themselves. The officer recounted that he prepared the Naval Hospital for "severe casualties," then set out for Camp Chorrera, where the exercise took place. Thirty minutes after the maneuver began on February 21, the marines were sprayed by air with CNB tear gas. "Three men were evacuated because of gas burns on the first day," he wrote. Two more men were evacuated the next day, and by the third day, "all the lesions are getting progressively worse (approx. 60 hrs. after exposure). There are two other casualties—one already described; the other one has gone 'Over the Hill.'" A week later, several men were still in the hospital with "burns approaching third degree." On the night of March 3, one of the marines tossed a live shell into a campfire and shot himself in the arm. A driver was to take the man to the hospital but instead overturned the jeep he was driving. "Very few dull moments," the officer commented wryly.[20]

THE SAN JOSE PROJECT

By the end of 1943, the risk of Japanese or German attack had dropped sharply, and the garrison in Panama was reduced dramatically in size. One military observer spoke of "a war in which our participation so far has been conspicuously passive" and "moments of exceptional dejection," broken only by alerts that inevitably were false alarms. Luxury goods — silk stockings, French perfume, Scotch — were a redeeming factor for the boredom. They could be had in abundance from commissaries in Panama while rationing was the rule at home.[21]

The changing circumstances prompted Henry Stimson to write in late 1944: "The menace of a Japanese surprise attack which livened up the situation two and a half years ago now is dim in the distance as the Japanese fleet has been pounded to pieces across the Pacific."[22] Ironically, it was precisely during this lull for the troops in Panama that the Army established and carried out an ambitious chemical weapons program there.

The Allied victories in the Pacific war had come at no small cost. In November 1943, U.S. marines took Betio island after firing more than 3,000 tons of explosives at 4,700 Japanese soldiers, all but 17 of whom were killed. The United States lost nearly 3,000 troops, as well.[23] "The Japanese continued resistance in a suicide [*sic*] way after a military decision has been reached, sometimes makes the conquest of the Japanese-held islands costly in personnel and time," began a 1945 Army film promoting the virtues of gas warfare in the tropics. "When driven to desperation, the Japanese reaction against our troops has been a frenzy of attack, without thought of the cost to themselves. Illogical and unpredictable, they may resort to gas warfare without considering the cost. In that event, what will be the net result?"[24]

Japan had already used chemical weapons extensively during its invasion of China in 1937–42, resulting in some eighty thousand injuries and ten thousand deaths.[25] The cws decided to mount a test project to gain an understanding of how chemical weapons could be used in case of a land invasion of Japan and its occupied Pacific islands. Because enemy soldiers in the hot Pacific islands exposed more skin than did soldiers in other climates, U.S. military scientists believed that chemical weapons would be especially effective there, and would also lead to many secondary infections. "We are very interested in contaminating large areas of ground for a very long time," Brigadier General Alden Waitt of the CWS said.[26]

Colonel Robert McLeod of the CWS was assigned to find a jungle testing ground for chemical weapons somewhere in the Americas. The military sought a jungle site with "lack of human habitation, safety distances to nearby islands, tropical jungle, good water, absence of disease and poisonous snakes," and accessibility to nearby airfields controlled by the U.S. military. In October 1943, McLeod, accompanied by a geologist from the University of Chicago, searched up and down the coasts of Costa Rica, Nicaragua, Peru, Panama, and the Galapagos Islands of Ecuador. McLeod discarded Panama's penal colony on Coiba Island because the presence of prisoners might have "complicated our problems" and other areas because of the distance from airfields. Instead he settled on San Jose Island, the second largest of the Pearl Islands in Panama Bay.[27]

An internal military history offers insight into how the military understood the tropical terrain it was entering. Acknowledging that historians had written little about San Jose, and that the following story "may or may not be true," the Army recounts this "Frankensteinian folklore":

> Some eighty years ago, around 1857, an Englishman with his wife and young daughter built a homestead on the island, bringing also a stock of hogs. Indians came across the water from Darien and "scalped" the man and woman, but somehow the girl managed to escape into the jungle, where she was found soon afterward, white-haired and demented, by some kindly negroes from the neighboring island of Pedro Gonzales. Taking her along with them, they set sail for Panama, but she died en route. From that time on the island was unofficially marked "haunted," and natives could not be persuaded to return there.[28]

In another account of the same myth, also told by a military writer, the English family was survived by "one man whose chin was cut off and who continued to live around Panama City until after the turn of the century. Returning from the raid, one of the native chieftains tripped over a sharp tree stump and was impaled. The native mind seems to have seized on this as a manifestation of the murdered men's ghosts returning for revenge."[29]

For the military, the "native mind" was more conveniently located in story than in physical proximity, where it might "complicate" operations. But the story pointed up the dangers of entering a jungle "beset by gnarled and venomous manchineel trees," an "island of mystery" whose "beautiful little bays" and "kindly negroes" belied potential revenge and dementia.

Brigadier-General Egbert F. Bullene, who had been tapped to run the project, paid a visit to the island in November and reaffirmed it as a test site. But in a twist on environmental values, the Army's General Staff delayed approval of San Jose Island as a site for chemical tests until they were assured that the experiments would not harm rare flora or fauna. The National Museum in Washington testified that no rare wildlife existed on San Jose, after which the General Staff gave its go-ahead.[30]

The military acted quickly. On December 20, 1943, the U.S. consul proposed to conduct "certain chemical warfare tests under existing jungle conditions" for sixty-day renewable periods on San Jose Island. Under the terms of the 1936 treaty, the agreement had to be made with both the government of Panama and the island's private owners, a Panama City family led by Max Huertematte. A rental fee of $15,000 a year was agreed for the use of three hundred hectares for chemical warfare experiments. The United States also sought Panama's consent to build trails and wharves and to incorporate the agreement into the 1942 base agreement signed the year before.

The project formally began on January 6, 1944, two days after Panama gave permission to the United States to conduct "chemical warfare tests" on the island.[31] Within days, hundreds of Army engineers arrived on the island to clear roads and an airstrip and construct the many buildings needed for operations and housing. The project divided the island into eleven areas, six of which were laid in grids for target areas. The three largest target areas, made up of overlapping squares, measured about one square mile each.[32] The project would use much more than the agreed seven hundred acres, leading the Huertematte family to make claims for compensation after the war.[33]

More than one hundred thirty tests were completed, using mustard gas, phosgene, cyanogen chloride, hydrogen cyanide, and butane, as well as napalm-fueled flamethrowers.[34] At least one participant in the

5. Mustard-gas bombs were stored at Rio Hato Air Base in 1944. (National Archives.)

project claimed that nerve gas was also tested.[35] Although neither the United States nor Great Britain had developed nerve agents of its own by 1945, the British knew about the existence of nerve gas from a captured German war chemist as early as 1943. In April 1945, a captured shell showed incontrovertibly that the Germans had produced this new weapon. The British felt that some of the stocks of captured German nerve agent should be "retained for possible use in the Far East" in case the Allies invaded Japan, an eventuality for which the San Jose Project was preparing.[36] But it was after the war ended that nerve gas was tested in San Jose. At the end of 1945, a visiting general reported on "training being prepared for all personnel in properties of certain new chemical agents (German), preparatory to tests planned."[37] Eugene Reid, who was working in San Jose at the time, said that nerve gas "was the hot thing then."

Chemical bombs dropped on San Jose were stored at Rio Hato, an air base on Panama's southern coast from which test missions took off (see figure 5). In 1946, a chemical officer described the San Jose "ammunition dump" in Rio Hato as being in "terrible" condition.[38] In addition to using the island, the San Jose Project tested chemical munitions on the sea off Panama to determine their effectiveness against

Axis ships. According to one military map, this included chemical spray on Iguana Island, which was also used as a conventional-bombing range during the war.[39] San Jose Island had become, in the words of the *Chemical Warfare Bulletin*, a "Test Tube Island."

USING LIVE SUBJECTS

Many of the tests on San Jose Island used rabbits or goats to observe how lethal various methods of attack or how effective gas masks were. "They brought goats from Ecuador," said José Alsola, a Peruvian who worked on San Jose in 1946 clearing vegetation for paths and an airstrip. "They put those gases on them. The skin fell off the animals, they died, and they ended up cooked. The animal was red, red! Like it was cooked, burnt."[40]

A 1945 film produced by the Signal Corps about the project shows a comparative test with three goats — one with a U.S.-made gas mask, one with a Japanese gas mask, and one without any gas mask. With the goats tethered to stakes and the camera running, the area is gassed with mustard. Two of the goats writhe and fall, while the goat with the American gas mask survives "unharmed." One apparent purpose of this film was to reassure the soldiers viewing it that, in case of gas warfare with the Japanese, the United States would not only win but would have few casualties.[41]

But military and civilian researchers had long believed that tests on non-human animals alone were inadequate. "In toxic warfare, the most critical point in the evaluation of an item is its toxic effects upon enemy troops," wrote the Chemical Corps' medical chief, Colonel John R. Wood, shortly after the war. "Where possible, in field trials, enemy troops are represented by human test subjects."[42] A civilian scientist, writing about tests conducted in 1943 with blistering agents such as mustard, said simply that, because in animals "the reactions of the skin vary so greatly from species to species . . . , it was soon found that the only constantly reliable test object was man."[43] These chemical experiments on soldiers began before the attack on Pearl Harbor, as Cadenhead's experience shows. The United States had exposed more than sixty thousand soldiers to chemical agents at various sites by the end of the war. At least four thousand of these people were subjected to high doses of mustard gas or Lewisite (an arsenic agent) in gas chambers or in contaminated field areas.[44]

According to a study of the effects of the chemical experiments on humans by the Institute of Medicine, it was "already known by 1933 that certain long-term health problems resulted from sulfur mustard exposure."[45] But one could imagine that the experience of a global conflagration in which tens of millions of people were dying was changing the moral benchmarks of what was acceptable. Faced with the carnage that could result during a land invasion of Japan, Army officers and scientists might have reasoned, exposing a few hundred or thousand soldiers to chemical agents, short of lethal doses, was a lesser harm.

The changing moral climate certainly applied to responses to the wholesale bombing of cities, which President Roosevelt condemned at the beginning of the war in Europe as "inhuman barbarism." By March 1945, when the U.S. Air Force destroyed sixteen square miles of Tokyo by use of incendiary bombs, the ethical equation employed was very different.[46] By that time, according to polls taken in response to the use of chemical weapons by Japan in China, as many as 40 percent of people in the United States favored using gas against the Japanese.[47]

The prospect of gas warfare on the Pacific islands occupied by the Japanese gave rise to the formation of the high-level, tripartite Advisory Committee on Effectiveness of Gas Warfare Materiel in the Tropics in March 1944, with representatives of the U.S. Army CWS, National Defense Research Committee, and chemical branches from Canada and Great Britain. At the time, England was operating other field tests in India and Australia (both then British colonies), while the United States also ran a chemical test site in Bushnell, Florida, as well as in Panama. The militaries wanted to make sure that these widely dispersed projects were coordinated as the Allies prepared for possible gas warfare.

British representatives told the assembled group that the British General Staff "did not accept any tests with relation to such gas without human observers as final," because that was "the only way to get real results." The group agreed to make an effort to obtain such "observers." The committee also agreed to test British and U.S. munitions in parallel.[48] "It should be noted," says one history, that the soldiers "might more accurately be described as Observees rather than Observers. But the word 'observer' has served a useful function by preventing the use of words or terms with unflattering connotations, e.g.

'guinea pigs.' The word 'observer,' it was noted, helped to interest the enlisted men who came from the mainland to aid in the tests." Four out of every five "observers" in the chemical shoots suffered from burns.[49]

Canada's director of chemical warfare, Elmer Maass, again raised the issue of obtaining human subjects, which were in short supply in May 1944. The medical chief of the CWS affirmed that such tests were essential for evaluating liquid and vapor agents. He also noted that attempts were being made "to correlate nonpersistent agent dosage with physiological effects on man in civilian prisons." Maass insisted that, unless human subjects were found, Canada's military participation in the San Jose Project would be withdrawn. General Bullene promised to approach General George Brett, chief of the Panama Canal Department, about the problem.[50]

The generals' solution lay at least in part with soldiers, who were then stationed in abundance throughout Latin America: Puerto Ricans. Puerto Ricans had played a large role in the U.S. military presence in Panama since they were first made citizens and conscripted into the Army, just weeks before the United States' entrance into World War I. At the end of that war, nearly four thousand Puerto Rican soldiers were camped in the Canal Zone.[51]

At the onset of World War II, the military draft was reactivated in Puerto Rico, bringing more than sixty-five thousand recruits into the U.S. military. Some of the Puerto Rican troops were based at Ecuador's Galapagos Islands, but the entire 65th Infantry Regiment, a regular Army unit from Puerto Rico, arrived in Panama in January 1943. It would be followed by two Puerto Rican regiments of the National Guard. Although a number of "continental" (that is, Anglo-Saxon) units were deactivated or redeployed elsewhere in 1943 and 1944, the Puerto Ricans stayed on.[52]

Officers tended to place less trust in Puerto Rican "insular troops" than in continental soldiers. As one general explained in 1946, the Puerto Ricans had "low intelligence quotients" and a "tendency toward emotional instability," and "the majority of the Puerto Ricans in the military service here do not understand their relationship to the Government of the United States sufficiently well to be expected to serve and sacrifice in the interest of the nation at large with the same willingness and enthusiasm as do our soldiers who were born and reared on the continent."[53]

As the San Jose Project got under way in late 1943, two chemical companies of continental soldiers were replaced with a Puerto Rican company.[54] One of the San Jose tests, carried out between August 9 and August 15, 1944, sought "to determine whether any difference existed in the sensitivity of Puerto Rican and Continental U.S. Troops to H gas [mustard]."

A preliminary test involved ten Puerto Rican troops and ten continental troops and was followed by a larger test involving forty-five Puerto Rican soldiers and forty-four continental soldiers. The men, who were unfamiliar with the use of chemical agents, were "given a stiff course in gas discipline and the significance of H [mustard] lesions to casualty production," according to a project progress report. The tests involved applying liquid mustard to the under-surface of each subject's forearms and then observing for three days. A summary of the test produced by Defense Secretary William Cohen in April 1998 implied that some of the men were hospitalized after they "sustain[ed] severe body burns or eye lesions." Men with less severe burns were simply returned to their barracks and expected to meet company formations (see figure 6).[55]

Some of the tests also served to train troops. In one exercise, called Sandfly, bombers dropped five tons of mustard gas onto a masked rifle company in the jungle, who then had to stay put for twenty-four hours. An Army historian reported "moments when panic or mass hysteria seemed close to the surface among the occupying troops."[56] A group of GIs was taken by boat to San Jose in March 1945 for an exercise — possibly Sandfly — that exposed them to casualty-inflicting levels of mustard gas. According to Charles McGinnis, a participant who developed chronic illnesses from the test and later died of cancer, more than two-thirds of the 133 soldiers had Spanish surnames and could not understand the instructions for the exercise. McGinnis remembered that he and his cohorts were dressed in heavy rubberized suits and told to put their bayonets in the ground and lean heavily on their rifles when the aircraft passed over head. The goats nearby "screamed and hollered and then died." He felt heat rising in his body, and when he looked up, "it was just like autumn with the leaves falling. Everything went black."

McGinnis and others were taken to a concrete-block building, where a man behind a glass window undressed him with mechanical arms. They were hospitalized for several days, watching the skin blister, then burst. Some of the men were blinded, McGinnis said. "We were in a hell of a shape. After that morning, it felt like a knot [in my throat]. I kept telling them, and they said, 'Nothing to it.' " McGinnis soon was coughing and choking whenever he spoke, and he later developed stomach and throat cancers. The Army commended McGinnis and the other participants for "subjecting themselves to pain, discomfort, and possible permanent injury," but did not grant benefits to McGinnis until the late 1970s.[57]

After 1945 activity on San Jose relaxed somewhat. USO women were brought over for the men's entertainment, officers brought their wives to live with them, and the Army showed movies in a theater built on San Jose (including films about Nazi atrocities). Latinos, who lived in a different camp from the Whites, were trucked to the theater, where they sat in the rear seats.[58]

But tests continued into that year and through 1947. For a time, the Army considered making the island into an Army-wide tropical testing station, one of a series that headquarters sought around the world "to provide tests for material under varying weather conditions, such as, tropical, frigid, wet, etc." On that basis the United States kept the island after the war ended, while other bases outside the Canal Zone were abandoned. When the War Department decided against using San Jose as a permanent Army-wide installation, the CWS nevertheless assumed that San Jose would be used permanently to test chemical agents.[59]

A shipment of mustard bombs reached the Canal Zone from New Orleans in March 1946. The USS *Colonial* carried another shipment of mustard gas in bulk containers from the Naval Mine Depot in Yorktown, Pennsylvania, to the Canal Zone two weeks later; the containers were then transported to an unnamed location in Panama in four trucks.[60] On San Jose Island, the medical officer noted in 1947, "chemical burns from the technical laboratories have been very common." He added optimistically that "more rigid discipline among technical personnel the last few months reduced these considerably."[61]

NATIONALISM INTERRUPTS THE EXPERIMENT

Popular movements against established authority gained ground and confidence during the war. By early 1945, student protests were the catalyst for the fall of President de la Guardia's government, which was ruling increasingly by decree, and the convocation of a constituent assembly.[62] This popular effervescence was occurring largely outside the conventional structures for decision-making in the country. This is one reason that U.S. diplomatic officers overlooked its significance. External factors also influenced the mood in Panama, including desegregation of the U.S. military, the liberation of European countries, and movements for decolonization in Asia, Africa, and elsewhere.

This was the backdrop in September 1946, when Panama's legislature called Foreign Minister Ricardo J. Alfaro to testify on the government's interpretation of the 1942 base agreement. Alfaro stated emphatically that the United States must return the bases to Panama by September 2, 1946, one year after Japan's surrender. Three months later, President Harry Truman turned to his aide Admiral Leahy and said: "Why don't we get out of Panama gracefully before we get kicked out?"[63] Some U.S. policymakers were especially sensitive to charges of military occupation on the eve of the United Nations' first sessions, when member nations had to declare whether they administered any territory whose people had not yet attained a full measure of self-government.

Instead of relenting, the military and the State Department persisted, informing the Panamanians that the United States "had no intention of disarming as we had after the last war."[64] The two sides continued to haggle over the duration of and payment for leases, finally settling in December 1947 on ten years for San Jose Island and Rio Hato and five years for fourteen other sites. The Army's first preference was to buy all of San Jose "if reasonable sale price can be obtained," but that was not the case.[65] Alfaro resigned in protest against the agreement.

The pact was signed on December 10, and students organized a street protest in Panama two days later. Police fired on the gathering, injuring thirty, including one youth who was paralyzed for life. "The capital was at that time a well integrated city," recalled one participant. "We felt solidarity and we guarded one another, all of us were responsible for the polity. The next day, tens of thousands of people came out into the streets condemning the aggression. . . . Thanks to the police's stupidity, the whole city repudiated the Filós-Hines Agreement."[66] Women in particular mobilized en masse against the accord, culminating in a December 16 demonstration of ten thousand women who marched to the National Assembly.

Inside, the president of the assembly announced — in what U.S. observers would later quote widely — that "ten thousand boys with knives" awaited their decision outside. Former Foreign Minister Alfaro testified against the accord, as did his predecessor and several Socialist Party deputies. The assembly then unanimously rejected the pact.[67] Spruille Braden, the fiercely anticommunist undersecretary of state, blamed communists for the loss of the bases.[68]

At midnight on December 23, 1947, personnel on San Jose Island received a "rather unwelcome Christmas gift," according to the project's diarist: they had to get out, with no new location to move to, by the end of January — "all made necessary by the failure of the Panamanian Government" to ratify the base agreement, in the diarist's words. "Beating the deadline date was not accomplished by working union hours," two of the project's officers wryly observed. After a holiday respite, civilians and soldiers alike worked around the clock to move sixteen thousand tons of goods that ranged from "baby high-chairs to diesel electric generators"[69]

DISPOSAL OF CHEMICAL MUNITIONS

The military kept fewer records on the disposal of chemical munitions stockpiled or used in tests during and after the war than on the tests themselves. As one participant in the San Jose Project commented, "We didn't worry too much about things like that at that time."[70] To understand the legacy of these tests, it is important to know the difference between non-stockpiled munitions, such as those fired on San Jose, and stockpiled munitions, which are kept in a controlled, contained manner where they can be continuously monitored and repackaged if in danger of leaking. Non-stockpiled weapons have not been contained or monitored, nor have they been kept safely away from public-access areas.

All chemical munitions, like conventional munitions, include a certain number of duds — that is, munitions that do not detonate when fired or dropped. It is these unexploded ordnance (UXO) that typically cause accidents in impact areas when people unsuspectingly pick up, step on, or play with them. The rule of thumb among explosives-disposal professionals is a 10 percent dud rate.[71]

On San Jose Island, thousands of chemical mortars and bombs were fired or dropped into eleven target areas, mostly on the north side of the island. In the eighteen tests for which declassified records exist, 4,397 mortars and bombs were used. If other tests averaged the same

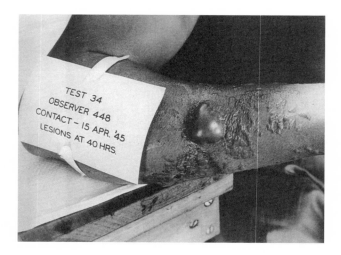

6. Chemical burns: Human "observers" were exposed to chemical agents to achieve "real" results from tests. (National Archives.)

7. San Jose Island in 2001: More than fifty years after the United States left, hundreds of containers that had held chemical agent remained. (Organization for the Prohibition of Chemical Weapons.)

number of munitions, that would mean that 31,267 chemical munitions were fired or dropped on San Jose. At a dud rate of 10 percent, that would leave 3,126 chemical UXO on San Jose Island.

The San Jose post diary reported that, even before the project was closed, barges left the island to dump chemical munitions at sea. On March 11, 1947, a tug towed a barge thirty miles from San Jose and dumped a load of munitions. Another barge-load of munitions was dumped at sea on August 19, 1947.[72]

The military's evacuation of the San Jose Project in early 1948 was carried out with haste, on a five-week deadline received from headquarters. A final barge was loaded with chemical munitions, which were then dumped at sea on January 12, 1948.[73] A summary of the San Jose Project written by the military for the White House in 1979 said that "known munitions were destroyed and detoxified" when the island was evacuated. But, the reported added, "In some tests, complete functioning of munitions could not be verified because of the jungle and marsh environment."[74] Canadian military reports in 2000 warned that mustard gas bombs may have survived below the soil's surface, and that heavy metal drums in which mustard was stored also may have endured the island's climate. In other words, both the United States and Canada were aware decades after the tests that chemical munitions remained on the land at San Jose Island (see figure 7).[75]

Stockpiled munitions that the military still hoped to use were moved into the Canal Zone. "The materiel owned by San Jose was stored wherever space could be found," two of the project's officers wrote. "Some of it was placed in the basements of barracks, more in an abandoned motor pool, and a toxic yard was established at the mouth of the Chagres River on the Fort Sherman Reservation."[76] The officers did not elaborate on this alarming declaration. The toxic materials at Fort Sherman were stored there for "rehabilitation," according to a later account, which may have meant leaks from munitions in need of repair.[77]

At least some of these munitions were moved again a few months later to Water Island on St. Thomas in the Virgin Islands, where the San Jose Project was rehoused between May 1948 and June 1950, when it was definitively laid down. Tugs left Panama on May 21 and May 26 towing three barges of "Technical Equipment," often a euphemism for munitions.[78] One of the barges carrying the chemical weapons developed a bad leak during the voyage to St. Thomas, took on water, and nearly sank.[79]

Some twenty-five years after the San Jose Project had left Panama, the island was owned by Earl Tupper, the inventor of Tupperware, who planned to build a resort on its lush bays. Tupper "wanted certification by the United States that there was no danger to people, life, or health in the waters around the island," recalled Fernando Manfredo Jr., then a treaty negotiator for Panama.[80] When one of Tupper's workers was burned in 1974, Tupper's son contacted an explosives-removal team.[81] The State Department never gave Tupper his certification, and he sold the island. Another quarter-century after Tupper's crew member was burned, Otto Probst and other owners were still struggling with San Jose's reputation as a no-man's land of chemical dangers.

Not long after the U.S. departure from San Jose Island, the Army's interest in chemical warfare in the tropics took new root in Panama, establishing chemical agent operations that were virtually continuous through the 1960s. In November 1952, the Tropical Test Team, a Chemical Corps unit of twenty personnel, arrived in Panama to set up shop again. Within three months, more than seven tons of chemical agents were being shipped to the Canal Zone from Mobile, Alabama.[82]

From February 1953 to February 1957, the team conducted tests of distilled mustard gas every three months at Curundu in the Canal Zone. The tests included pressure tests of one-ton containers of mustard, as well as freezing of the distilled mustard.[83] Toxic materials were stored in a large open building in Cerro Tigre, and munitions were kept nearby in igloo-type magazines. According to a 1956 report, "The chemical demolition area, located on a knoll on the Chiva-Chiva Trail, is utilized for large-scale testing of screening smoke devices and for a few tests of hazardous materials. This section, *which is also used for the disposal of all materials of a hazardous nature*, is restricted and well marked to prevent the entry of unauthorized persons."[84]

The report clearly indicates that the tests included detonation of chemical mines and added: "The toxic gas building at Cerro Tigre is used for limited testing of toxic gases and liquids."[85] In April 1998, a visit to Cerro Tigre showed that the area had grown up with vegetation, without fences or signs. The area apparently was no longer restricted or well marked.

On June 11, 1957, stevedores in the Canal Zone unloaded a shipment of sarin nerve-agent projectiles from the SS *Suzanne Bound*.[86] Three hundred fifty-one shells containing two pounds of sarin apiece were tested by leaving them exposed to the tropical air. Men periodically extracted agent from some shells to test its purity, and all of the shells reportedly were shipped back to the United States in 1960.[87] In 1958, the Chemical Corps outlined a test plan for some six hundred gas masks in Panama, which were to employ live CK gas as part of the tests. The document describes how gas-mask canisters would be stored in Panama's humid tropical environment for periods ranging from two to fifty-two weeks, subjected to tests of lethal CK gas, then destroyed.[88]

During the same period, the military conducted chemical activities that made soldiers stationed in Panama violently ill. Joseph Oppedisano served with the Army in Panama from 1956 to 1958. On January 4, 1958, he said, the entire island of Flamenco where he was stationed — located at the Pacific entrance to the Panama Canal — was defoliated. "We had about ten million fish die. They got stuck on the rocks and made a stink," he said. Oppedisano thought it was a secret military test. He and other soldiers on the island became ill and were hospitalized. One of those soldiers, Israel Jewetz, testified, "The areas where we were barracked were sprayed with chemicals every day to control insect populations and prevent malaria and yellow fever outbreaks." Oppedisano developed hairy cell leukemia as a result of his exposures.[89]

In 1961, the Chemical Corps participated in a transport exercise called Swamp Fox I, which took place primarily in the Darién region of Panama, not far from Colombia. The exercise involved firing 58 CN tear-gas grenades in the jungle.[90] Other activities involved testing small amounts of live chemical agents such as mustard and sarin, which were probably kept in glass vials in laboratories. From November 1960 to February 1962, the Chemical Corps' Tropic Test Activity in Panama tested twenty kits designed to detect contamination of food by chemical agents, including sarin, mustard, and cyanogen chloride.[91]

BIRTH OF THE TROPIC TEST CENTER

Pressure within the Army to establish a tropical test station began in the early 1950s, after the United States had lost San Jose Island. Ten years later, in 1962, the Army established a research and development office in Panama, which was expanded two years later into the U.S. Army Tropic Test Center (TTC). The Kennedy administration's mandate for counter-terrorist warfare, and the U.S. escalation of the Vietnam War, further stimulated military interest in the tropics. The TTC brought together a number of disparate activities that had tested equipment under jungle conditions throughout the 1950s.[92]

Colonel Pedro Florcruz, brought to Panama from the Defense Atomic Support Agency in 1964, established the TTC as a full-fledged research-and-development organization. Florcruz approached the Canal Zone governor, Major General Robert Fleming, who made available to him all lands in the Canal Zone that had not been licensed. The Navy also gave the TTC some lands. "It was virgin forest, so we could test without worrying about safety," Florcruz said. In all, the TTC used fifty-five sites, all but one (Rio Hato) in the Canal Zone.[93]

Documents show at least four tests in Panama with live chemical munitions from 1964 to 1968 (VX gas mines, rockets and projectiles, and sarin rockets).[94] The tests were part of a range of tests under arctic, temperate, desert, and tropical conditions to which chemical munitions were usually subjected.[95] Some tests in 1964-68, known as "environmental tests," involved subjecting munitions or equipment to specific environmental conditions (usually tropic, desert, arctic, or temperate) for specific periods of time to understand how those climates affect the materials. Environmental tests did not necessarily include firing munitions.

Periodically the TTC staff went out to the Cerro Tigre toxic yard, where most of the chemical munitions were stored, and took samples of the nerve agent to see whether it had been diluted through storage in the tropical heat. Richard Dow, a chemist who participated in nerve-agent tests in Panama in 1965-66, recalled how he and a colleague poured the agent into a five-hundred-gallon tank of decontaminant solution after testing samples from the munitions. All this was consistent with the test plans, some of which Dow had designed. After the solution was agitated for twelve to eighteen hours, it was drained into a gravel pit under the tank. Dow estimated that a hundred pounds of sarin and VX agent were disposed of using that method during the year and a half he was in Panama.[96]

In the case of the VX-filled M-23 mines, the test aimed to "determine the effects of environment on the storage and functioning of the ABC-M23 mine in the climates represented by the Arctic, Desert, Temperate and Tropic Test Sites," according to the test plans. Twenty-four VX mines were shipped to each site in July 1964 after undergoing engineering tests at Dugway Proving Ground. The M23 mine is just five inches high and thirteen inches in diameter, but it carries more than ten pounds of VX agent. Because ten milligrams of VX agent constitutes a lethal dose, each of these VX mines theoretically had enough nerve agent for nearly half a million lethal doses.

The mines were stored outdoors on pallets during the test; storage cycles ranged from thirty days to nearly two years, depending on the "storage cycle" assigned to each mine. Monitoring of the mines during storage included periodic sampling and analysis of VX agent and leak tests. Finally, each mine was detonated, according to TTC veterans.[97]

TTC documents offer mixed evidence on whether the mines were detonated with live agent. But the test participants remember clearly. James McLaughlin was one of a handful of chemical test officers stationed in Panama from 1963 to 1965 responsible for what he described as a "blizzard" of tests. His team blew up the VX mines on the muddy coastline near Fort Kobbe and the Panamanian town of Veracruz. "The seawater would dissipate it," McLaughlin remembered. "See, we went out at low tide. Then, when the tide came in, you might have ten, fifteen feet of water down at the bottom of it." The VX agent in the mines would have hydrolyzed quickly in the water into relatively harmless compounds.

Although an interim report and final report on the VX mine tests both say that agent was drained out before the detonations, McLaughlin is sure that is not the case. McLaughlin's insistence and his account of the TTC's early operations throw suspicion on the written documentation's description. Test results were sometimes altered to meet the expectations of commanding officers. Chemical testers were responsible for a high volume of tests, worked with little supervision, and were under intense pressure to turn out specific results. In one case, the men took samples of nerve agent, each time standing in full rubber suits in the tropical heat. When two attempts did not yield the same results as the Arctic and Desert Test Sites had obtained, the test officers penciled in the numbers the commanding officer wanted, without conducting the test again.[98] The TTC's commander, Colonel Florcruz, confirmed that the warheads were detonated on a site in the Canal Zone: "Some chemical munitions were detonated. Afterward the area would be inspected. And signs were posted."[99]

McLaughlin himself was apparently hit with chemical agent on November 24, 1965. He and another soldier had just arrived at the

Cerro Tigre compound, where chemical weapons were stored. His gas mask was off. Suddenly, he said, "my legs gave out and I grabbed the fence. . . . My legs didn't work right, my eyes didn't work right. . . . Everything gets dark, your pupils constrict." A medic who had worked at Dugway Proving Ground told him that he probably had a cumulative dose of agent rather than a sudden one, which would have killed him. Thirty-six years later, McLaughlin still had spells that he called the "wobblies," which prevented him from driving long distances or on bridges. "From that day on," he said, "it's never gone away. I still get it."[100]

The four nerve agent tests represented only part of the Tropic Test Center's use of chemical agents during the period. The Tropic Test Center also used a site on a firing range in the canal area to test tear gas grenades in 1965, and the military had constructed a chemical test site nearby during the same period.[101] Shipping records show that the United States sent three tons of lethal vx nerve agent in 1964 for testing in Panama — more than three times what was needed for tests conducted by the Tropic Test Center between 1964 and 1968.[102] TTC officers test fired M55 rockets filled with a simulant for sarin gas into the ocean from a beach site near San Lorenzo, an old Spanish fort on the Atlantic coast.[103]

The Army also continued to use live gas in troop training, including in what was known as the "mustard confidence test." This consisted of putting a small drop on soldiers' forearms to show them what mustard gas could do. The mustard was kept, together with canisters of phosgene and AC gas, at Cerro Tigre. Once, Dow and a coworker were instructed to prepare a sample of mustard. Pressure had built up in the canister, and when Dow inverted it to pour out a sample, "the canister started to sputter and spit," Dow said. His partner, who was not wearing rubber boots, moved away, but liquid landed on his boot and then disappeared. "Around mealtime in the afternoon, my friend began to experience a burning pain in his foot and removed his shoe to find the top of his foot had turned white from exposure to the agent." The man spent two weeks in an Army hospital waiting for a blister that held a quart of liquid to heal.[104]

In another test, troops wearing gas masks and treated fatigue jackets and pants hiked through clouds of live tear gas. A sergeant asked for volunteers, promising weekend passes, which was "better than cleaning latrines which was the fate of the non-volunteer," said John Ronco, a test participant who was stationed in Panama from 1966 to 1968. The men had to put what looked like charcoal packets in their boots. "I could feel the burning," said Ronco about the ten-mile march through gas, then "smoke and something strange." The packet in his boot broke, leaving a deep blister and — years later — a tumor in his heel. "After three surgeries on my neck, groin, and heel I'm a little angry with the military," he wrote.[105]

According to Florcruz, there was a small burial site for chemical waste in the Canal Zone, located on the Pacific and eastern side of the canal. "Those items would just deteriorate and be part of the soil," Florcruz believed. The site was remote and double-fenced and unlikely to be breached by intruders, he said. McLaughlin heard about a different site — a dense marshy ravine on Cerro Tigre "where no one goes in on a bet," in which he and co-workers believed 155-millimeter chemical shells had been dumped. A number of the shells were missing from storage, he said.[106]

The TTC's experiments with lethal chemical weapons were conducted without Panama's knowledge and prompted special security requirements. During the four-day riots in Panama City and Colón in January 1964, during which Panamanians and U.S. soldiers were killed and Panama severed diplomatic relations with Washington, the Army moved chemical munitions from Cerro Tigre to a more secure location in Corozal until the unrest ended. McLaughlin said that he and others filled converted flame-throwers with CS gas, a crowd-control agent, for use by troops against Panamanians.[107]

In about August 1968, Army headquarters ordered a worldwide moratorium on chemical weapons tests, according to Roy Blades, a TTC project manager hired to review documents of the tests. Blades said that when the TTC expedited the order, some chemical items were burned in fifty-five-gallon drums, while others were encased in concrete and buried at sea.[108] The TTC still had twenty-seven sarin and VX warheads on hand, so they were placed in fifty-five-gallon drums that were filled with concrete and dumped at sea off Panama's Azuero peninsula.[109]

In November 1969, Congress prohibited deployment, storage, and disposal of lethal chemical and biological agents outside the United States unless the host country was first notified. For overseas locations under U.S. jurisdiction, the law required prior notice to Congress.[110] But some testimony indicates that live lethal-agent tests were conducted in Panama anyway.

In 1971, Dr. Erimsky Sucre was on his way home from a visit to patients when he and his assistants felt strange. Driving their jeep on a remote Panamanian road with the windows open to the humid air, they passed the Empire range and began to have trouble breathing. It was "a sensation of lack of oxygen," said Sucre, a medical doctor, that reminded him of carbon-monoxide poisoning. He stopped the jeep, unable to drive, and saw a U.S. soldier with his gas mask on. The soldier, a Puerto Rican, took off his mask and told the group not to drink water. As their asphyxia passed, Sucre felt a burning on his face that lasted another hour. He knew it was not tear gas, he said, because he had experienced tear gas in street protests.[111]

WEAPONS RESEARCH MEETS DISEASE RESEARCH

In the 1950s, the Gorgas Memorial Laboratory spun off a new biological-research organization, the Middle America Research Unit (MARU), which studied diseases that had dual civilian and military applications. MARU "handled some of the deadliest and most infectious diseases known to medicine at the time," according to Carl J. Peters, a scientist who worked there in the 1960s. Peters emphasized the measures taken to contain the agents that the MARU technicians were working on but noted that one lab technician accidentally contracted Bolivian hemorrhagic fever at the lab and died within a few days.

One disease in particular that MARU worked with was Venezuelan Equine Encephalitis (VEE), a naturally occurring virus that incapacitates but generally does not kill its human victims. Instead, VEE begins abruptly with high fever, chills and aches, and an intense aversion to light, then typically is gone within a week or two. In Central America in the 1960s, VEE attacked horses and mules, leaving many dead, and MARU sought to stem the disease's migration toward the United States through development of a vaccine. But, Peters wrote,

> Nobler designs aside, the U.S. government had other reasons to be interested in VEE. The symptoms in humans are so incapacitating that VEE had been seen as a potential biological weapon. The army wanted to develop different categories of biological warfare agents: incapacitators as well as killers.

With a relatively short incubation period of two to three days, VEE could be an ideal incapacitator: neutralizing an enemy population right before a battle without risk of killing innocent civilians or committing wartime atrocities. With that as a plan, the army had developed a vaccine to protect our troops in case an enemy tried to use it on them, or presumably in case the wind blew the wrong way the day they tried to use it on someone else.[112]

Exercises to test the military usefulness of VEE were carried out in Vietnam in the 1960s and on deserted islands in the Pacific, but they were put aside because allied troops could not be protected.[113]

The Army authorized MARU to test a live-attenuated vaccine on horses in the field, and Peters has described such tests on Costa Rica's Pacific coast. The Gorgas Laboratory also studied VEE among humans in rural areas from 1960 to 1962 and in both rural and urban communities in 1968, as well as in laboratory animals during the same periods. The studies included testing live vaccines of VEE on animal subjects.[114]

VEE persisted for long periods in Panama. Troops training at Fort Sherman in 1981 contracted it, an exposure that was linked to VEE when the military was actively experimenting with the virus in 1970. The Walter Reed Army Institute of Research reported: "Exposure was linked to training in October in an area of Fort Sherman that was previously implicated over ten years ago. An intensive serological survey identified five cases presenting with fever, chills and headaches."[115]

Biological agents could have more direct military applications, as well. News accounts in 1977 cited intelligence sources who claimed that in 1971 U.S. intelligence agents brought Swine flu from Fort Gulick (which then hosted the U.S. Army School of the Americas) in Panama to Cuba, where the flu apparently contaminated a large number of pigs. The United Nations Food and Agriculture Organization called the epidemic of swine flu that hit Cuba in 1971 the "most alarming event" of that year. According to the accounts, an intelligence agent was given a sealed, unmarked container and instructed to deliver it to an anti-Castro group in Panama. Cuban exiles interviewed for the report said that they received the container off Bocas del Toro in Panama and took it to contacts on the small island of Navassa, from which it was shipped to Cuba in late March 1971. The first Cuban pigs contracted the flu around May 6.[116] Cuban authorities slaughtered half a million pigs to contain the epidemic.[117]

In 1972, the United States became one of the first parties to the

Biological Weapons Convention, which outlawed efforts to "develop, produce, stockpile, or otherwise acquire or retain" biological weapons. The U.S. military subsequently converted stockpiled biological agents into harmless fertilizer.

AGENT ORANGE

Shortly after the documentary record for the TTC's nerve-agent tests ends in 1968, the Army began to use another toxic agent in Panama: Agent Orange. A veteran who took his medical claim to the Veterans Administration wrote that he saw U.S. Special Forces drop Agent Orange on Fort Sherman in 1969 or 1970 and "watched the jungle disappear over the next few days." The veteran, an Army engineer whose duty was to take water samples, also found high levels of Agent Orange in coral reefs on the Pacific side of the canal. Gatun Lake, where he witnessed the spraying, spills out of the canal into the Pacific reefs. In 1999, he was suffering from peripheral neuropathy, a disease common among veterans exposed to Agent Orange.[118]

In 1999, Pamela Jones, the widow of another Army veteran who had served in Panama, was awarded benefits by the Veterans Administration because of her husband's exposure to Agent Orange in Panama in the early 1970s. At Jones's benefits hearing, Charles Bartlett, the former head of the government's Agent Orange litigation project, testified that several hundred barrels of Agent Orange had been shipped to Panama in the mid-1960s for tests. After the tests, he said, the barrels remained in Panama for use in controlling weeds. Jones's husband developed severe acne on his back and face within days of his exposure and later died of non-Hodgkins lymphoma, another disease typical among those exposed to Agent Orange.[119]

At least nine witnesses confirmed that the military had sprayed heavily with Agent Orange in an area of Fort Sherman known as the "drop zone" in the late 1960s and early 1970s. The "drop zone" is located near a popular beach, recreation center, and sporting club on the shores of Gatun Lake. The revelation was important because it established that Southeast Asia was not the only place the United States exposed soldiers, and perhaps others, to Agent Orange. Until Jones won her claim, the Veterans Administration had institutionalized Agent Orange-related benefits for those who fought in Vietnam but excluded others from consideration for such benefits.[120]

According to Raul Duany, spokesman for the U.S. Southern Command, if Agent Orange was sprayed, "it wouldn't pose a threat today because it should have dissipated by now." However, the dioxin in most Agent Orange—the toxin that causes disease—remains in the soil for decades. The retired officer who ordered the use of Agent Orange in Vietnam as a defoliant contradicted Duany's claim. "It does not dissipate," said Admiral Elmo R. Zumwalt Jr. "If it's true that Agent Orange was tested in Panama, it is clear that the spokesman was wrong about the residual stuff."[121]

Army policy required the use of only simulants at chemical test sites after 1980. In the 1980s, chemical activities included tests of gas masks and defensive exercises.[122] However, the military also acknowledged "limited, controlled laboratory testing of some tear gas agents" in Panama after 1979.[123]

By the 1990s, the Army's interest in chemical weapons was focused on herbicides for use in the drug war and defending soldiers against chemical agents. The Tropic Test Center continued to test equipment designed to detect and defend against chemical agents under tropical conditions. "There has been a significant increase over the past two years in testing of this type of equipment," the TTC wrote in July 1997.[124] As we will see, the Army also expended considerable energy to keep records about chemical weapons tests carried out on San Jose Island and in the canal area from coming to light.

3 ☆ THE NUCLEAR CANAL

In the 1950s and 1960s, the United States planned to excavate a sea-level canal in Panama with nuclear explosions. Today, most people find this hard to believe. At the time, it was not secret but part of a series of ideas meant to redeem the splitting atom from its Hiroshima and Cold War legacies. The plan was to set off two hundred fifty to three hundred hydrogen bombs in the Darién region of Panama, near the border with Colombia, with each explosion carrying explosive power between twenty and two thousand times that of the bomb in Hiroshima in order to build a sea-level waterway without locks. The project would displace forty thousand people, mostly Kuna Indians for whom the area was their homeland; shatter windows up to five hundred miles away; and possibly cause damage to the existing canal from earth slides.

The episode illustrates how tropical Panama was a target of opportunity for scientists intent on completely transforming the environment to fulfill U.S. strategic aims — largely oblivious to the cost to the tropics' resident life. In the case of Project Plowshare, the federal program for nuclear excavation that sponsored the idea, nuclear engineers would accomplish this transformation in the hostile environment of the tropical isthmus.

U.S. officials and scientists openly and publicly discussed plans for nuclear excavation. Unlike the secret chemical weapons tests the military conducted in Panama, the prospect of a nuclear canal was an object of pride. Until political and technical obstacles got in the way, the nuclear canal represented a hope that both the terror of nuclear blasts and the remaining wilds of a savage jungle could be transformed through sophisticated technology into a new pathway for civilization. But despite tens of millions of dollars and fourteen years spent determining the feasibility of a nuclear-excavated canal in Panama or Colombia, the Interoceanic Canal Study Commission concluded in December 1970 that nuclear excavation was not viable. Lacking the cost advantage of the nuclear canal, no sea-level canal route or construction method was cost-competitive. The idea was quietly buried.

Several broader social and political projects converged in the effort to build an isthmian nuclear canal. First, after World War II the Panama Canal Company concluded that a new sea-level canal would be needed both to protect against the possibility of a surprise attack with atomic weapons and to keep pace with the growth of shipping traffic through the canal. A sea-level canal, the company and military officers reasoned, could recover more quickly than a lock canal from an enemy military attack and could accommodate more and wider ships, as well as aircraft carriers being built for the Navy.

The second project was the advent of the "peaceful atom" — specifically, the attempt to apply nuclear explosives to industrial and civil uses. Nuclear scientists, working in offices far from the tropical isthmus, conceived of engineering projects that would use the power of nuclear explosives to strengthen the United States' economic position and help sustain the record levels of consumption seen in the post–World War II era. Their ideas ranged from nuclear-excavated harbors to the "liberation" of natural gas through atomic explosions, and were part of Project Plowshare, under the aegis of the Atomic Energy Commission (AEC). The first underground hydrogen-bomb test in 1957 further stimulated the project, giving rise to an entire scientific subindustry known as "nuclear cratering."

Project Plowshare was conceived at a time of overarching optimism about the positive power of atomic energy. In addition to using "peaceful nuclear explosions" for excavation, natural gas and oil production, and mining, the United States planned in 1957 to build hundreds of reactors for electricity generation, to use irradiation as a pesticide and a food preservative, and to power merchant ships. Many of the men who drove these "Peaceful Atom" programs had worked on the Manhattan Project. "The opportunity to turn the menacing technology of nuclear explosions into something so beneficial was irresistible, especially for those of us who had worked in the wartime atomic bomb project," wrote Glenn Seaborg, chairman of the AEC.[1] In the end, no industrial uses were found for nuclear bombs, and Project Plowshare died from falling on its own sword.

These two projects came together in the idea to excavate a sea-level canal on the Central American isthmus using nuclear explosives. The attraction of the idea from the start was that it was cheap — about one-third the cost of conventional excavation. Because soil was ejected during the explosion, it did not have to be removed by men with machines.

A third social-political project eventually collided with the nuclear-canal idea, however: environmental consciousness. This took form in the late 1950s in the movement to stop atmospheric nuclear tests, culminating in the Limited Test Ban Treaty ratified in October 1963. The environmental movement continued through the 1960s, turning its attention to radiation generated by commercial nuclear power. The development of Project Plowshare also coincided with the negotiation of two other major nuclear-arms–control treaties: the Non-Proliferation Treaty and the Treaty of Tlateloco, banning nuclear weapons in Latin America. The negotiation of these treaties generated political conditions that were averse to the nuclear-cratering tests necessary to determine the nuclear canal's technical feasibility, especially its seismic implications and geologic stability. Moreover, the Limited Test Ban prohibited any tests that caused radioactive debris to cross national borders. Nuclear excavation in Panama certainly would have sent measurable fallout into neighboring Colombia.

Nuclear excavation of a sea-level canal on the isthmus, however, had also become the driving motor of Project Plowshare. As the chairman of the powerful Joint Committee on Atomic Energy put it in 1965, the nuclear canal was "the one thing that has given this thing life and the one thing that has more or less enthused this committee to provide the money for Plowshare. Once you have ruled that out, I am afraid interest is going to drop off."[2] When the technical and political viability of the nuclear canal could not be demonstrated, Project Plowshare eventually withered.

In addition, the Vietnam War and other events generated widespread distrust of the government in general. The political attrition and logistical demands of the war took their toll on the nuclear-canal pursuit, even though supplies to Southeast Asia were shipped through the canal in large quantities, strengthening the U.S. military's rationale for constructing a canal with greater shipping capacity.[3] Simultaneous with the psychologically traumatic defeat of the United States by a sophisticated peasant army in Vietnam, the U.S. military was forced to concede an inability to overcome the engineering and political obstacles to a sea-level canal.

Finally, especially after riots in Panama City and Colón in January 1964 and in 1966, Panamanians increasingly sought sovereignty over the Canal Zone and all of the isthmus. For the United States, managing relations with Panama became increasingly difficult as a result. One of the virtues of a sea-level canal, from a management perspective, was that it reduced the number of humans needed to construct, operate and defend the canal — and thus reduced the problems associated with dealing with Panamanians.

Panama wanted control over any new canal and was less willing to bear the risks of a construction project controlled by the United States. Such a sea-level canal would have made the United States' long-term presence in Panama feasible. Without it, the canal increasingly became a liability in Cold War politics. And without direct U.S. control of the canal, military bases on its banks were becoming less politically viable. The nuclear canal project's collapse thus set the stage for the United States' eventual withdrawal from Panama.

THE DREAM OF A SEA-LEVEL CANAL

The French made the first attempt to build a sea-level canal in Panama from 1880 to 1889. The project was undertaken by Ferdinand de Lesseps, the engineer who had succeeded at Suez, but was ultimately overcome by a combination of disease, financial mismanagement, and the challenges of the sea-level design itself. When the United States took over the canal works in early 1904, the first Isthmian Canal Commission's plan was to create a sea-level waterway modeled on the Suez Canal, which had been built in a dramatically different terrain and climate. It was not until the second canal engineer, John F. Stevens, piloted the lock-canal idea through the politically treacherous waters of Washington, D.C., in 1906 that the plan for a sea-level canal was abandoned.[4]

The idea of a sea-level canal was revived periodically, but it was typically dismissed as too expensive or unworkable. A third set of locks appeared to be a more feasible option and would meet many of the same needs for increased traffic, defensibility, and size to accommodate the largest Navy ships. A Congressionally funded study of new canal locks led to actual dredging in 1939, but the effort was suspended in May 1942 amid other demands of the war and suspension of programs for larger battleships, for which the new locks were designed.[5]

The development of long-range air power and nuclear weapons led Army and Navy officials to conclude that the lock canal could not be defended against a determined modern attacker. A new sea-level canal would be easier to defend and less expensive to operate than a locked canal. And abandonment of the third locks project spurred advocates of a sea-level canal. Studies mandated by Congress and completed in 1947 examined thirty routes, from Ecuador to Mexico. The studies discarded all but eight of the routes as impractical and found that a sea-level canal in the Darién region bordering Colombia — known as Route 17 — would cost $5.1 billion dollars. Nevertheless, as late as October 1956, the Joint Chiefs of Staff concluded that though it was desirable militarily, construction of a sea-level canal was not politically feasible.[6]

NUCLEAR CONCEPTION

The Suez Canal crisis of November 1956 prompted nuclear scientists to think about excavating a second sea-level canal at Suez using nuclear explosives, which could provide a technical solution to the political impasse created by Egypt's bid to nationalize the waterway. Edward Teller, who is often called the "father" of the hydrogen bomb and who became the political protector of Project Plowshare, called the Suez crisis the "political trigger" for the nuclear-canal project. The advent of fusion bombs, which produced a smaller percentage of radioactive byproducts, also stimulated nuclear scientists to explore the potential of nuclear excavation, as well as a variety of other industrial applications.[7]

The same month that the Suez Canal's closure generated political interest in alternative canals, a specialist in high-explosive cratering at the Sandia Laboratory in Albuquerque — which, like Livermore, was under contract with the AEC — produced a classified study "Earth Moving with Nuclear Explosives." The scientist, Luke Vortman, had been intrigued by a Canadian project that used explosives to remove a hazardous rock in the middle of a navigation channel. His paper explored the use of nuclear explosives to excavate three routes across the isthmus: Sasardi in Darién, Panama, and Rio Truando and Cupica in northern Colombia. Vortman calculated that nuclear excavation of a sea-level canal along Route 17 in the Darién would offer $1.74 billion in savings compared with conventional excavation methods.[8]

In the summer of 1956, Harold Brown, director of Livermore Laboratory, had written to the AEC proposing to study a broad range of projects that would use nuclear-bomb explosions for industrial purposes. At the classified conference, held on the lab's premises on February 6–8, 1957, twenty-four scientists presented papers on how "clean" hydrogen bombs could open the way for earth-moving projects such as canals and harbors, underground production of power, use of thermal energy generated by nuclear explosions to produce electricity, and breeding new isotopes that could be used for bombs or other uses. In his keynote address, Teller was enthusiastic about the opportunities created by less radioactive explosives: research, mining of oil, "digging canals, making harbors, or removing obstacles" to navigation. Vortman's paper on nuclear excavation of an isthmian canal, presented at the symposium, caught the attention of many participants.[9]

The first underground nuclear-explosive test, conducted in September 1957 and dubbed "RAINIER," spurred debate among scientists about verification of underground atomic tests using seismographic equipment.[10] The test had been motivated by a desire to prevent delays brought about by unfavorable winds for above-ground tests, which, according to the test director, Gerald Johnson, made that approach "costly [and] inefficient and tended to be dramatic with all its adverse public reactions."[11] But RAINIER also stimulated interest among nuclear scientists and AEC officials in a wide range of industrial uses of nuclear explosions. "The results from the RAINIER test gave the Plowshare Project a tremendous boost of enthusiasm," according to Milo Nordyke, a scientist at Livermore who later directed the lab's studies of nuclear cratering. "Before RAINIER, all the ideas for peaceful uses were based on theoretical conjecture. . . . RAINIER validated many of the concepts that had been only sketchy ideas in scientists' minds."[12]

Independent of the AEC investigations, in mid-1958 the Canal Company contracted the San Francisco engineering firm of Parsons, Brinckerhoff, Hall, and MacDonald to do a study of a third set of locks for the existing canal as well as a new sea-level canal across the isthmus. Parsons, Brinckerhoff heard in the press about the AEC's Project Plowshare, especially the plan to excavate a harbor in Alaska with nuclear explosives known as Project CHARIOT.[13]

The Canal Company authorized the engineers to meet with the AEC. During their meeting with Commissioner Willard Libby on July 10, 1958, Libby said that nuclear excavation would require evacuating people up to five miles from the explosions and a buffer of twenty-five miles from large towns and cities, thus disqualifying the current Canal Zone route from consideration for nuclear excavation. The AEC passed Vortman's paper to the engineers and made Gerald Johnson, an associate director at Livermore Lab, the key contact for canal studies. Livermore scientists, working with Vortman, carried out the nuclear study for the Parsons, Brinckerhoff report, which was completed in February 1959.[14]

In the meantime, President Eisenhower ordered a moratorium on atmospheric nuclear-weapons tests beginning November 1, 1958, which was to last three years. The canal engineers and scientists were forced to pursue the nuclear canal through theoretical desk studies and experiments with conventional explosives. Eisenhower does not appear to have intended to stymie canal studies, and he directed the army to incorporate the nuclear approach in engineering studies of the construction of a new sea-level canal.[15] In June 1959, he also approved an agreement with Panama for cooperation on research in industrial uses of atomic energy.[16]

But both atmospheric tests and canal relations with Panama were becoming increasingly sensitive, and Eisenhower was not ready to go public with the initiative: A press statement about his directive was scrapped, and the Canal Zone's governor was ordered not to talk about the nuclear plans in open Congressional hearings.[17] Instead, the State Department agreed in July to study the international complications of nuclear canal excavation, believing that negotiations with Panama for permission to carry out the project "could be further complicated by communistically-inclined propaganda sources."[18] The officials were referring to increasingly militant demonstrations against the U.S. canal enclave, including protests in November 1959 that resulted in U.S. troops injuring forty Panamanians.[19]

The Canal Company meanwhile was proceeding with its own studies. The result of its collaboration with the Livermore Lab was "Isthmian Canal Plans — 1960," which looked at five routes: Tehuantepec in Mexico; Greytown-Salinas Bay in Nicaragua; the San Blas route forty miles east of the existing canal; the Sasardi-Morti route in Panama's Darién; and Atrato-Truando in northern Colombia (see map 2). "In view of the distinct economic and operating advantages," the study concluded, "it is recommended that first priority be given to a sea-level canal excavated by nuclear methods, and that second priority be given to a sea-level canal constructed in the Canal Zone by conventional methods."[20]

The study found that the cost of nuclear excavation of all of the

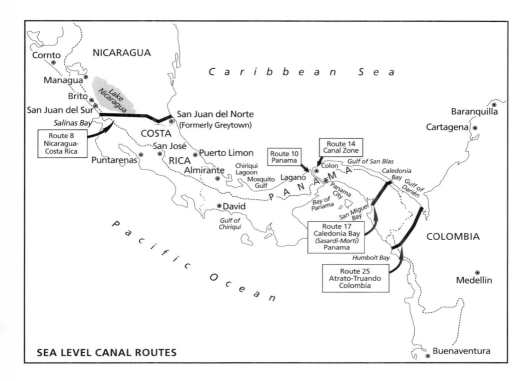

SEA LEVEL CANAL ROUTES

Map 2. Principal proposed routes for a sea-level isthmian canal. (U.S. House of
Representatives, *Fifth Annual Report of the Atlantic–Pacific Interoceanic Canal
Study Commission.*

routes would be several orders lower than that by conventional excavation, and expressed a strong preference for a Panama route.[21] For
Route 17 in Panama's Darién, known as the Sasardi-Morti Route, for
example, the engineers estimated an engineering and construction cost
of $750 million. For Route 25, along Colombia's Atrato River, the cost
was estimated at $1.225 billion. These estimates became the basis of
public and official discussion of a possible second isthmian canal for
the next ten years.[22]

Eisenhower's cabinet approved the study's recommendations to explore nuclear excavation and sea-level routes in Panama, Colombia,
Mexico, and Nicaragua on April 29, and the National Security Council subsequently became "seized of the entire Isthmian Canal problem." The study was classified.[23]

A board mandated by Congress to study the canal's long-term needs was reaching some of the same conclusions. The board focused on projections of ship traffic through the canal and the costs of various plans, but did so without the benefit of the Livermore studies of nuclear excavation. Thus, the least expensive option for a sea-level canal of which the panel was aware was a route in the Canal Zone projected to cost $2.287 billion (see table 3). Based on predictions of canal traffic through the year 2000, the panel concluded that "a sea-level canal cannot be justified economically in the near future unless it can be built much more cheaply than under any plan so far proposed. As of now, the only hope for an economically justifiable sea-level canal appears to be excavation through as yet unproven nuclear means."[24]

In December 1960, the National Security Council recommended going forward with the nuclear-excavated canal while acknowledging that nuclear cratering would not be feasible within fifty miles of a densely populated area. Eisenhower adopted a policy to develop nuclear explosives for excavation "as consistent with U.S. nuclear testing policy," and investigate "the physical, biological and psychological effects of nuclear explosives under conditions to be encountered at the canal site."[25] With the results of their study given political legitimacy by the White House, officers in the Army Corps of Engineers and scientists from the Livermore Lab began to put into place institutional supports for a nuclear-excavated canal.

In April 1962, President John Kennedy ordered a five-year technical and economic investigation into the construction of a sea-level canal to determine "the feasibility, costs and other factors involved in various methods of excavation." The technical studies were to be carried out jointly by the AEC and the Department of Defense. The Army was to submit a funding request to Congress for field studies of canal routes, "including at least one in Panama and one in Colombia." The Army Corps of Engineers created a Nuclear Cratering Group that worked directly with Livermore Lab scientists on the studies.[26] The AEC carried out the first atomic test for nuclear cratering, known as "Sedan," on July 6, 1962, at the Nevada Test Site. The Sedan explosion was a one-hundred–kiloton shot, or eight times the explosive power of the atomic bomb dropped on Hiroshima, and gave engineers the first empirical evidence on nuclear cratering's feasibility.

With this much optimism on the technical front, the Army also moved to ensure that other agencies would have the political nerve for the project. It asked the State Department to examine the international

Table 3. Nuclear canal economics (construction-cost estimates for sea-level canal)

Route	Length (miles)	Maximum elevation (feet)	1947 estimated costs (millions)	1960 estimated costs (nuclear) (millions)
Route 1: Mexico (Tehuantepec)	125	810	$13,000	$2,300
Route 8: Nicaragua (Greytown-Salinas Bay)	140	760	$4,100	$1,900
Route 14: Panama (Canal Zone)	46	—	$2,483	$2,287
Route 16: Panama (San Blas)	37	1,000	$6,200	$620
Route 17: Panama (Sasardi-Morti)	46	1,100	$5,132	$770
Route 25: Colombia (Atrato-Truando)	102	950	$5,261	$1,200

(John W. Finney, "A Second Canal?" [*New Republic*, March 28, 1964]; House Committee on Merchant Marine and Fisheries, "Report on a Long-Range Program for Isthmian Canal Transits," [H.R. 1960].)

complications that would result from using nuclear explosives for the canal. Similarly, and with prescience about the project's political obstacles that he must have rued later, Teller told Kennedy in December 1962 that the technical studies for a nuclear-excavated canal "will take less time than it will take you to make the right political decision."[27]

In January 1963, Representative Herbert C. Bonner, who had chaired a study of the canal's long-range needs in 1960, introduced legislation to authorize the Canal Company and the AEC to conduct on-site surveys to permit site selection for construction of a possible new sea-level canal.[28] Only days later, the Canal Company's Army engineers received news of a freeze on nuclear shots at the Nevada Test Site — shots that were critical to establishing the project's technical viability. The freeze "would appear to complicate our picture," an Army officer wrote to the Nuclear Cratering Group at Livermore. As another Army engineer central to the project wrote, "Overcoming the political problems [of Plowshare] is going to be a long, slow process."[29]

By April, when a "reconnaissance" team of fourteen scientists and

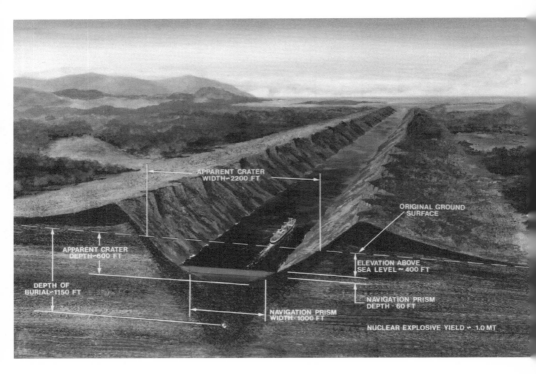

ORIGINAL GROUND SURFACE

APPARENT CRATER WIDTH~2200 FT

APPARENT CRATER DEPTH~600 FT

DEPTH OF BURIAL~1150 FT

ELEVATION ABOVE SEA LEVEL ~ 400 FT

NAVIGATION PRISM DEPTH · 60 FT

NAVIGATION PRISM WIDTH~1000 FT

NUCLEAR EXPLOSIVE YIELD ~ 1.0 MT

8. Nuclear-excavated canal: Army engineers and scientists at Livermore Laboratory believed that a sea-level isthmian canal could be constructed using 275 nuclear explosions for one-third the cost of excavation through conventional means. (Archives, Lawrence Livermore National Laboratory.)

engineers from the AEC, the atomic labs, and contractors visited Panama, plans for a field study in the Darién and in Colombia were already well advanced. The plans ranged from radiological safety to a "medico-ecological study," which aimed "to study the primitive people (Cuna Indians) of the region before they are influenced by the incoming civilization associated with the proposed isthmian highway." The team also included in its findings concerns about the effects of air blast from nuclear explosions, as increased use of air conditioning and enclosed buildings would soon "make Panama vulnerable to the same 2-millibar blast overpressures which are safety limiting for larger U.S. towns and cities."[30]

But four months later, on August 5, Washington signed the Limited

Test Ban Treaty, which changed the political and legal context for Plowshare. The treaty prohibited any nuclear test that "causes radioactive debris to be present outside the territorial limits of the State under whose jurisdiction or control such explosion is conducted." The commitment caught canal officials by surprise and angered Panamanian representatives, who had not been consulted about the United States' becoming party to the treaty. Panamanians, who tend to see treaties as literally binding, reportedly felt betrayed.[31]

AEC Commissioner Glenn Seaborg had testified to Congress that the treaty need not affect Plowshare experiments within the United States, hinting that the Soviets — who had their own program for industrial uses of nuclear explosives — would be amenable to an exception to the provision against radioactivity crossing borders. In so testifying, Seaborg finessed the question of whether Plowshare would be prohibited by the treaty in the hope that, if enough international enthusiasm for nuclear excavation were generated, a revision of the test ban would be possible.[32]

Even as the test ban threw a host of doubts onto the viability of a nuclear canal, scientists at Livermore fed the excitement of Panama Canal Zone Governor Robert Fleming in late 1963 with cost estimates for a nuclear-excavated canal as low as $400 million, saving nearly half the cost indicated by the 1960 study.[33] Events in the Canal Zone would soon make negotiations for a new arrangement between the United States and Panama — for both the existing canal and a newly excavated one — dramatically more urgent.

CANAL STUDY COMMISSION: A RESPONSE TO CRISIS

Panamanian demands for a fundamental revision of the 1903 agreement were also affecting U.S. considerations of the uses of a sea-level canal, beyond questions of cost, width of ships, or vulnerability to sabotage. A sea-level canal would require a workforce for operations and maintenance only one-tenth the size of that needed for the existing canal, with its troublesome neighboring populations. And in the event that negotiations led to a reduced U.S. military presence in the Zone, military bases serving U.S. hemispheric policy interests (such as the training of Latin armies at the School of the Americas) could be moved away from the Panamanian agitators in Panama City and Colón. The prospect of construction of a sea-level canal outside Panama, moreover, would give U.S. negotiators greater leverage in responding to Panamanian demands for treaty revision. In other words, a sea-level canal apparently allowed the United States to solve not only problems of canal-traffic capacity but also long-term political and military problems as well.

Between 1959 and 1964, U.S. policy toward Latin America as a whole was dominated by fears, inspired by the Cuban revolution, that the region would slip out of Washington's hegemonic control. Simultaneously at home, people who looked much like Panamanians were upsetting the violent balance of segregation in the South. By the end of 1963, news outlets around the world for years had been showing young people of color taking direct action for civil rights in the United States, culminating in the massive march on Washington in August 1963. The movement had met with state violence in Birmingham, where police clubbed protesters and a church bombing left four girls dead in October 1963. A month later, President Kennedy was assassinated in Dallas. This was the turbulent context in which the most severe crisis in U.S–Panama relations to date erupted in January 1964.

As a concession to growing nationalism in Panama, Kennedy and his vice president, Lyndon Johnson, had developed a policy initiated by Eisenhower that allowed the Panamanian and U.S. flags to be flown together at selected locations in the Canal Zone. At Balboa High School, a resistant administration flew neither flag, and U.S. students responded by raising the U.S. flag on January 9, then surrounding the flagpole. Students from Panama's National Institute marched to the school, Panamanian flag in hand. Details of the resulting standoff were disputed, but after the Panamanians' flag was torn, the confrontation that began that afternoon exploded. Twenty-four Panamanians and four U.S. soldiers were killed during four days of street fighting. Rioters burned the buildings of the U.S. Information Agency, the PanAm and Braniff airlines, and the Goodyear and Firestone tire plants. Panama's President Roberto Chiari broke off diplomatic relations with the United States and demanded that the two countries renegotiate the 1903 canal treaty.

President Johnson sent Thomas Mann, a fellow Texan and blunt talker, to Panama for discussions. The United States insisted that no treaty talks could take place under the threat of force, but Mann returned empty-handed. "We could not solve the dangerous situation which now exists unless we came up with a long-range plan to satisfy

Panamanian demands," he insisted in his report to Johnson. Mann's solution was to negotiate with Colombia and Nicaragua to allow a sea-level canal across their territories. Washington could then go back to the Panamanians, who would "be prepared to make a satisfactory deal with us."[34]

The flag riots certainly set in motion a long-term planning process but on a much bigger scale and on different terms than Mann envisioned. The two countries reestablished diplomatic relations in April and agreed to talks "to seek the prompt elimination of the causes of conflict between the two countries without limitations or preconditions of any kind." Johnson appointed Robert Anderson, another Texan and a former Treasury Secretary, to lead the U.S. negotiating team.[35]

Johnson's main impediment to reaching agreement with Panama was a domestic U.S. constituency that saw the Canal Zone as integral to U.S. identity. But after he won a landslide electoral victory in November, the way was cleared to address the fundamental conflict: sovereignty over the Canal Zone. In December, following a recommendation from Anderson and fearful of trouble in Panama on the first anniversary of the riots, Johnson made a decisive announcement. The United States would enter negotiations for "an entirely new treaty on the existing Panama Canal" and, at the same time, would press forward with Panama "and other interested governments [for] plans and preparations for a sea-level canal."[36]

In September, Congress had finally authorized $17.5 million for a comprehensive exploration of sea-level–canal construction, including site studies in Panama and Colombia. The legislation established the Atlantic–Pacific Interoceanic Canal Study Commission, which would carry out the most sustained study of a nuclear-excavated canal. President Johnson appointed Anderson to chair the commission as well as lead negotiations with Panama. The canal study commission's work was coordinated by an Army colonel and West Point graduate named John Sheffey and covered a vast range of disciplines. "The investigation involves the most complicated combination of political, military, economic and technical problems imaginable," Sheffey wrote to a friend, "but it is at the same time the most interesting work I have ever done."[37]

The field studies, authorized by a secret exchange of notes between Panama's Foreign Minister Fernando Eleta and U.S. Ambassador Charles Adair on February 15, 1966, began formally the following month and involved thirteen federal agencies (six of them military) and twenty-seven principal contractors.[38] The number of Canal Commission personnel in the Darién eventually reached 170.[39]

An early but unheeded voice of realism during this time was that of James H. Stratton, an Army colonel who had coordinated many of the 1947 studies. He pointed out that the infrastructure and military development needed on any route remote from population centers would bring the costs of a nuclear-excavated canal to roughly the same as those projected for converting the lock canal to sea level. In an essay published in the influential journal *Foreign Affairs*, Stratton cited AEC Chairman Seaborg's estimate that the program to develop nuclear-excavation technology would cost $250 million, and said, "At least part of this cost should be considered a charge against a sea-level canal." Stratton's critique of the "dubious savings" to be realized from nuclear excavation represented a minority and prescient voice.[40]

The nuclear-canal studies focused on four problems of nuclear excavation that worried engineers: radiation, air-blast effects, ground shock, and slope stability. The National Security Council's 1960 objective of studying nuclear excavation's psychological effects was largely ignored. The engineers quickly discarded the Mexican and Nicaraguan routes because conventional excavation was prohibitively expensive and nuclear excavation would expose large populations to radiation and other effects. Consistent with Mann's idea of using other routes to pressure Panama into accepting a treaty that was more acceptable to Washington, the commission did not publicize this dismissal of routes in Mexico and Nicaragua, while extensive field studies for nuclear excavation were undertaken in Colombia near the Panamanian border.

RADIATION AND NUCLEARIZATION

Livermore scientists calculated that nuclear excavation would still need to occur fifty miles or more from populated areas and that the people living in that range would need to be evacuated for their safety. The canal studies also examined secondary effects of nuclear excavation, in addition to direct human exposure — that is, of radioactivity carried to other parts of the world via animals serving as food; radioactive contamination of the environment generally, both land and water; the social consequences of relocating native people; the risks of disease resulting from environmental changes produced by the project; and predicting the economic consequences of those environmental changes.[41]

To determine how far from the nuclear shots radioactive materials would travel, the commission measured wind and rainfall rates. In 1964, construction plans called for evacuation of only part of the Pearl Islands for just two months. By the end of the canal studies, the exclusion area extended to most of the Kuna *comarca* (territorial) islands as well as all of the Pearl Islands on the Pacific. A report by the Oak Ridge National Laboratory eventually concluded that a "definitive assessment of radiological safety is not possible" for nuclear excavation of a sea-level canal. The report also noted that radioactive debris trapped below ground could be flushed out in time, and that there was no effective solution to this possible problem.[42]

The nuclear scientists were undaunted. The initial promise offered by underground nuclear tests, in their view, was the great reduction in release of radioactivity into the atmosphere relative to the earlier open-air shots. Further, the fascination with atomic power extended beyond excavation to means for providing power to the excavation project. G. Corry McDonald, an engineer based at Sandia Corporation in New Mexico, published a proposal to use the government's surplus nuclear-power plants to provide power for the construction project. McDonald calculated that the cost of transporting reactors would be lower than even the bill for shipping diesel fuel for conventional power generators. He also asserted that nuclear reactors would provide permanent illumination to the canal after construction.[43]

Army engineers had an opportunity to test the thesis when a floating nuclear power plant, called the *Sturgis*, was towed from Virginia to Gatun Lake in the Canal Zone in July 1968. The aim of using the reactor was to alleviate pressure on the need for electrical power provided by canal waters to Panama, so that more water would be available for ship passages, thus extending the capacity of the existing canal. Because water reserves were one limitation on the number of ships that could pass through the canal, *Sturgis* could delay the need for a new, sea-level canal. The portable reactor went on line on October 5, 1968 and provided power to the Army for its ongoing land operations.[44]

The economic feasibility of a sea-level canal in the Darién hinged nearly entirely on the method that would be used to cut through the clay shale soils of the Chucunaque Valley, a twenty-mile stretch on Route 17. If nuclear excavation worked, the canal could be built for close to the optimistic cost estimates the AEC had given. But if those soils gave way to chronic landslides under the destabilizing impact of atomic blasts, then the Chucunaque Valley would have to be excavated using far more costly conventional methods, making the whole project more expensive than was merited by the expected growth in canal traffic.

When the field studies began, the only geological study of soils along Route 17 had been made in 1947 by a geologist named Thomas Thompson. His study was cursory — only eight pages of text — and reached conclusions about the soils that later were shown to be mistaken.[45] In their 1959 desk study, Livermore scientists dismissed the need to take preliminary boring samples along Route 17, claiming that "sinking . . . the holes required to bury the devices will provide all information needed during the progress of the work."[46]

The creation of the Army Corps' Nuclear Cratering Group in 1962 led to increased attention to just how nuclear cratering would work, not only through test shots conducted in the United States by the AEC, but in reconnaissance of the Darién by Army officers. The corps sent Major William Wray, who had been detailed to Livermore for work on nuclear cratering tests in 1961, to Panama in September 1963.[47] Wray began to ask some disquieting questions. "The more I think about the problem of slope stability in the deep cuts we would plan to make," Wray wrote in March 1964, "the more I am concerned about the likelihood of major failures requiring the movement, by conventional equipment, of some rather large quantities of rubble." Writing to his counterpart Lieutenant-Colonel Ernest Graves at Livermore, he pointed out that the detonations of up to thirty-five megatons planned to excavate the Continental Divide would not only damage previous cuts made during excavation, but "would correspond to an earthquake with an intensity of XII (or even worse)" and "would suggest some effects that are not comforting to think about." He concluded, "We must acknowledge the problem and try to place some sort of price tag on this rather special contingency."[48]

Wray put his finger on the engineering problem that would dog proponents of the nuclear canal to the very end. When the field studies began in earnest in 1966, bore holes found soil samples consisting primarily of clay shale along twenty miles of Route 17. In environments as wet as the tropical Darién, clay is highly unstable and subject to frequent slides. The ground's stability would also be undercut by strong currents through the canal and heavy rains. In that circumstance, the side slopes of the canal had to be made much flatter than the slope anticipated from the use of a single row of nuclear-explosive charges.[49]

The military engineers went back to work. In 1968, the Nuclear Cratering Group experimented with one-ton high explosives in clay shale soils in Fort Peck, Montana, and concluded, "A system of three-row-array detonations offers a solution to the problem of obtaining flat slopes in the Chucunaque Valley clay-shale." The solution, however, added enormously to the amount of nuclear megatonnage that would be exploded. For the twenty-mile segment of the Chucunaque Valley alone, the concept required 231 explosions with a total yield of 69.2 megatons.[50] Thus, the economical solution to the slope-stability problem exacerbated the difficulties of radiation and air blast posed by the project. The commission's final report concluded that "attempts to excavate stable slopes in deep cuts in clay shale rocks by explosive procedures are so unlikely to produce acceptable or safe results that further investigations or tests in this direction are not recommended."[51]

GROUND SHOCK AND AIR BLAST

To understand how air blast from the explosions would travel in the upper atmosphere, the canal studies launched a program of rocket firings from the Canal Zone to measure wind and air density thirty to sixty kilometers above the ground in Panama. The Army lent the Canal Study Commission a site in Fort Sherman, and military personnel shot rockets with radar-reflecting payloads every week from March 1966 to early 1968.

The rocket shots showed that focusing the air blasts' pressure — similar to the way a magnifying glass focuses the sun's rays — would cause nearly six thousand windows to break as far away as San Jose, Costa Rica, and in Bogotá. Jack Reed, a meteorologist with Project Plowshare, determined that the number of broken windows could be reduced if engineers chose days for nuclear salvos when high-altitude winds moved away from populated areas — winds that occurred on one out of every three to six days. Even during calm periods, however, Reed estimated that air-blast focusing from nuclear shots on Route 17 would break about fifteen hundred window panes. If canal builders neglected the upper-wind effects, damages would be increased by a factor of five to fifty.[52] "Livermore howled and screamed over my conclusions," according to Reed, and tried to take the project away from him, but his conclusions were never refuted.[53]

The other potential impact that the nuclear scientists took very seriously, although it received much less public attention than radiation, was ground shock — that is, the seismic effects. The initial assessment largely dismissed the seismic risks: Urban populations were well beyond the damage range for prospective nuclear blasts, the 1964 studies concluded.[54] But by early 1966, the working group formed to study ground shock reached the judgment that "at the upper limit of projections there may be loss of life, the present canal may be put out of commission, and severe property damage, such as the structural collapse of multi-story apartment buildings. This damage may be comparable to that experienced from an earthquake disaster." The group projected that detonations would be equivalent to earthquakes up to 8 on the Richter scale and could produce landslides in the canal and damage to buildings as far away as Venezuela, Ecuador, and Costa Rica. The group pointed out that Panama City had not seen a major earthquake since the early 1600s, before significant building had occurred.[55] A contractor studying the seismic effects estimated that repairing the damage from excavation blasts of five to thirty megatons would cost up to $218 million.[56]

As the working group grappled with the uncertainties of the detonations' seismic impact, they realized that they needed more data to predict ground motions. Such information could be obtained from test explosions in the kind of clay shale found on the Darién route, using either conventional high explosives or nuclear blasts. In September 1966, the group had proposed to James Reeves, manager of the AEC's Nevada Test Site, that "plans be started now to prepare for a nuclear detonation on either or both Routes 17 and 25." They believed that the test could be contained completely underground for the seismic studies, but that a cratering test would be more useful for the studies of radiation and air blast. Reeves responded that "funding limitations rule out a nuclear calibration shot."[57]

The following May, the working group reiterated its assertion that a one-hundred–kiloton nuclear "calibration" test in the Darién or similar clay shale soils was "vital to determine feasibility." The tests, they said, should proceed "with a gradual escalation of yields approaching the maximum yields required for canal construction or until significant damage thresholds are reached in a city too large to be evacuated."[58]

While the military undertook studies in the Panamanian Darién, the AEC was attempting to show Project Plowshare's technical viability through continued nuclear tests in the continental United States. Studies of public attitudes in the United States, Panama, and a dozen other countries showed that nuclear excavation would have greater acceptance if the United States showed its technical feasibility on U.S. soil first.[59] Otherwise, it would appear the United States was using Panamanians as guinea pigs. But the AEC faced perennial political obstacles to obtaining approval for the nuclear shots, slowing the development of knowledge of nuclear cratering.

PANAMA'S RESPONSES

In early June 1967, General Harry Woodbury of the Army Corps of Engineers, who advised the Canal Study Commission, raised the prospect of a cratering experiment in Panama with Foreign Minister Fernando Eleta. Eleta at that time was in the midst of negotiations for the canal and bases treaties. According to the account by the John Kelly of the AEC, Eleta strongly endorsed the idea and suggested the U.S. proceed along those lines.[60]

Eleta went further. According to Kelly, he indicated to Woodbury that "it would be quite useful politically, if not technically, to do some kind of nuclear shot in Panama during the course of the canal studies." Eleta's technical adviser on the canal studies, the nuclear physicist Simón Quiros Guardia, also supported the idea of a nuclear test in Panama and said that he believed Panama would request such a shot. Kelly, however, wrote to the AEC commissioners that he believed a nuclear test in Panama was "extremely unlikely unless the Government of Panama makes a very high level, very strong, request for such detonation."[61]

Why a nuclear explosive test in Panama might be "useful politically" can be better understood in light of public and private responses to the project within Panama at the time. Many people were skeptical that nuclear excavation could ever work safely. Atmospheric nuclear tests conducted by the French in the Pacific in May 1966 provoked outrage in South American capitals, and a Chinese test the same month resulted in reports of radioactive fallout in India, Japan, and the United States. Clearly, atomic explosions had the potential to vent radiation beyond national borders. Panamanian newspapers dedicated extensive coverage to these developments.[62] The legislature declared that the French test could contaminate Panama; the previous year, it had called on Eleta to report on whether the United States had atomic warheads in the Canal Zone, to Eleta's great discomfort. A Panamanian treaty negotiator was forced to announce that no sea-level canal would be built if nuclear explosions put Panamanians at risk.[63]

Critics of the nuclear canal pointed out that, while U.S. engineers were preparing to detonate nuclear explosives in Panama, Americans at home were building millions of atomic-fallout shelters.[64] "The whole subject is regarded in a very emotional light," wrote a U.S. embassy officer about Panamanians' attitudes in early 1967. Few people had enough information to distinguish between an atmospheric nuclear test and a nuclear cratering explosion, which theoretically would trap most of the bomb's radioactivity in the ground.[65]

Some key Panamanian officials harbored serious doubts in private, as well. F. J. Morales, a civil engineer appointed to advise Panama on the canal studies, told U.S. officials in 1966 that he was

> strongly biased in favor of conventional excavation in the present Canal Zone and that it would take extremely persuasive demonstrations to convince him that "he should not move his wife and children out of Panama if the U.S. undertook nuclear canal excavation." He further emphasized that he intended to advise the Treaty Negotiators not to agree to a sea-level canal option which would leave the future choice of nuclear or conventional canal excavation to the U.S.[66]

Morales's advice was heeded. On June 21, 1967, two weeks after Kelly described Woodbury's conversation with the Panamanians favoring nuclear tests in Panama, Eleta and Anderson, the U.S. negotiator, initialed three treaties. One of the treaties addressed the construction of a sea-level canal in Panama; the other two dealt with the existing canal

9. Yabiliquiña and the Colonel: Kuna *saila* signs an agreement to permit a weather-monitoring station on an (uninhabited) island in San Blas, while Colonel Alex Sutton (second from the right) looks on. The Kunas opposed the nuclear-excavation project after field studies began in Darién in 1966. (National Archives.)

and military bases. The sea-level–canal treaty gave Panama the right to veto nuclear methods of canal construction. It was leaked to the press before either side could obtain political approval, however, and the treaties were neither signed nor ratified.[67]

"ROSARIES OF BITTER PAINS"

Kuna leaders in the Darién were initially wary of Army scouts for the canal project and made early reconnaissance of the route difficult. They subsequently signed an agreement to allow a weather-monitoring station on an uninhabited island in San Blas (see figure 9).[68] But when Army engineers brought large amounts of heavy earth-moving equipment in to clear a swath of land from coast to coast in March 1966, the Kuna cacique Yabiliquiña led a delegation that publicly protested and took the case to Foreign Minister Eleta in Panama City.[69] "We are and will continue to be happy without a sea-level canal in San Blas," Yabiliquiña said, worried about the canal project's effects on Indian traditions.[70] Officials with the Canal Study Commission emphasized that "special attention . . . should be given to the Kuna Indian problem as this matter may easily be blown out of proportion by other groups."[71]

Receiving only bland reassurances from Eleta, Yabiliquiña became more adamant. "We Kunas will not go back a single step in our struggle against having the canal built in our land," he told a reporter in May. He said that the Kunas would not benefit from the canal; instead, they would be "exploited" and "enslaved." Clearly fearful of the effects of the projected atomic blasts, Yabiliquiña said the Kuna islands "are long rosaries of bitter pains; our land is one long mournful song."[72]

REASONS FOR PLOWSHARE'S DEMISE

When the Canal Study Commission submitted its final report to President Richard Nixon in December 1970, it concluded that "nuclear excavation of a sea-level Isthmian Canal is not now feasible."[73] After fourteen years of investigation, the mobilization of thousands of people and dozens of agencies, and the expenditure of tens of millions of dollars, the United States laid the nuclear-canal plan to rest. The White House completely cut funding for nuclear excavation in 1971, and Project Plowshare itself was eliminated in 1978.[74]

What killed the nuclear-canal project? "The environmental dissenters that we still have around today . . . raised some serious questions," said Vortman. "It was clear that there was sufficient opposition, that these things wouldn't be done."[75] Harold Brown, the project's initiator, concluded simply that "the political negatives associated both with radioactivity and with nuclear explosions meant that any program to carry out such explosions never really had a chance."[76]

The AEC met an even more fundamental challenge from within to its premises about the health risks of radiation. The 1962 Sedan cratering test in Nevada had generated radioactivity whose effects were being felt in the atomic establishment (see figure 10). Robert Pendleton, a University of Utah radiologist, had taken a group of students to measure background radiation in rock formations in the mountains southeast of Salt Lake City, some five hundred miles from the Sedan explosion. The students witnessed a large dusty cloud — not unusual in that desert — but quickly found that radiation levels rose to a hundred

10. Sedan crater: The largest man-made explosion in the continental
United States at the time, the 100-kiloton Sedan explosion on July 6, 1962,
left a crater in the Nevada desert 300 feet deep and 1,200 feet wide. It gave
nuclear scientists their first empirical information about nuclear cratering.
(Archives, Lawrence Livermore National Laboratory.)

times higher than the normal background level. His team measured high levels of iodine-131 in milk and in humans in Utah and presented their findings in *Science* magazine later that year.[77]

A few months later, Livermore director John Foster asked the nuclear physicist and medical researcher John Gofman to direct a biomedical division at the lab that principally related to nuclear weapons and Project Plowshare. According to Gofman, who had been a protégé of Seaborg, Foster told him that the AEC was "catching hell" for the findings on iodine-131 in milk resulting from the Sedan shot. A biomedical program would allow the AEC to show that it was attending to concerns about potential health risks from radioactivity.[78]

The plan for canal workers was to allow whole-body radiation doses up to 5 rems per year.[79] Gofman and a colleague developed studies indicating that these levels, applied to the whole program of commercial nuclear reactors, would cause up to thirty-two thousand additional deaths from cancer, and that exposure to any radioactivity could be harmful. As a Livermore scientist, Gofman had a great deal of public credibility, and his claims spurred an environmental movement that had effects on Plowshare projects across the board. He became known within Livermore and the AEC as "the enemy within."[80]

The controversy over radiation generated by proposed Plowshare projects was not unique to the nuclear canal in Panama. Plowshare proposals to "liberate" natural gas with underground nuclear explosions in Pennsylvania and Colorado met with strong and growing citizen opposition.[81] At the same time, the AEC was fighting another rear-guard action against arms controllers. The Limited Test Ban Treaty already restricted nuclear detonations on the isthmus. This, together with the negotiation of other nuclear-weapons treaties, increased the political and legal restraints on developmental tests for nuclear cratering within the United States. Early cratering tests had spread radioactivity over significant distances. A Plowshare cratering shot at the Nevada Test Site in April 1965, buried 280 feet underground, for example, had pushed a radioactive cloud across the Canadian border. The Soviets protested. "It was much more important [for the United States] to reach an agreement with the Soviet Union on nuclear explosions than it was to make a canal through Panama with these explosions," Eleta said later.[82]

Negotiations between 1965 and 1967 for the Treaty of Tlateloco, which banned the deployment of nuclear weapons in Latin America, made the State Department even more sensitive to the political effects of nuclear explosions that might generate radioactivity in the atmosphere. According to both Eleta and Simón Quiros Guardia, it was Tlateloco, which was signed in February 1967 and entered into force in April 1968, that effectively chilled prospects for the nuclear-canal project, because it prohibited the presence of nuclear weapons in Latin America.[83]

Another conflict with arms-control objectives was the inability to verify that nuclear cratering tests were for "peaceful" — that is, non-military — purposes. In fact, the Plowshare engineers' interest in the program was not always solely in the civilian applications of nuclear explosives. A Plowshare manual "Military Engineering with Nuclear Explosives" detailed the most effective ways to blow up bridges, airfields, dams, tunnels, and piers, using the same methods of nuclear cratering that were to be used for the canal.[84] The Canal Study Commission's final classified report concluded that these methods would boost weapons development: "Both the device and the effects technology are applicable to the strategic and tactical use of nuclear weapons."[85]

It was this tension between arms-control objectives and the Plowshare program that prevented the AEC from receiving approval for any nuclear cratering tests at all between 1965 and 1968, critical years for the nuclear-canal studies.[86] Johnson administration officials, worried about the impact of the tests on nuclear-arms–control negotiations, delayed and postponed the tests. President Nixon, although reportedly a personal supporter of Plowshare, was, like Johnson, preoccupied with the war in Vietnam.[87]

RETURN OF THE RATIONAL ENGINEERS

The demise of the nuclear canal appears to have been inevitable, given the political and technical obstacles to its completion. A more pertinent question may be why it was pursued for so long and with such high-level seriousness. The project was introduced in 1956, when U.S. premises about atmospheric atomic tests were very different from what they became a few years later. The nuclear technicians who championed the project were largely insulated from the political and social changes going on in the United States and especially in Panama.

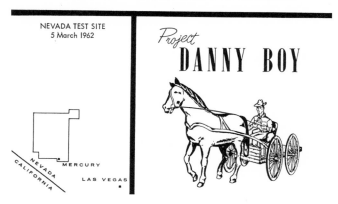

NEVADA TEST SITE
5 March 1962

Project **DANNY BOY**

NEVADA
CALIFORNIA
MERCURY
LAS VEGAS

11. Project Danny Boy: The graphic representation of
this nuclear-cratering test in 1962 evokes the nuclear
engineers' image of themselves as pioneers in a wilderness
inhabited only by themselves and animals.
(National Archives.)

Teller, one of Plowshare's greatest proponents, "had the idea that
Livermore was one of the islands of sanity and that the rest of the
world outside was in trouble," according to John Gofman.[88]

As U.S–Panama relations over the existing canal and sovereignty
grew acutely conflictive, the sea-level canal — whose economics were
only feasible through nuclear excavation — became a pawn in a superpower negotiation strategy. The establishment of the Atlantic–Pacific
Interoceanic Canal Study Commission, together with the 1965–67
negotiations for new canal treaties, injected new life into the nuclear-
canal project.

We may also understand the persistence of the nuclear-canal idea in
light of the image of engineers as a civilizing influence on the tropics.
Typically, the language used by those engineers was stripped of emotive content and connotation. Atomic explosions were "events"; the
bombs themselves were "devices." Such language had the effect of

making the act of blowing up huge areas of earth seem more rational than the emotive associations with bombs.

In Project Plowshare's salad days, journalists sometimes burnished the heroic image of the nuclear engineers with gushing prose. "Atomic scientists with their imaginations unlocked and the sky the only limit, offered a dizzying array of peaceful uses for nuclear explosives," wrote a *San Francisco Chronicle* reporter in a 1959 front-page story. The engineers' ideas "created a vista of a whole new world," where nuclear blasts would "churn up unlimited water supplies, . . . mine huge ore bodies, and . . . blow up hurricanes before they can wreak their damage."[89] The nuclear scientists rarely expressed such reverence for the tropics. Instead, the AEC's language reflected the view of nature as hostile: atomic blasts would be used to dislodge "menacing rocks" and establish "reluctant oil wells"—a stark contrast to "the imaginative mind of man" that had conceived of nuclear excavation (see figure 11).[90] When military engineers encountered soil conditions that were not propitious for nuclear excavation, they did not conclude that the nuclear method was problematic. Instead, as Lieutenant-Colonel Hughes of the Nuclear Cratering Group wrote, it was the clay shale soil found in the Chucunaque Valley—nature itself—that was "troublesome."[91]

The indigenous Kunas clearly had a different understanding of the tropical forest and its ecology from that of the Army engineers. Colonel Alex Sutton, the Army engineer who led the site study in Darién, described a trail as "made hazardous by vicious black palm thorns." Sutton expressed frustration at the attention required to convince Kuna representatives to allow the field studies to go ahead. "Their superstitions and customs hold not only certain birds and animals sacred, but types of rocks as well," he wrote—sacredness that may have been relative to the plans to blow up those rocks with atomic explosions. Sutton expressed little hope that the worldviews could be reconciled, only that arrangements might be made: "Advance preparation with these people by understanding and sympathetic representatives should be made in order to avoid a major problem and much adverse publicity."[92]

Policymakers believed that Latin Americans were especially susceptible to bouts of emotion on nuclear issues. "The Mexicans are notably skittish on nuclear matters and easy prey to alarm over fallouts, real or fancy," Secretary of State Christian Herter wrote in 1960.[93] A White House aide conceded in 1965 that radioactive fallout from nuclear excavation was inevitable, and that "there will undoubtedly be a widespread fear on the part of the uneducated, uninformed, and superstitious population."[94]

AEC Commissioner Willard Libby touted nuclear explosives' "potential in civilization-building," to which "the general public sometimes reacts unthinkingly."[95] The Army engineer Walter Fade, in a speech lauded by his peers at the Albrook Officers' Club in late 1964, declared that safety problems of radioactivity "are not well understood by the general public. . . . The wide acceptance of the Nuclear Test Ban Treaty is ample testimony to the general nature and seriousness of this problem." Fade advocated aggressive public relations "to overcome the political and psychological resistance that will be encountered" during nuclear excavation.[96]

Extensive national and international propaganda efforts to promote the benefits of atomic energy apparently had little impact on the "skittish" and "superstitious" Latin Americans and their environmentalist counterparts in the United States. According to air-blast specialist Jack Reed, Plowshare's downfall was caused by "politics, hysterical antinuclear attitudes."[97] Emotion ruled.

Twenty years later, after the watershed decision in the 1977 canal treaties to transfer the canal and military bases to Panama, the tropical forces of irrationality as represented in Panama would again meet the civilizing forces of the U.S. military. In that encounter, the object of contention was illegal drugs, not nuclear excavation, which by then had long been forgotten.

4 ☆ PLAYING THE DRUG CARD

"Once the negro has formed the [cocaine] habit he is irreclaimable. The only method to keep him from taking the drug is by imprisoning him." —Edward H. Williams, M.D., *New York Times*, 1914

"At the top of the list of the world's drug thieves and scums." —Dan Rather, CBS News, on General Manuel Noriega, 1989

After the Cold War ended, a new rationale for U.S. military intervention and bases in Panama became dominant: the drug war.[1] This was most overtly a basis for U.S. military policy in Panama during two periods. The first, in 1987–89, occurred during the crisis that led to the December 20, 1989, invasion of Panama in which General Manuel Noriega was captured, and focused on Panama and its military forces as targets. The second, in 1995–98, took place as Washington and Panama attempted to negotiate a post–1999 military presence in Panama under the rubric of a Multinational Counterdrug Center (MCC), and aimed at maintaining a military infrastructure in Panama to serve regional objectives. These negotiations faltered because of resistance in Panama and in the region to keeping military bases on the isthmus.

From 1987 to 1989, the debate focused narrowly on Manuel Noriega and his involvement in drug trafficking. The drug war focused on internal ethnic minorities and foreigners who were identified as both users and sellers of drugs that threatened U.S. citizens with violence, addiction, and temptation. Although evidence was widely available showing that the vast majority of cocaine users were White, the criminal-justice system and media focused on Black and Latino users and street vendors. The racial dimensions of the drug war, as they were expressed by U.S. leaders and the media, created a greater political imperative to confront Noriega and Panama than would have been the case if the most salient media images had been of White traffickers and addicts. Even though average U.S. citizens did not make the decisions about the invasion, the intervention was politically driven by the need to boost domestic support for President George Bush. Thus, the images of Panama and drugs that shaped public opinion in 1988–89 were important determinants of the decision to invade.

The negotiations for a continued military presence in Panama during the later period were largely ignored by the U.S. media and were low on the White House agenda. But the talks were fundamentally shaped by the sanctions and invasion of 1987–89 and by the larger shift of U.S. policy in the region toward a rhetoric on drugs. The invasion carried an implicit threat of attack if Panama did not bend to Washington's desire, yet it also left a deep wound and tapped Panamanians' resentment of the United States' impositions and suspicion of its intentions. Both implicit threat and resentment would be present in U.S–Panama relations leading up to and during the Counterdrug Center negotiations.

PANAMA AND DRUGS IN THE NORTH AMERICAN MIND

The association in Whites' minds of Panama and Black people with drugs and inebriation predates by far the crisis in U.S–Panama relations of the late 1980s. When the Canal Zone became prohibitionist in 1920, Panamanian clubs and bars took up the slack in the alcohol trade, setting the stage for Panamanians to be seen as a corrupting influence on U.S. soldiers. During World War II, the Canal Zone was a rest and recreation port for hundreds of thousands of GIs returning home from the Pacific, when they had the chance to sample Panama City's canteens and nightlife. In the popular 1973 song "Panama Red," Jerry Garcia, lead singer of the band Old and in the Way, identifies Panama with a personified drug that has come into town: "Then he'll rob your head [while he] keeps well hidden underground"; under his influence, "everybody's acting lazy / Falling out and hangin' 'round." In the U.S. imagination, Panama is a source and way station for the life of the senses.

Because the primary response to illicit drug use in the United States has been punitive, constituencies vie with one another in the political arena to lessen the negative consequences to them of drug enforcement. White drug users as a class have greater resources and leverage with which to reduce those consequences by avoiding the criminal-justice system entirely or drawing on influence and legal defense. Furthermore, because of social inequalities, drug abuse has taken a greater toll on Black and Latino communities than it has on White communities. This has sometimes led Black and Latino leaders to support punitive measures strongly, even though they affect Blacks disproportionately. White fears of people of color high on narcotics thus have been reinforced by the communities' own needs to "do something" about the substances ravaging some of their members.

From 1900 to 1918, fear of cocaine use by Southern Blacks was closely linked to the rise of alcohol prohibition: Whites feared that, when liquor became scarce, Blacks were turning to cocaine. According to this reasoning, Blacks' inhibitions were being unleashed by the drug, leading them to transgress the bounds of Reconstructionist segregation. "It has been authoritatively stated that cocaine is often the direct incentive to the crime of rape by the negroes of the South and other sections of the country," wrote Hamilton Wright in a 1909 report to the Senate on the International Opium Commission. Cocaine drove "humbler negroes" to abnormal crimes, he said.[2] Dr. Christopher Koch reiterated the danger of attacks on White women resulting from the "cocain-crazed negro brain" in 1914.[3] A study of 2,119 Blacks admitted to the Georgia State Sanitarium between 1909 and 1914 found that only three were addicted to narcotics, but this did not stem the alarm over Southern Blacks' using cocaine.[4]

The most fantastic claims about Black "cocaine fiends" were that their marksmanship improved under the influence of cocaine, and that they became impervious to gunshots to the chest — allegedly the reason that police in the South began using heavier-gauge, .38 caliber revolvers.[5] Thus, alarm over cocaine use was employed to justify more repressive tools against Blacks in the South. Other ethnic groups were also targeted by Whites as drug users who posed a danger to the social order.

The propagation of the image of "cocainized negroes" coincided with the period of disfranchisement of Blacks in the South, use of Jim Crow laws, and a large number of lynchings. It was also during this time that the debate over narcotics in the United States first turned to the idea that the drug problem was imported from other countries and cultures, and that it was not indigenous to an overconsumptive U.S. culture. "Projection of blame on foreign nations for domestic evils harmonized with the ascription of drug use to ethnic minorities," according to the historian David Musto.[6]

During the Cold War, the Caribbean Defense Command headquartered in Panama (which was renamed the U.S. Southern Command, or SouthCom, in 1963) was the nerve center for U.S. military activities and relations with armies throughout Central and South America. The command's major functions in Panama were intelligence, training, and developing informal relationships with Latin American military officers that would serve U.S. interests as the officers ascended to power in their countries.

In 1943, the Caribbean Command set up the Inter-American Air Force Academy (IAAFA) on the Canal Zone's Albrook air base, where it trained Latin American pilots how to survive if grounded in the jungle. In 1946, the School of the Americas was established to train military officers and enlisted men in a wide range of skills and doctrine. Initially, most of the students were U.S. soldiers, but after 1954 a majority of students were Latin American. The U.S. schools in Panama brought about "respect for the producers of the equipment, acceptance of U.S. ideas and doctrines, and probably friendships with Americans and positive feelings for this country," according to a U.S. officer writing in *Military Review*.[7] The School of the Americas trained 57,000 Latin American military, policemen, and civilians, including 3,554 Panamanian National Guardsmen, from 1950 to 1986.[8] The IAAFA trained more than 20,000 Latin American troops between the end of World War II and the 1989 invasion, before moving to Texas.[9]

Fears stimulated by the Cuban revolution and other Latin American social movements led to an expansion of U.S. programs for what was dubbed internal defense — that is, military operations against conationals. In response to President Kennedy's intense interest, the training carried out in Panama shifted to emphasize Special Forces and counterinsurgency. The Inter-American Police Academy was established for that purpose in Fort Davis in 1962.[10]

Cold War paranoia revived metaphors about Latin Americans from an earlier, more explicitly racist period, leading military doctrine to absolute imperatives about the need to train militaries in the region. Major-General William Yarborough, addressing the military's chemical warfare proponents in 1964, dwelt on the need for allied armed forces to "show up higher on the popularity poll among the peasants and workers." The general's drawings illustrating the movement of

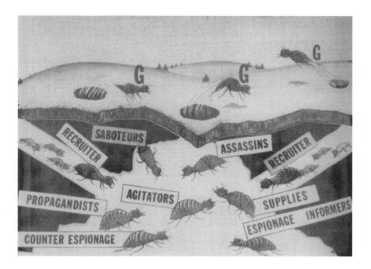

12. Insect subversives underground, 1964. (*Armed Forces Chemical Journal*, December 1964.)

insurgency vividly conveyed how he saw the terrain. The first picture, designed to help explain the "tactical problem faced by a conventional force in dealing with guerrillas who refuse to stand and fight," shows a town nestled in a valley. Underneath the ground's surface are cavities housing huge striped insects with pincers that jump out of openings in the soil. Each opening is marked "G." The second drawing (see figure 12) looks more closely at one of these cavities (a "cell"), labeling the insects: SABOTEURS, AGITATORS, ASSASSINS, RECRUITER, SUPPLIES, PROPAGANDISTS, ESPIONAGE INFORMERS, and COUNTER ESPIONAGE. To show how insidious the guerrilla influence is on the insect world, large RECRUITER insects are depicted leading small, baby insects into the cell.[11]

By 1968, the Southern Command had become preoccupied with guerrilla insurgencies in Bolivia, Colombia, Guatemala, and Venezuela, had 103 military advisers in Brazil, and generally subordinated relations with Panama to "hemispheric internal defense."[12] The following year, 70 percent of the curriculum at the School of the Americas consisted of counterinsurgency training.[13] There, Panamanian cadets played "guerrillas" in exercises while U.S. soldiers took the part of counterinsurgents.[14]

The School of the Americas also served to share intelligence among the hemisphere's armed forces. In the 1970s, for example, Latin American officers used a secure telephone system at Fort Gulick to coordinate intelligence for Operation Condor, a counterinsurgency operation by Southern Cone militaries that included international assassinations of dissidents and suspected subversives. The phone system was "used mainly by student officers to call home to Latin America," wrote Robert White, U.S. ambassador to Paraguay, in 1978, but it doubled as a means for conveying confidential messages.[15]

In addition, Panama became the home base of Mobile Training Teams (MTTs) — military trainers who visited other Latin American countries. Some MTTs taught combat skills, but many were charged with a wide variety of tasks aimed at civilians and known as civic action. From the 1960s through the Central American wars of the 1980s, civic action was a key component of counterinsurgency strategies that tried to get on the right side of the peasant "sea" in which the guerrilla "fish" swam, and many of its operatives were Special Forces soldiers. During the 1990s, the military used civic action in Latin America to train National Guardsmen in road building, construction, and medical-assistance missions that they were prohibited from undertaking inside the United States. The Army Corps of Engineers' history with the canal made Panama convenient for stationing the engineers to be deployed for civic action in the region.

During the 1970s, SouthCom played a small overt role in U.S. policy for the hemisphere and was even considered for elimination, but with the election of Ronald Reagan and the U.S.-led military drive against the Sandinista government in Nicaragua and guerrilla forces in El Salvador, SouthCom received an infusion of attention and resources.

The 1977 Canal Treaty authorized the presence of U.S. troops and bases in Panama during the treaty's life (through 1999) for canal defense, not for other military missions in the hemisphere. Nevertheless, Panama — especially once Noriega took power after the death of Omar Torrijos in 1981 — gave the United States important support for wars in the region. Panama's support included use of its territory for joint military maneuvers and covert training; use of U.S. bases for logistical supply and intelligence flights to El Salvador and Honduras; and training of troops from the region in the School of the Americas, where more than eighteen hundred Salvadoran soldiers took courses in combat tactics, intelligence, logistics, and other military subjects from 1982 to 1984.[16] According to Duane Clarridge, who was chief of the Latin America division of the Central Intelligence Agency (CIA), Noriega helped the CIA set up a short-lived training camp for the Nicaraguan Contras' Southern Army in 1983.[17] Noriega also provided Oliver North with a pair of demolition experts who helped blow up a munitions-storage dump in Managua, Nicaragua, in March 1985, which rocked the capital.[18]

In February 1985, four thousand ground, sea, and air troops from the Panama Defense Forces (PDF) and the United States participated in exercises in Panama's interior — outside the canal area — to lend "realism to the guerrilla insurgency scenario." PDF, Army, and National Guard units carried out road-building exercises on Panama's Azuero peninsula from January to May of the same year.[19]

From the fourteen U.S. bases in the canal area, SouthCom carried out other regional military operations. U.S. officers shuttling from Panama to El Salvador were used to circumvent the limit of fifty-five military advisers in El Salvador imposed by Washington officials who were wary of deeper involvement in the war there. Beginning in early 1983, four heavily armed and equipped reconnaissance aircraft were permanently deployed to Howard Air Force Base, from which they made nightly low-level flights over guerrilla-held territory in El Salvador. Their infrared photographs were transmitted to Salvadoran military units, who used the information to carry out combat operations in areas controlled by the guerrillas and their civilian supporters. Other aircraft at Howard made supply runs to Nicaraguan Contra camps in Honduras. SouthCom was also responsible for coordinating the frequent military maneuvers that took place in Honduras from 1983 to 1987.[20]

The National Guard (later PDF) was handsomely rewarded for its institutional cooperation with the United States. Military rule in Panama from 1968 through the 1980s was overlooked by Washington, initially in the drive to obtain a canal treaty. In 1984, massive electoral fraud in the presidential contest led to the inauguration of Nicolás Ardito Barletta, a protégé of Secretary of State George Shultz, who attended his inauguration. From 1980 to 1987, Panama received more than $47 million in U.S. military equipment, training, and loans — more than three times what it had received from 1946 to 1979. By 1983, the National Guard had formally become an army, which provided a rationalization for the increase. Noriega became chief of the PDF the same year. Even after the U.S. military pipeline was cut off in

June 1987, Washington continued to authorize sales of military equipment to Panama — even increases in such sales.[21]

CULTIVATING PANAMANIAN MILITARY LEADERS

Among those recruited by U.S. military intelligence as a spy in 1955 was a young officer named Omar Torrijos. The Army paid him $25 a month, for which he continued to inform U.S. agents until 1969 on subjects ranging from "labor unrest" and "student activities" to "political issues" and "Soviet–Chinese penetration."[22] During the 1964 flag riots, Torrijos took part in suppressing the unrest in Colón, where he was flown from the rural province of Chiriquí. The influence of the 470th Army Intelligence Group on Panama's National Guard was very strong in the 1960s, and one operative of the 470th even helped Torrijos plan the 1968 coup and sheltered his family during the takeover.[23]

U.S. Army officers first recruited Manuel Noriega as an informer in the mid-1950s. His career had been stalled by problems with alcohol and violence against women until 1964, when Torrijos picked him as his intelligence officer in Chiriquí. Noriega took courses in intelligence and counterintelligence at the School of the Americas in 1967 and trained for psychological warfare at Fort Benning.[24] As chief of intelligence for the National Guard from 1970 to 1983, and de facto military ruler from 1983 until 1989, Noriega became a key figure in the growing institutional relationships between the U.S. and Panamanian militaries.

Critics of the School of the Americas have documented a long list of graduates who have gone on to commit atrocities against civilians or assume dictatorial powers in their countries. Panamanian soldiers such as Noriega had an experience that differed from that of students from other countries, however. In Panama, not only was the School of the Americas near at hand until 1984, but U.S. Army intelligence agents were assigned to work with Noriega and other National Guard officers, effectively extending the U.S. military education of those officers far beyond a few courses at the school.[25]

Except for brief periods, Noriega's value to intelligence agencies as a source of information about governments and militaries throughout the region, including in Cuba — as well as concern with other issues — took priority in Washington over problems with his involvement in cocaine trafficking. The CIA paid Noriega more than $1 million for his services, and he received at least $162,000 from the Army and the Defense Intelligence Agency.[26] U.S. agencies knew about Noriega's involvement in the drug trade as early as 1972, when the Bureau of Narcotics and Dangerous Drugs considered assassinating him. During Jimmy Carter's administration, U.S. officials continued to receive evidence about Noriega but suppressed it in the bid to gain support for the ratification of the Canal Treaties. In 1983 and 1985, the Reagan White House had intelligence reports about meetings with cartel managers in which Noriega gave permission to manufacture cocaine in Panama and offered to mediate turf disputes among traffickers. According to Norman Bailey, then a staff member on the National Security Council, "This wasn't a smoking gun. It was a 21-gun salute."[27]

It was not until the Iran–Contra scandal erupted in late 1986, forcing out Noriega's allies Lieutenant-Colonel Oliver North and CIA Director William Casey, and Panama's internal crisis erupted in June 1987, that Noriega began to fall from favor. These events came after Noriega had cut many of his ties to the Medellin cartel. He was eventually convicted on charges of drug trafficking that occurred between March 1982 and July 1984.

The indictments of Noriega for drug trafficking were issued in February 1988 by grand juries in Miami and Tampa, and they both framed and jump-started the political conflict with Panama that led to the invasion. U.S. economic sanctions against Panama instituted less than a month after the indictments were purportedly designed to push Noriega from power. SouthCom simultaneously put in place the first contingency plans for an invasion and increased the number of U.S. forces in Panama. "Under pressure from Washington, [SouthCom chief Frederick] Woerner had quickly learned that the [Joint Chiefs of Staff] preferred inaccurate information to no information at all," according to a military history of the crisis.[28]

The sanctions provoked shortages of basic goods and a sense of crisis, and incidentally diminished money laundering, but they did not topple Noriega, who used them as cause for emergency measures amid nationalist rhetoric. At the same time, the presidential campaign of George Bush faced criticism for the connections he made with Noriega when he was CIA chief and vice president. The Reagan–Bush policy thus was caught between punitive action and the unwillingness to negotiate with a trafficker indicted by a U.S. court. It had no exit except escalation.[29]

The crack-cocaine scare burst onto the scene in 1986, concurrent with Noriega's divorce from his Washington patrons. Attempting to draw political advantage in the days before midterm elections, Congress passed the 1986 Anti-Drug Abuse Act, the first of several federal mandatory minimum prison-sentencing laws for drug offenders.

The 1988 election campaign escalated national rhetoric both on drugs and racial identification of crime. The Bush campaign ran TV ads with the face of Willie Horton, an African American man convicted of a rape and murder, who had been furloughed from state prison in Massachusetts, where Bush's Democratic opponent Michael Dukakis was governor. Horton had committed another crime while on furlough, and the ad effectively exploited Whites' fears while sending the message that Black offenders would be put back in cages under a Bush administration. The Anti-Drug Abuse Acts of 1986 and 1988 and the Drug-Free Schools and Communities Act of 1989 were the fruit of the new rhetoric and extended the penalties for drug users and sellers.[30]

For the use of large-scale military force, however, no internal offenders provided the same target of opportunity as did a foreign enemy. Overseas, the armed forces could be massively deployed without provoking a constitutional crisis. The mass media provided a kind of blueprint for U.S. military action in Panama. Typical of the media's construction of policy choices was a *Newsweek* cover story that appeared within a month of Bush's election titled "The Crack Nation" — that country "in our midst, but not a part of us" and distinct from "people of normal human appetites." (NBC had already aired a prime-time feature titled "Cocaine Country."[31]) The *Newsweek* story's nine photos made abundantly clear who the residents of this Crack Nation were, and they were nearly all Black. If crack users truly represented a nation, surely that nation's sovereignty would have to be violated to address the danger.[32]

The story immediately following proposed several remedies. It led with a statement by the onetime drug trafficker Carlos Lehder calling cocaine "the Third World's atomic bomb." The article did not say whether Latin Americans were purposely deploying cocaine to destroy the lives documented on previous pages, but it did call on the new administration to make some hard decisions and asserted that "America's cocaine problem in fact has been caused by the Colombian cartels and their U.S.-based accomplices: attacking the enemy high command is good strategy."[33]

The first year of the Bush presidency represented the high-water mark of the drug war's racially punitive thrust. The 1986 and 1988 mandatory minimum sentencing laws were yielding an unprecedented level of incarceration of youth of color. During 1989, for example, 92 percent of those arrested for drug offenses in New York City were Black or Latino. Nationally, 35 percent of all Black males aged sixteen to thirty-five were arrested during that year. Although Black men represented only about one-seventh the population of White men, more were in prison or jail than their White counterparts.[34]

Mainstream media participated in the intense campaign focused on crack. The *New York Times* published an average of 101 stories about drugs each month in 1989 (compared with 36 articles per month in 1985), fueling anxiety in Congress and among the public about the problem. The media's stories in 1989 emphasized drugs as a "plague" and "foreign scourge." The coverage also reflected a preoccupation with crack as a phenomenon of Black neighborhoods that threatened to metastasize into White communities, despite scant evidence that drug abuse grows across social classes. "A Plague without Boundaries" was the headline of a *Time* magazine story that appeared just six weeks before the Panama invasion; a plague that respects no sovereignty would have to be met with comparable methods.[35]

In Panama, meanwhile, Noriega had suspended the results of elections held in May 1989, leading to internal protests and an attempt by Latin American leaders to resolve the crisis. The Organization of American States organized a team to mediate a solution, but the United States hardly supported the effort. Instead, it deployed two thousand more troops, including a Delta force trained in covert action, with orders to travel on Panamanian roads and ignore PDF roadblocks and orders. President Bush openly called for Noriega's ouster.[36]

Some of the most widely broadcast images of Panama in 1989 before the invasion were guaranteed to evoke racial fears about dangerous Panamanians. In the wake of Noriega's cancellation of the election results, in which his candidates had been soundly defeated, opposition parties organized protests in Panama City, and the PDF violently repressed them. Vice-presidential candidate Guillermo Ford's bodyguard was killed, spattering blood all over Ford's white shirt. In an image that was widely reproduced in military publications, TV cameras caught dark-skinned people — identified by network-news broadcasts as "government goons" — beating the bloodied Ford, who is White, with sticks as he tried to flee. Another image repeated on the U.S. airwaves showed a defiant and triumphal Noriega waving a machete, a symbol of Central American identity and a sharp contrast to the gringos' high-tech tools of war. All of these images served to evoke the historical idea of savages challenging the forces of civilization represented by the United States and its military.

In September 1989, President Bush made a major, televised, prime-time speech — his first — focusing on crack, in which he held up to the camera a baggie containing the drug that had been purchased from a young African American man in Washington. By this time, the media's coverage of crack, and the fact that the sale had occurred in the majority-Black city of Washington, D.C., thinly coded the inference that the problem was Black. Bush's aides had the Drug Enforcement Administration agents lure a suspected drug dealer across town to Lafayette Park in front of the White House for a crack sale. The arrest and its presentation gave the false impression that Black sellers were brazen (or foolish) enough to venture close to the White House territory to sell crack.[37] The speech illustrates how internal ethnic minorities had become politically expendable props in the drug war at the time. Shortly after President Bush's televised speech, an ABC poll found that 64 percent of those surveyed believed that drugs were "the most important problem facing this country today."[38]

On October 3, Panamanian military officers attempted a coup against Noriega that was brutally put down. With the officers' execution and Noriega's continued stay in power, President Bush came in for heavy criticism by both the mass media and Congressional leaders, who by then openly shared the aim of ousting Noriega from office by whatever means available. Senators and editorialists called the administration's failure to topple Noriega Bush's "wimp factor." General Colin Powell, who had just returned to Washington to take up the post of Chairman of the Joint Chiefs of Staff, had never witnessed such intensity of acrimony in a foreign-policy battle. "My God, what has happened to this town?" he asked himself. He told the reporter Bob Woodward that the political class was acting like a lynch mob.[39] The stage was set for a greater escalation in the confrontation between the United States and Panama. From that point forward, the machinery of invasion was in motion, seeking only a trigger.

On December 16, a marine intelligence unit ran a roadblock near PDF headquarters, speeding in the direction of Noriega's office. The unit was known as the "Hard Chargers" and had a reputation for using dangerous tactics. PDF soldiers fired on the vehicle, killing First Lieutenant Robert Paz. A U.S. soldier and his wife who had witnessed the incident were taken into PDF custody, where he was reportedly beaten and she threatened with rape. According to one account, it was "Noriega's men mistreating a family, a woman, a noncombatant" that caught the Pentagon leadership's attention more than the shooting of First Lieutenant Paz.[40] An unstated piece of information that must have been present for U.S. planners was that many officers in the PDF were dark-skinned, a legacy of Torrijos' populist policies. Here were accusations of Panamanian military violence and sexual harassment by Black men in an area historically controlled as a U.S. reservation, and in a period of elevated emotions about drug use by Blacks. The incident was the tripwire the Bush administration had been waiting for, and within twenty-four hours Bush ordered a full-scale invasion.

The images of Panamanian violence contributed to the impression that Noriega was an unusual threat, though neither his repression of internal opposition nor abuses of foreigners ever matched the violent ferocity and killing occurring at the same time in neighboring Colombia, El Salvador, or Guatemala. In November, Guatemalan security agents had kidnapped, tortured, and raped Diana Ortiz, an Ursuline nun from the United States, before she escaped. There is no record that military or cabinet officers in Washington even registered the act, much less used it as a trigger for military action against the Guatemalan military. Similarly, world attention focused on El Salvador a few days later when guerrillas launched a major offensive on San Salvador and the Salvadoran army responded, in part, by assassinating six Jesuit priests. The armed forces also systematically arrested international humanitarian and church workers, in some cases torturing them before they were released. But the generals in those countries had not been indicted in U.S. federal courts for their crimes.

REASONS FOR THE INVASION

Besides the imperatives generated by the drug war's racially charged dynamic, a number of other factors contributed to the invasion and its timing. First, under the Canal Treaties, January 1, 1990, was to be the first day on the job for a Panamanian as administrator of the Panama Canal Commission (although the United States would retain a majority on the commission's board through 1999). The treaties called for Panama to name an administrator and the U.S. president to confirm him or her. Noriega had nominated Tomás Duque, who had been found unacceptable by President Bush. With a new government in place in Panama, an administrator acceptable to Washington would be found.

Second, the invasion was a showcase for the Pentagon's post–Cold War missions. Three months before, the Berlin Wall had fallen — and with it much of the domestic political rationale for the United States' worldwide military supremacy. Ronald Reagan, like other presidents before him, attributed many conflicts in Latin America to interference from Soviet and Cuban interlopers, a Cold War version of the Monroe Doctrine. Reagan's hyperideological presidency gave way to the conservative pragmatism of George Bush, and as Eastern European nations overturned their party bureaucrats, Americans became newly aware of addictive drugs as an evil, an "other." With the collapse of Soviet and Eastern European socialism and the contraction of Cuba's international presence, only a new set of threats could justify U.S. military action in Latin America. President Bush's launching of the drug war in September filled much of the gap.

Some SouthCom military officers were astute enough to realize in 1987 that the drug war could be pitched publicly to replace the anticommunist crusade in Latin America. The political usefulness of that crusade was in decline as a result of grassroots mobilizations across the country for human rights in Central America, and the military sought "a weapon with which to regain the moral high ground we have appeared to have lost," wrote Colonel John D. Waghelstein, who coordinated U.S. military advisers in El Salvador, in 1987. "A melding in the American public's mind and in Congress of this connection [between the drug trade and insurgency] would lead to the necessary support to counter the guerrilla/narcotics terrorists in this hemisphere. Those church and academic groups that have slavishly supported insurgency in Latin America would find themselves on the wrong side of the moral issue."[41]

In 1989, Congress made the Defense Department the "single lead agency" in the federal government for the detection and monitoring of drug trafficking in the hemisphere. The part of the drug war dedicated to interdicting drugs was itself growing in emphasis and budget. Other countries and agencies would be responsible for arresting and prosecuting traffickers, but the military became an increasingly important player in the drug war. The invasion served to accustom everyone involved — Latin Americans, Congress, the U.S. public, and the Pentagon itself — to the military's new declared role. General Maxwell Thurman, assigned to Panama in September 1989 to take charge of invasion preparations, called the drug war "the only war we've got."[42]

Third, by September 1989, military leaders in Washington concluded not only that they could not make Noriega behave, but that they no longer had any meaningful influence on the other PDF leaders. SouthCom therefore decided to eliminate the entire Panamanian military and made "their primary military objective the disarming and dismantling of the Panama Defense Force."[43] The United States would establish a new police force, to be constructed and indoctrinated directly by the U.S. military.[44]

In planning to eliminate the Panamanian armed forces, Pentagon leaders must have been well aware that they would be doing away with the force projected to defend the canal after the U.S. military's withdrawal under the terms of the Canal Treaties. The Pentagon had infused significant training, funds, and equipment into the PDF based on the theory that it would take over the responsibility for canal defense from the United States. By expanding the operation from a drug bust to the destruction of an army, the United States took away the entity on which post–1999 canal planning had rested. The invasion thus paved the way for later negotiations to keep a U.S. military presence that could defend the canal after 1999. This may have been a fourth objective, although the evidence in documents released to date is circumstantial.

Reagan and others during the Canal Treaty debates had already staked out an objective of keeping troops in Panama. The Bush administration largely adopted the 1988 foreign-policy blueprint of the conservative Santa Fe Committee, which stated: "Once a democratic regime is in place . . . discussions should begin on a realistic defense of the Canal after the year 2000. Those talks should include the United States' retention of limited facilities in Panama (principally Howard air base and Rodman naval station) for proper force projection throughout the Western Hemisphere."[45] The absence of a Panamanian military would be used by Congressional boosters of the military presence as a rationale in resolutions approved by the House and Senate in 1990 and 1996 urging first President Bush, then President Clinton, to negotiate continued military bases in Panama.[46]

THE INVASION

"If you just looked at television, the most violent thing American troops did in Panama was play rock music," the political media consultant Robert Squier told *Newsday*.[47] Yet the U.S. invasion on December 20, 1989, was the most violent event in Panama since Colombia's Thousand Days War ninety years earlier, and it was certainly the most traumatic event in the lives of most of those who were directly affected by it. Eighteen thousand Panamanians lost their homes during the midnight attack and lived in makeshift shelters for months. At least 516 Panamanians were killed during the invasion, according to official Pentagon figures; an internal Army memo estimated one thousand civilian casualties.[48] Some church and human rights observers believed that there were many more deaths. Troops detained more than five thousand Panamanians and kept them in prison camps.[49] The destruction occasioned by the attack, in addition to looting in the chaos that followed, caused more than $1 billion in damage, which compounded losses suffered during twenty-one months of sanctions.[50]

The United States used simultaneous and overwhelming force far beyond that necessary to subdue the PDF, which had only three thousand trained soldiers. Much of the force was directed at targets in heavily populated areas. The military for the first time deployed the $50 million F-117A Stealth bomber, which is invisible to radar, although Panama had no radar defenses. (It was later learned that the Stealth missed its bombing target in Rio Hato by more than three hundred yards.[51])

Most of those displaced and killed during the invasion lived in El Chorrillo, the neighborhood next to PDF headquarters that burned to the ground, although many Panamanians died from gunfire and rocket attacks, as well. The *chorilleros* were mostly Blacks and Mestizos whose families lived in tenement buildings that had been built for West Indian laborers during the canal-construction era. The impoverished community of San Miguelito was also bombed. Across town at Punta Paitilla, wealthy Panamanians watched the invasion from their condominiums in expensive high-rises. At nearby Paitilla Airport, Navy SEALS were ordered to undertake a risky operation to disable Noriega's personal jet at close range to avoid damage to nearby residences from crossfire; four SEALS lost their lives in the operation. No such care was taken with the PDF headquarters next to El Chorrillo, where U.S. forces bombed from the air. There, tracer bullets and flares contributed to the conflagration that incinerated the community and many people who were trapped inside.[52]

Across the isthmus in Colón, the Caribbean port populated mostly by Afro-Caribbean Blacks, the victims were similarly dark-skinned. When looting of city businesses threatened to move into the gated warehouses of the Colón Free Zone, armed businessmen began shooting at the looters, killing three. The businessmen asked for military help and were joined by U.S. troops on December 22. When the shooting was over, one U.S. soldier and fifty-one Panamanians — including civilians, members of the paramilitary Dignity Battalions, and soldiers — were dead. Under an agreement with the soldiers, the merchants kept their guns.[53]

The names of the twenty-five U.S. soldiers killed during the invasion rolled across TV screens around the world. Yet a register of Panamanians killed during the invasion has never been published, even in Latin America.

Through accumulated media images before and during the invasion, Noriega came wholly to represent the tropics' primitive and hostile forces and the object toward which so much military fury was directed, although both the motives and the effects were much wider. Given the rising fear of crack cocaine's savage effects on people in the United States that year, it was not difficult to channel public and media outrage at a trafficker and focus attention on him to the exclusion of other issues. Thus, although military objectives focused on dismantling the PDF and installing the new civilian government, U.S. media coverage zeroed in on the invasion's initial failure to find Noriega, who was on the lam until December 24.

The manhunt for Noriega brought out the old metaphors of Panamanians as savages (see figure 13). ABC News anchor Peter Jennings characterized Noriega as "one of the more odious creatures with whom the United States has had a relationship." Other journalists turned to metaphors of jungle animals that recalled the myths of

13. "Bush versus Noriega." (Cartoon by Victor Juhasz, *New York Times*, December 31, 1989.)

"cocainized negros" who were immune to bullets. "Noriega seemed almost superhuman in his ability to slither away before we got him," anchorman Bill Beutel told TV viewers in New York.[54]

When soldiers searching for Noriega found materials used in Santeria, a popular religion in Caribbean cultures, they used them to suggest that Noriega worshiped the devil. SouthCom told reporters soon after the invasion that 110 pounds of cocaine were found in Noriega's so-called witch house. All this played big as "voodoo" on TV news and on the front pages, invoking more racial stereotypes. The *Los Angeles Times* excelled at picturing Noriega as an "other" worthy of military rage: "Vats of blood. Animal entrails. A picture of Adolf Hitler. Spike-heeled shoes. More than 100 pounds of cocaine. All were part of the bizarre scenes encountered by American troops as they stormed Noriega's inner sanctum."[55] A month later, when the "cocaine" turned out to be tamales, the military's admission of deception was a footnote at best.[56] More important, the "witch propaganda," like the drama of finding the general, served to divert attention from the fact that the military operation had other objectives besides Noriega — and that it had affected many thousands of people who had nothing to do with him.

North Americans had no individual political celebrities besides Noriega to frame their understanding of Panamanian politics and public life. Few U.S. citizens could name the Panamanian president installed during the invasion, and fewer still knew who succeeded him in 1994. They might have known that the salsa singer and actor Ruben Blades or the baseball pitching star Mariano Rivera were Panamanian, but they came to know these figures through the U.S. entertainment industry, not as people formed by Panamanian society.

The result was a tendency to identify Panama with Noriega, and it was logical to invade the country to hunt him down and take him to court. Other Panamanians were alternately seen as victims of this drug trafficker or as paying this price for purportedly harboring the general.

Equally important, no individual U.S. soldiers or commanders ever became the subject of such intense emotional scrutiny or personal comment as did Noriega. Media reports on the invasion did not focus on Generals Maxwell ("Mad Max") Thurman or Carl Stiner, the SouthCom chief and operational head of the invasion, respectively, as responsible for the hundreds of killings produced by the action. The Pentagon's policy during the invasion of restricting access to graphic images of blood and gore, including the wounds of U.S. soldiers, had an impact beyond limiting public recoiling from the human consequences of the invasion. It also reinforced the view that North Americans are not so visceral, not animals. The visceral emotions associated with the conflict belonged to Panama.

AFTERMATH AND CONSEQUENCES

With Noriega and the PDF overthrown and combat continuing, Panama had no government. After two or three days, U.S. troops stepped in to run affairs and execute the Pentagon's post-invasion operation, code-named BLIND LOGIC. The military assigned officers to oversee twenty-two Panamanian government ministries and agencies, effectively running Panama for several months.[57] The military further disabled the civilian government by seizing fifteen thousand boxes of documents from Panamanian government offices and denying civilian officials access to them for years.[58] An incident that illustrates the relationship between the military officers and their Panamanian charges occurred in January, when President Guillermo Endara agreed to meet in the presidential palace with several labor leaders. "Inside the building, we were going up the stairs with Endara, when a U.S. colonel called to us from the top of the stairs, saying, 'No one can go upstairs.

Go and look for another room.' . . . Upon hearing this, Endara turned around, and we all went back down. He said to us, 'Why don't we sit down in this little room.' "[59]

The invasion radically altered the calculus of power in Panama's relations with the United States for all political leaders but especially for the Revolutionary Democratic Party (PRD) founded by Torrijos and later dominated by Noriega. The invasion had demonstrated the impotence of Panama's institutions, divided before the invasion between those co-opted by Noriega's nationalist discourse and those in the opposition who welcomed intervention if it brought electoral democracy.

The acceptance of the invasion by the U.S. media, Congress, and public also had important implications for U.S. policy toward the isthmus. The Clinton administration was unrepentant about the 1989 invasion. "The U.S. government takes responsibility for its actions no matter what administration did it," State Department officer David Noble said about the invasion in 1996. "If Noriega were still there, everyone would be saying, 'Why do you support him? Why aren't you doing something about him? How can you get him out?' "[60] The State Department's conclusion ratified the impunity with which the invasion was carried out and reinforced Washington's assumption of its right to invade Panama, overturn its government, and dismantle its armed forces, at enormous human cost to some of the country's dark-skinned communities.

The invasion was also a moment of catharsis in attention to Panama. Panamanian attorney Miguel Antonio Bernal pointed out, "Noriega's arrest ended the American media's interest in Panama and ushered in an era of American apathy. This neglect has hardly been benign."[61] Media coverage of cocaine and crack also declined precipitously after the invasion, as if Noriega's capture had brought down the whole cocaine enterprise. In fact, the use of Panama as a transshipment point for cocaine and a platform for money laundering remained at similar levels after the invasion.[62] But with such intense attention shone personally on Noriega, the resumption of drug traffic went virtually unreported in the United States. A collective forgetting had begun.

After 1988, the axis for U.S. policy in Latin America and the Caribbean was the drug war. Between 1988, when the drug-war debate set the stage for the invasion of Panama, and 1995, when Washington and Panama first began negotiations for a post–1999 U.S. military presence, the U.S. counterdrug bureaucracy was institutionalized and underwent significant growth. In pure budgetary terms, the Defense Department's funds for counterdrug surveillance nearly quadrupled between the fiscal years 1989 and 1993, from $212 million to $844 million.[63] President Bush's Andean Initiative, a five-year program announced in September 1989 that aimed to cut the coca supply in half, featured $2.2 billion in mostly military aid to Colombia, Peru, and Bolivia, which was administered by SouthCom.

General Thurman reassigned the command's brightest officers to a new Counternarcotics Operations Center. He submitted dozens of proposals for drug-war programs to agencies in Washington, "jump-starting" the drug effort, according to a State Department official. One analyst familiar with SouthCom described the drug war as a shark's mouth that devoured everything, while the war in El Salvador and the invasion of Panama were the shark's dorsal fins.[64]

The U.S. overseas antidrug strategy did not aim to reduce the quantitative supply of illegal drugs. Instead, the objective was to increase the cost of the drug, both for producers and for consumers. The idea was to elevate the costs of production and transportation in South America so that these costs would be passed to the market, dissuading purchases. But studies by Peter Reuter, an economist with RAND Corporation, show that the earnings and costs to traffickers in Latin America represent only 5 percent of the consumer price—a percentage that does not affect demand by drug users.[65]

Drug trafficking also became a rationale for possible direct U.S. intervention on the isthmus. After the Persian Gulf War of 1991, the Pentagon proposed seven war-fighting scenarios in which U.S. troops might intervene in the future. The only scenario in Latin America was in Panama, under the hypothesis that "former drug-dealing Panamanian Defense Force leaders who have connections to narco-terrorist elements of the Revolutionary Armed Forces of Colombia" would threaten the canal. The scenario called for simultaneous airborne and amphibious landings at Panamanian ports.[66]

In August 1992, SouthCom established the Joint Air Operations Center on Howard Air Force Base, a set of computers staffed by twenty to twenty-five airmen at a time whose mission was to track unauthorized flights throughout the Andean and Central American region. The center, which became the centerpiece of the proposed post–1999 military presence in Panama, coordinated intelligence from a web of ground- and ship-based radars and aircraft that were widely dispersed throughout the region. The center at Howard had representatives and military pilots from Peru, Colombia, Venezuela, Ecuador, and Brazil. The center and its associated radar sites would monitor forty-five thousand flights annually in Latin America. Only one hundred fifty of those flights (.3%) were suspected of being involved in drug traffic; of those, twenty-one were shot down or forced to land.[67]

The military strategy to fight drugs was a failure on its own terms. Between 1988 and 1995, the amount of land planted with coca leaf in Latin America grew from 186,000 hectares to 214,800 hectares, an increase of 15 percent. The street price of cocaine in the United States remained stable, and the purity of heroin actually increased. In 1996, the amount of land planted with coca leaf in Colombia went up by 32 percent. This was primarily due to the so-called balloon effect: when one part is squeezed, the substance moves elsewhere. In Bolivia and Peru, coca leaf was planted on only 1 percent of the land where it can be cultivated. As the General Accounting Office reported, "when air interdiction efforts have proven successful, traffickers have increased their use of maritime and overland transportation routes."

The explanation for the persistence of the military's interdiction strategy, despite its lack of success, can be glimpsed in an encounter with one of its proponents. In 1997, I pointed out in a meeting with Deputy Undersecretary of Defense for Interamerican Affairs Maria Fernandez that by nearly any concrete measure of drug-war success — street price of cocaine, supply in the United States, acreage planted with coca leaf — the supply-side strategy against cocaine was ineffective. Fernandez responded, "That's a philosophical difference," although the argument had been made purely on tangible measures. Military planners, however, are accustomed to addressing threats outside the United States and focusing problem-solving externally, on others, while trying to seize and destroy tangible manifestations. For them, the critique of the interdiction anti-drug strategy as being ineffective is a philosophical matter.[68]

The military's counterdrug mission became the axis for discussions lasting three years to keep U.S. military troops in Panama after 1999. Unlike the campaign in 1988–89, U.S. Latin American drug policy from 1995 to 1998 was not centrally focused on trafficking or money laundering in Panama — except perhaps as rhetorical leverage for a deal with Panama. It was focused instead on Colombia, Peru, and Bolivia, the countries identified in the Andean Initiative as "first-tier" nations for the fight against cocaine transshipment. The language was different from the earlier period, as well. For the most part, the vitriolic personal rhetoric against a single figure such as Noriega was gone and replaced with abstraction. Military spokesmen gave their understated attention to the somewhat sterile activities proposed for U.S. personnel. "They're a bunch of people on computer screens or radios and telephones," said Colonel David Hunt about the facility around which the United States proposed to structure its post–1999 bases in Panama. "It's all done with electrons."[69]

Article XIII of the 1977 Panama Canal Treaty specifically provided for the transfer to Panama without charge of all U.S. military facilities by December 31, 1999, and Article V of the companion Neutrality Treaty called for the departure of all U.S. troops from the isthmus by the same date. While the U.S. Senate was ratifying the treaties, however, Senator Sam Nunn attached a reservation stating that nothing would prevent the two countries from reaching an agreement for a post–1999 U.S. military presence in Panama. This reservation was included in the ratification instrument signed by Panama, although it was not part of the package approved by Panama's electorate in the treaty plebiscite.

Article 319 of the Panamanian Constitution provided that any international agreement for use of the canal or the lands on its banks must be approved first by the Legislative Assembly, then by a majority of Panamanian voters at least ninety days after the assembly vote. This provision fundamentally conditioned all of Panama's actions during the negotiations in 1995–98. Panamanian negotiators could not take executive action; instead, they would have to submit any agreement to a political process.

Conditions in Panama initially seemed to favor continuing U.S. military bases. Beginning in 1991, polls showed that a solid majority of public opinion — from 60 percent to 80 percent — wanted U.S. military bases and troops to stay in Panama after the transfer of the canal in 1999.[70] The polls were reported widely not only in Panama but also in the mainstream U.S. media under headlines such as "Yankee Don't Go Home."[71] Despite the polls, the continued presence of the U.S. military was not a major issue of public discussion in Panama in the early 1990s. President Endara, who was sworn into office on a U.S. military base while bombs rained on Panama City, did not have the political legitimacy to negotiate continued bases with Washington — and later would oppose attempts by his successor to do so. The United States waited until the PRD — a party founded by Torrijos and thus carrying significant nationalist credentials — was back in power.

The May 1994 elections put the PRD back in the saddle. President Ernesto Pérez Balladares, a banker by training, had been campaign manager for Noriega's candidate in 1994 and received only a plurality of the votes cast (33 percent). In August 1995, General Barry McCaffrey, chief of SouthCom, publicly called for keeping up to five thousand U.S. troops in Panama.[72] During Pérez Balladares's first state visit to Washington the following month, Clinton raised the prospect of keeping U.S. bases after 1999. Pérez Balladares responded that Panama would need to see some economic benefit from a continued presence. The two sides agreed to begin formal negotiations by the end of November.[73]

The talks got off to a rocky start. The Clinton administration's low level of commitment to a continued military presence in Panama was evident from the beginning. "People here are not willing to expend a lot of political and financial capital" on the negotiations, one official said at their outset.[74] Officials worried about the precedent set only a few years earlier, during negotiations with the Philippines for U.S. bases, which were not only drawn out but resulted in a rejection of extending the military's stay.

In the early phases of discussions, official and public attention focused on the economic benefits of the military bases. Ambassador William Hughes was frustrated by the debate's focus on rent or no-rent as the central question. "When I arrived in Panama" in November 1995, Hughes said, "I wasn't off the plane more than a few days when it became clear that the national dialogue in Panama was very shallow. It was rent or no rent."[75] Colonel Richard O'Connor then announced publicly that the United States would not pay rent for the bases. Foreign Minister Gabriel Lewis was enthusiastic about keeping bases, but the lack of rent undercut support for a deal, and he asked Hughes to delay the talks. Panama's postponement had put the issue on the back burner for the White House. After Michael Skol, the U.S. negotiator, retired in January 1996, no new negotiator was appointed for nine months. Other forces took up the debate about the bases' economics.[76]

SouthCom asserted — and the U.S. media reiterated — that the bases "pumped" $450 million into the Panamanian economy, which was sometimes claimed to represent 13 percent of the country's gross national product. (In a $7 billion economy, the direct income of $300 million represented 4.5 percent. The bases employed only 0.6 percent of the national labor force.) Opponents pointed out that the reduced military presence under consideration would employ even fewer Panamanians. The United States was making the case that its mere presence provided ample economic "compensation."

But in 1996, pollsters began to ask Panamanians what they thought about a military presence if the United States did not pay for the privilege of keeping bases in the country, and support dropped considerably, to 37–49 percent.[77] The White House and Pentagon refused to consider rent or "indirect" compensation, such as trade agreements or aid packages, for budgetary reasons and because of the precedent it would set for other countries in which the United States ran bases. "It has to be something that they and we see in our national interest," a National Security Council official insisted.[78] Meanwhile, Panamanian Foreign Minister Lewis Galindo, who sometimes "may have forgotten which side he represented," according to both U.S. and Panamanian officials, became ill and resigned in May 1996.[79] He was replaced in June by Ricardo Alberto Arias, who was more circumspect about an agreement, believing that Panama needed to gain more from any deal if it was to be accepted in Panama. Finding no common ground on the issue of compensation, Pérez Balladares announced in November 1996 that U.S. military bases were off the table, and that only a "civilian-run" MCC would be discussed.

PANAMA'S NARCO-VULNERABILITY

To understand why the MCC would be more politically acceptable than "bases," it is important to know the context of U.S. drug policy in the region in 1996. Partly spurred by election-year politics, as well as by the appointment of General Barry McCaffrey as drug czar in January 1996, Washington heated up the drug war. In March, the State Department de-certified Colombia's cooperation in the drug war and shortly thereafter revoked the U.S. visa of Colombian President Ernesto Samper, who had been accused of accepting campaign funds from cocaine traffickers. A State Department official threatened that if Panama did not "take vigorous steps to clean up its financial sector, it [would] become more difficult for the United States to back international financial activity through that country." Assistant Secretary of State for International Narcotics Matters Robert Gelbard also said that Panama was "at great risk" of drug cartels' "taking power" after the withdrawal of U.S. troops in 1999.[80] Ambassador Hughes claimed in a hearing before Panama's Legislative Assembly on April 8 that the Darién province bordering Colombia hosted two hundred secret air strips and that the cartels continued to launder money in Panama, although he gave no evidence for the claims.[81]

These actions were not lost on Pérez Balladares. George Bush had made drug trafficking the principal rationale for the 1989 U.S. invasion of Panama that targeted Noriega, who had controlled the PRD, over which Pérez Balladares now presided. The Panamanian president knew the cost of stepping over an unspecified line and falling out of Washington's favor. Much depended, wrote the Panamanian priest Nestor Jaén, on "the expressed or latent interest of the United States in the bases. If this interest is great, then all the pressures will go in that direction and there will be grave danger that Panama gives in even on points where it should not. Unfortunately that is our history, and we don't escape its logic."[82] Negotiations for a continued military presence would not take place between equal partners.

In June, Pérez Balladares sheepishly admitted receiving $51,000 from a Cali cartel figure during the 1994 presidential campaign.[83] The news threw the country into turmoil. Within four weeks of this admission, while the scandal of the narco-checks still dominated the Panamanian press, Pérez Balladares publicly offered the United States free use of Howard Air Force Base after 1999 for the "counter-drug center."[84]

The base negotiations throughout were caught between two irreconcilable positions: the U.S. Southern Command, supported by Senator Jesse Helms and other conservatives who demanded unilateral U.S. control for any post–1999 presence in Panama, and the sovereignty and environmental concerns of Panamanians and other Latin American leaders.

In the meantime, negotiations for the MCC continued to be subjected to cost-benefit analyses on both sides. For Panama, the potential benefits were thought to include income from services and supplies, Panamanians employed by the military, and purchases by U.S. personnel (estimated at $35 million for each one thousand soldiers). The U.S. military also conducted road-building and medical-training operations in the countryside at a level beyond what it did in the rest of the region. Last but not least, having the U.S. military near at hand historically had served Panamanian political elites as a security blanket when they faced domestic trouble. For example, the government had called in U.S. soldiers in December 1990 to put down a police rebellion.

The costs to Panama included lost opportunities for commercial uses of the strategically located bases, the environmental impact of military operations, and the political costs from alienating nationalist sectors. For some Panamanians, sovereignty was linked to the country's right to charge rent for use of national territory. Critics also pointed out that Howard Air Force Base, which Pérez Balladares offered for use without charge, was valued at $1.5 billion by the president's economic advisers — or more than a third of the value of all the U.S. bases combined. Howard had the largest potential for civilian use, said Fernando Manfredo Jr., who oversaw the creation of a master plan for civilian use of the bases.[85]

For the United States, the benefits included faster and cheaper air access to the Andean nations, where the drug war primarily was being fought, than was available from U.S. bases in Puerto Rico or the United States. For such access, the military's priority was keeping the air strip at Howard Air Force Base. The computer center that "moved electrons" could be run from Thailand, Colonel Hunt acknowledged: "They would just have to work at night." The bases also were and could continue to be a center for military training, ranging from the

Jungle Operations Training Center on Fort Sherman, used for U.S. and Latin American military forces, to a riverine training facility on Rodman Naval Station. The bases in Panama had a psychological benefit, as well: they invoked memories of the days when Uncle Sam was indeed sovereign on the isthmus. "The old hands that work on Panama," mused one U.S. officer, "are used to the way things have been, with maids, service, and don't want to accept change."

The costs to the United States included the direct expenses of maintaining bases, the political contradiction of keeping bases in Panama while closing bases at home, and — if rent or economic benefits were to be provided — the precedent established for other nations that were hosting U.S. bases around the world. The reticence about costs was shaped by the Pentagon's bureaucratic structure. SouthCom, the most vocal champion of keeping the bases, is a joint command that does not own assets. Instead, the service branches are responsible for funding operations and new requirements. In the case of Panama, the Army from the beginning "non-concurred" — that is, dissented — from paying the costs of maintaining a presence in Panama, whereas the Air Force was willing "to belly up to the bar," in the words of a treaty implementation officer at the Pentagon. The difference most directly affected Fort Sherman and Fort Clayton, run by the Army.[86]

As they played out, the negotiations suffered a series of setbacks that delayed and prolonged the process. And the longer the process took, the more organized opposition to the military became. At the same time, as nonessential facilities shut down, the withdrawal gathered institutional momentum within the military. After SouthCom's headquarters moved to Miami in March 1997, for example, Panama and the talks became more remote for SouthCom leaders.

The MCC, which dominated U.S–Panama relations in 1997, presented its own set of problems. First of all, what was it? Panamanian leaders insisted that the MCC was not a military base but acknowledged that it would require upward of two thousand soldiers, sometimes referred to as "technicians," to operate. Pérez Balladares had rejected military "bases" unless they paid rent, so why was his government proposing something so similar under another name? The counterdrug mission proposed for the center essentially was being run out of Howard Air Force Base already, highlighting its continuity with the military bases. Opponents persuasively argued in the press that the center was a "disguised military base." Suspicions about the MCC's real intent were strengthened by the secrecy and exclusion of opposition parties, and even PRD officials, from information about the negotiations. They were reinforced in February 1997, when a U.S. Senate staff report revealed that former Foreign Minister Gabriel Lewis Galindo had reached an "understanding" with Ambassador Hughes about selling the military presence as part of the MCC, which would serve as "a political umbrella or even a cloak for a continued U.S. military presence."

In September 1996, with Republicans harshly criticizing the Clinton administration for its lack of energy in the war on drugs, the appointment of Ambassador John Negroponte as lead negotiator for a base agreement with Panama was leaked to the press, less than a week after the Senate had passed a resolution supporting a post–1999 military presence. Negroponte was known for the role he had played in imposing U.S. bases on Honduras during the Nicaraguan Contra war in the Reagan years and for resigning from the National Security Council in 1973 to protest concessions in the Paris Peace Agreement with Vietnam. Nationalists and peace activists criticized Negroponte as a cold-warrior who would impose bases on Panama.

The political foundations for the talks then suffered a series of rapid setbacks. In late September, all political parties and organizations from a wide spectrum of Panamanian civilian society met under the United Nations' auspices to reach consensus on the future of the canal area. The gathering's statement rejected continued military bases as an "obstacle" to national development.[87] The first cracks were appearing in the attempt to legitimize a continued military presence through popular acceptance or on economic grounds.

Panamanian officials were emphatic that the MCC would involve the participation of other Latin American countries. Such participation was necessary to give Panama domestic cover when it sought legislative and popular approval for the agreement. But regional support was weak, at best. In October 1996, a meeting of the region's defense ministers in Argentina had rejected a Panamanian proposal to support the Counterdrug Center. And although Panamanian media reported in 1997 that Colombia, Brazil, and Mexico had been incorporated into the negotiations, Panama had only given those countries some information about the center and had not even sought out their views.

During this time, opposition to the negotiations grew. The Fellowship of Reconciliation (FOR) and the human rights group Service for

Peace and Justice in Panama had initiated a campaign in 1994 to convert the bases in Panama to civilian use. After the Pérez Balladares–Clinton meeting in 1995, other human rights, labor, and student groups in Panama also began to raise their voices against a continued military presence. So, too, did a sector of businessmen, including Roberto Eisenmann, publisher of the newspaper *La Prensa*, who had earlier supported the abolition of Panama's army. Political elites on both sides badly miscalculated the depth of opposition, which mushroomed during the course of the negotiations.

At the beginning of July, the FOR released news that the United States had tested weapons containing depleted uranium in Panama, as well as chemical weapons. The information was based on military documents and the testimony of a whistle-blower who had been under contract to the Pentagon. The story unleashed a minor feeding frenzy in the Panamanian press, prompting a series of denials and retractions by U.S. officials and promises by Panamanians that they knew nothing of the tests and were investigating. The story broke on the eve of the start of "formal" negotiations for the MCC and just after the Army's Tropic Test Center (TTC), which had conducted both the depleted-uranium and chemical weapons tests in Panama, had quietly submitted a proposal to stay in Panama after 1999 as an academic nonprofit organization. The problem of contamination generated by U.S. military activities would prove to be a thorn in the negotiation process. In the case of the TTC, the revelations irrevocably disabled the center's image as a civilian science outfit, its director later admitted.[88]

In September 1997, Negroponte retired and was replaced by Thomas McNamara, a former ambassador to Colombia. At this point, the negotiations moved into high gear, as both sides were working against the clock. For Washington, structuring an arrangement into the military budget became increasingly difficult as the months passed. For Panama, any agreement would need to be submitted to the assembly and to a plebiscite. To avoid being entirely politicized, this had to occur before campaigning began for the May 1999 national elections. Although other deadlines for an agreement had come and gone, both governments said they would either conclude negotiations by the end of the year or there would be no deal.

McNamara proved to be a skilled negotiator — perhaps too skilled. Reflecting after the fact, U.S. and Panamanian participants in the talks believed that the United States pressed for so many concessions that the end result became politically infeasible in Panama, where it had to receive approval. According to Panamanian negotiator Jorge Ritter, U.S. negotiators were uninterested in the deal unless they received everything they asked for. At the beginning of the talks, he said, the Pentagon favored a continued presence, and the State Department opposed it. By the end of the talks, the State Department was trying to make a workable agreement, while the military passively or actively opposed an agreement.[89]

Ambassador Hughes believed that forces within the Pentagon were trying to sabotage the negotiations. "[SouthCom chief General] Wesley Clark was airborne sometimes as much as twice a week trying to get the MCC back on track," Hughes said.[90] According to an officer based in Panama during the negotiations, Clark agreed to concessions during his tenure (mid-1996 to mid-1997) that diminished considerably the military's interest in a deal. "Wes Clark gave away about half of what was on that table for nothing, even before we got to formal negotiations," the officer said. The core of the concessions was a reduction in the number of troops who would be stationed at the bases from five thousand to two thousand five hundred and a reduction in the number of bases from seven to three.[91]

It was at this moment that Pedro González went on trial for the murder of Zak Hernández, a Puerto Rican soldier stationed in Panama in 1992 who was picked off in an ambush on the eve of a visit by George Bush. González was the son of one of the PRD's most powerful leaders, Gerardo González, president of the Legislative Assembly and an opponent of the U.S. military presence. Physical evidence and three witnesses tied the younger González to the crime, but a jury acquitted him on November 2. U.S. officials were outraged and saw implications for a continued military presence if "soldiers could be killed with impunity." But defense lawyers had tapped a deeper well of feeling in Panama by invoking the hundreds of Panamanians killed during the invasion, implicitly saying that Hernández was getting payback for what his kind had given. If it was going to go that way, and soldiers stayed in Panama, then it would be a long time before the ledger was evened up.

Negotiators did not let this get in their way. On December 23, Washington and Panama announced an "agreement in principle" on a counterdrug center, with Howard Air Force Base as its core, for twelve years. The final texts, they said, were still being finished. No other

Latin American countries participated in the announcement. The agreement established the MCC's control of all of Howard Air Force Base, port facilities and buildings on Rodman Naval Station, Fort Kobbe, buildings and lands on Farfan Naval Station, Panama Canal College, seven buildings in Corozal, Galeta Island, and unspecified firing ranges and training areas. The counterdrug center found it necessary for its operations to include hundreds of housing units, swimming pools, movie theaters, playing fields, chapels, gyms, schools, and a post office, as well as Howard's airstrip and other military facilities. Under the draft accord's provision for bombing ranges, Panama's police force would have become the "owners" of the ranges, but their military use would continue. Use of the firing ranges could be shared with Panamanian government agencies, although Panama had no armed forces.

In the case of a conflict among members of the counterdrug center, Panama would have had no recourse to the United Nations, the Organization of American States, or any other "foreign" body to mediate the dispute. Furthermore, Panama would be prohibited from enacting new laws or enforcing existing laws that might regulate or "interfere" with the counterdrug center's activities. U.S. officials would exercise criminal jurisdiction over U.S. personnel in the MCC who violated security laws. In addition, soldiers and other MCC personnel would be exempt from all taxes, tolls, and customs inspections within Panama.

Any semblance of a consensus fell apart within days of announcing an agreement, in both the elite and grassroots spheres. When McNamara arrived in Panama after the holiday to initial the agreement, Foreign Affairs Minister Ricardo Alberto Arias emerged from a briefing of Brazilian, Mexican, and Colombian officials to say that their review and support of the document must be obtained before Panama signed on.

Five days later, on the thirty-fourth anniversary of the flag riots — a day of commemorating Panamanian martyrdom at the hands of U.S. troops — a broad new grassroots coalition formed, the National Movement for the Defense of Sovereignty. The event illustrated how the anti-base movement in Panama had gathered strength and momentum, with hundreds of activists showing up for meetings and thousands for a protest against the military accord. Former President Jorge Illueca, who once was president of the UN General Assembly, joined the movement, adding considerable prestige.

There were also divisions within the government and the ruling party. A meeting of leading figures examined the agreement's text in mid-January and "tore it apart," according to one participant. Both this group and other countries were especially peeved about the agreement's provision for "other missions" in the region besides counterdrug actions—a potential gaping loophole for U.S. intervention. Foreign Affairs Minister Arias said that Panama opposed the agreement's provision for military missions unrelated to counterdrug operations, "and other countries we consulted also objected." Panama also objected to the United States' insistence that Panama not have jurisdiction over crimes committed by U.S. soldiers. Instead, Panama insisted on the right to end the agreement after three years, instead of the twelve years agreed in December, if it became a cause of conflict between the two countries. Arias met with White House officials on January 21 and told them that the bilateral base agreement had to be renegotiated for "internal" reasons, or that the two countries would have to drop the project.[92] Three days later, the *New York Times* came out against the Panama base proposal in an editorial, saying: "It is dismaying to see Congress and the Clinton administration return to a strategy that has failed and could harm Latin democracies."[93]

Even more devastating was the publication of a full draft of the agreement in Mexico's *El Excelsior* on January 27. This leak "killed [the MCC]," according to a U.S. military officer involved in the negotiations. "It made it impossible for Panama to accept any agreement."[94] According to the draft agreement, which Panamanian and U.S. officials said had been revised, no party could withdraw from the center until the year 2012. The framework agreement set up the center's structure as a multilateral entity, but it was up to Panama, not Washington, to negotiate separate bilateral agreements to include other countries in the center. The draft caused understandable indignation in Panama, exacerbated by the fact that it had not been published there first. Mexican officials also harshly criticized the "exclusivity" of the pact negotiated by the United States and Panama, saying that it gave "excessive responsibility" to the U.S. military for the antidrug center's security.[95]

Activists' suspicions that the center was a cover for SouthCom's traditional operations was confirmed by a Pentagon report that was leaked in January as the accord was unraveling. The Special Forces stationed in Panama, known as SOCSOUTH, had not even considered a location outside Panama until Arias's ultimatum in January. The "current plan and only option SOCSOUTH seriously considered is to remain in Panama," the Pentagon said.[96] The Panamanian counterproposal to reduce the term to three years was clearly unacceptable to the United States. That is where the project stalled.

After several months of pessimism, the project's fate was definitively sealed in September, when Pérez Balladares lost his bid to be allowed to run for reelection. On September 24, the governments formally laid down negotiations. The Pentagon then scrambled to find other "forward operating locations" in the region, including in Ecuador, Aruba, Curacao, and El Salvador. Most Army troops stationed in Panama moved to Puerto Rico.[97]

POSTMORTEM

In the aftermath, some blamed the military for the failure of the negotiations. U.S. negotiator Thomas McNamara concluded that "there was a miscalculation, prevalent among the military, that the Panamanians would, in the end, accept a large U.S. military presence despite the intense opposition within the ruling elite," which "made negotiations more difficult."[98] "The Pentagon thought it was a 'gimme' and it blew up in their face," said Jack Vaughan, a former U.S. ambassador to Panama.[99] "Both sides made the mistake of centering everything in the post–1999 relationship on the [counterdrug] center," reflected a U.S. military official. Without the center, he said, everything after December 31, 1999, created "panic."[100]

For their part, some military officers blamed Panama. The Panamanian government's "reneging" on the MCC also brought back the old animal metaphors. "Arias was a snake," said one officer close to the negotiations. "He lied to Hughes, mostly about the MCC."[101] Helms accused the Pérez Balladares government of "playing petty domestic politics."[102] Such "domestic political" considerations included taking into account the objections of opponents of the bases, who successfully articulated economic and environmental grounds for the military's withdrawal. They invoked concerns of sovereignty and national dignity, as well as the history of U.S. intervention in Panama. Other Latin American countries were also important to the outcome. Finally, having a calendar for the treaty commitment helped the anti-base struggle. It meant that the anti-bases movement had only to prevent an agreement from being approved before time ran out—qualitatively different from the more difficult task of forging a new one.

With the U.S. military definitely leaving, the two governments turned their attention to the legacy the bases would leave behind. Panamanians worried that unexploded bombs, chemical agents, and other environmental hazards on the former bases would saddle them with a series of risks whose full dimensions were still hidden. Washington already was turning its attention elsewhere. It was a recipe for prolonged conflict.

5 ☆ THE POLITICS OF ENVIRONMENTAL COVER-UP

> The presence of U.S. bases in Panama has saved 80 percent of lands still controlled by [the Department of Defense] — in stark contrast to the deforestation which has occurred, most of it in the past fifteen years, on many of the neighboring lands outside U.S. control.
> — U.S. Southern Command statement, 1996

> The current approach by this administration is to try to sneak off into the night quietly with as little appropriations and effort as possible.
> — Robert Pastor, 1998

> Does the U.S. live up to its moral commitments in Panama? That is the basic question. — Juan Carlos Navarro, 1998[1]

Although it is less than fifteen miles from Panama City, Andrés Romero's home is far from what is commonly called "civilization." With no vehicle of his own, he must take a bus to Arraiján on the Pan-American Highway and from there catch another transport to the town of Emperador. It takes Romero an hour and a half to get home from his job doing outdoor maintenance for the Panama Canal Commission. Situated atop a hill that overlooks green, forested valleys and distant hills on one side and the rural community of Huile on the other, the building has no electricity. But the spot receives a cooling breeze and is surrounded by sumptuous natural beauty.

During the 1970s, Romero was in the habit of walking to the fence between Panama and the Canal Zone to sell oranges or chocolates to the soldiers or trade them for American cigarettes. One June day in 1977, on his way back from the fence, he found a canister on the ground. Curious, he picked it up and brought it home. There, with his three- and five-year-old children nearby, he set to trying to open the thing with his hands. It exploded, throwing him across the yard and burning all the hair off his face and arms. A nephew ran for help, and Romero was rushed to Santo Tomás Hospital, where he remained for two months.

Romero's wife was not able to visit him every day, and the day he was released he took a public bus home. She saw him walking up the hill and asked, "Is that you?" She barely recognized him. "It's me," he said.[2]

Less than a month later, Jimmy Carter and Omar Torrijos signed the Panama Canal treaties. The treaties obligated the United States to remove all threats to human life, health, and safety on U.S. military lands "insofar as may be practicable," before departing Panama in 1999.

The transfer to Panama of explosive ranges riddled with bombs, mortars, rockets, and other dangers, and how to interpret the treaty's "practicable" clause, would become the single most contentious issue in implementing the treaties. The United States tried to limit its liability for cleaning up the ranges, fearful of setting a precedent for other overseas U.S. military facilities. "It's all about money," said two different senior U.S. officers about the reasons that the United States did not do more. Panamanians wanted the United States to clean up the bases and ranges, but when U.S. officials withheld information or excluded Panama from decision making, higher-level Panamanians were wary of pressing the United States until late in the process. In the end, the United States left more than one hundred thousand pieces of unexploded ordnance in Panama.[3]

The Panamanian government hesitated to raise the contamination issue because of two principal fears. The first was that public discussion of the bases' environmental problems might scare away investors considering projects on the reverting lands, because it meant uncertain liability for those obtaining concessions to the facilities. The other related to the United States and became more prominent as Pérez Balladares's government increasingly put its political capital into an agreement to keep the military in Panama. In the way that U.S. military environmental policy was framed, cleanup was an inherently conflictive issue and required diplomatic confrontation to protect Panama's interests.

I must make a disclaimer — or a claim — here, because I was involved in this controversy through my work with the Fellowship of Reconciliation (FOR). As a researcher, I helped uncover information that, by his own account, blindsided U.S. Ambassador William Hughes. As an informal adviser to Panamanians inside and outside the government, I became a reference for both technical and political insights into cleanup of military bases in Panama and elsewhere. And as an activist, I helped organize efforts to call the U.S. government to accountability for the explosives it was leaving behind in Panama and to full disclosure of information that would shed light on these environmental dangers.

Throughout, the military assumed the right unilaterally to define and redefine treaty terms and ideas crucial to the outcome and to co-opt environmentalist values to the institution's purposes. Removal of explosives was defined as "containing" or "controlling" them. "Practicable" cleanup was determined not according to whether it could be done but according to how long it would take, even as the military continued to bomb the ranges until nearly the end of the treaty period. Most insidiously, forested lands contaminated with unexploded ordnance became "preserved" areas. In effect, U.S. environmental policy in the canal area was to protect forests against Panamanian civilians — by mining them.

Romero's accident was part of a longer history of nearby communities' experience of unexploded ordnance on the three active firing ranges in Panama, each of which lies on the western and less populated bank of the canal. Before the canal was built, especially during the canal-construction period, the Panama Railroad gave rise to bustling towns, including Empire, on what would later be the canal's west bank. When Gatun Lake was flooded for the canal, the railroad was relocated to the other side. As one observer noted in 1913, "Proud Culebra and haughty Empire, stranded on a railless shore of the canal, will wither and waste away and even their broad macadamed roads will sink beneath a second-growth jungle."[4]

Beginning in the 1930s, that second-growth jungle became a vast practice area for the U.S. Army known as Empire Range. The Air Force's Balboa West Range was established contiguous to Empire in the early 1950s and used for bombing exercises on a dozen different targets, as well as in a 3,150 acre impact area. In addition, Navy special forces used an inlet from the canal called Bailamonos for live-fire training.[5] Until 1971, the Army used Rio Hato for various kinds of training that involved explosives, including a depot for storing mustard gas. During the century of U.S. occupation, military activities combined with agricultural uses to eliminate the primary forests in

Fort Sherman on the west side of the Atlantic terminal of the canal.[6] The United States also used Iguana Island, off Panama's coast, for bombing practice during World War II, leaving large tracts of the island off-limits to the tourists who flocked to its white-sand beaches.

The explosives left behind by this history of military use led to a pattern of accidents. According to the Panamanian Foreign Ministry, twenty-one Panamanians died between 1979 and 1996 from ordnance accidents on or near the range lands.[7] Panama's National Police recounted eighty-six official reports of encounters with grenades and bombs between 1993 and 1997, most of them on former military bases.[8] The military placed signs warning civilians not to enter the area, but that did not stop U.S. youth growing up in the Canal Zone from using parts of the ranges as their playground. "The water was so nice and cool under all those big jungle trees," reminisced one Zonian about his youthful visits to swimming holes on the Empire Range.[9]

Official Army reports of range accidents that killed Panamanians tended to be cerebral and clipped. "At approximately 1330 hours on 28 February 1989, Mr. Gouldburn, Range Operations Assistant, informed me, Mr. Stoeberl, that there had been a range accident and there were several persons wounded," began a one-paragraph account.[10] The men killed and injured by the explosive were not named. The anonymity and sense of remove from the tragedy served the military's later efforts to limit its liability for cleanup.

Another case demonstrates who was most affected by the abandoned explosives. During Panama's political crisis and economic embargo from 1987 to 1989, many Panamanians lost their jobs and had to improvise means of getting income. Some would brave the risks of the firing ranges by going there to gather metal, then take the metal to recycling centers in the city. Six-foot-long cluster bombs, for example, are made of aluminum, which is highly prized for recycling.[11]

Algis Amores, then twenty-one years old, and his brother-in-law Domingo Julio Avila, twenty-six, were among those made unemployed by the crisis in 1988. On May 28, they headed from their home in Cerro Silvestre, in the town of Arraiján, to Empire Range to look for aluminum. When they brought a metal object back to the house, Anibal Villarreal, the young men's fourteen-year-old cousin, tried to open it with a hammer to see what was inside. Domingo stood beside Anibal, while Algis fed a rabbit close by.

Algis remembers only that there was an explosion, and everything

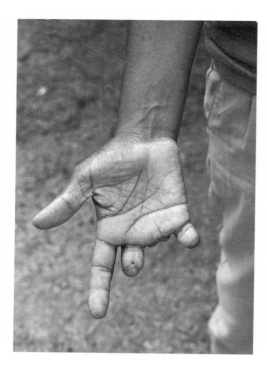

14. The hand of Algis Amores, injured on firing range. (Photograph by Rafael Pérez Jaramillo.)

went red. He lost three fingers and an arm, today replaced with a prosthesis (see figure 14). Domingo and Anibal died in the blast. The incident remained a painful memory for the community, where Algis continued to live with his mother, Gladys de Amores. "They ought to deactivate all those bombs," she said, "because it's true: They can just stay there."[12]

Panamanians' fears of contamination on the bases were exacerbated by the off-limits status of the Canal Zone enclave. The restricted access Panamanians had, and the culturally strange habits of foreigners, fed the idea that the United States was conducting all kinds of experiments. This fear was latent as long as Panamanian access was restricted to those brave or foolhardy enough to enter the remote terrain of the ranges.

But environmental issues were destined to become more prominent with the abolition of Panama's army after the invasion and once the United States established a calendar in 1993 for the gradual transfer of the remaining bases. Now, instead of becoming the property of the Panama Defense Forces, the bases would be controlled by civilians.

Many Panamanians saw the moment as a chance to end the canal area's enclave status and integrate it into the rest of Panamanian life and economic activity. This would require that the areas not be weighted with environmental risks to investment or community uses. The full exercise of Panama's sovereignty thus became tied to U.S. fulfillment of its responsibility to transfer the lands free of dangers to human health and safety. The Canal Treaties had spelled out this responsibility: They required the United States to "ensure insofar as may be practicable that every hazard to human life, health and safety is removed from any defense site or military area" at the time of U.S. withdrawal, and to consult with Panama concerning removal of such hazards. Another article of the Panama Canal Treaty required both countries to carry out actions, including military actions, "in a manner consistent with the protection of the natural environment of the Republic of Panama."[13] After the initial implementation of the Canal Treaties took place in 1979, only 17 percent of the remaining lands had passed to Panama by 1994. The remainder would be transferred to Panama at an accelerated pace from then through 1999.

Meanwhile, the United States experienced three major rounds of domestic base closures in 1988, 1991, and 1993. These closures had shown the extent and range of environmental and toxic problems present on many bases. More than 17,000 contaminated sites on 1,769 domestic bases had been identified by 1991, and the numbers were growing. The military had come under the jurisdiction of most major environmental laws, requiring a new level of institutional accountability, and Congress had created an account to fund base cleanup. The military's environmental budget peaked at $5.6 billion in 1994, before the new Republican Congress began to cut the programs.[14] But cleanup was slow going. Many projects bogged down in studies, and the military was notorious for jealously guarding information and documents, despite requests from state agencies.

From 1990 to 1993, the Pentagon announced plans to close or downsize 704 overseas facilities, some 38 percent of its basing infrastructure outside the United States.[15] The legislation governing domestic military toxic cleanup did not apply to overseas bases. Although a substantial body of international law exists to protect against discriminatory treatment, attempts by environmental groups to apply U.S. environmental law to U.S. actions overseas have generally failed in the courts. Compounding the problem, environmental concerns at bases outside the United States received little official attention. A 1986 General Accounting Office report on the DOD's environmental problems at thirteen facilities in seven countries found "inadequate hazardous waste management practices," but the report was classified.[16] The Pentagon was thus free to move on a track that was completely different from its response at domestic installations. The result was an environmental policy that placed the capacity to conduct continuing training and operations and the protection of U.S. forces as its first priority. A policy directive to fifty European base commanders in August 1990 was unequivocal: "Do not spend time looking for new problems. Do not execute abatement or mitigation actions" at known contamination sites, it directed, unless they imminently threaten public health.[17]

Financial claims by other nations and their citizens against the U.S. military were another institutional concern. At some installations, Army officials and DOD workers were fined and even indicted by local authorities for improperly dumping toxic materials.[18]

Prompted initially by complaints from Germany, Congress held hearings on the Pentagon's overseas environmental record, and the Pentagon budgeted $93 million for overseas cleanup in 1992, the vast majority for bases in Europe.[19] But cleanup costs for the Army in Germany alone were estimated at nearly $200 million.[20] In November 1991, the Senate of the post-dictatorship Philippines rejected a base treaty that would have maintained the Subic Bay Naval Station and Clark Air Force Base, the premier U.S. bases in the region. Nearly simultaneous with the Senate's action, a General Accounting Office report on Subic Bay documented problems with pollutants whose cleanup "could approach Superfund proportions."[21]

In the 1991 Defense Authorization Bill, Congress ordered the DOD to produce a comprehensive policy for overseas environmental compliance and cleanup. But what Congress had in mind were cost-saving measures. Representatives pressed the Defense Department to recoup costs at bases abroad by offsetting environmental claims against "residual value," the Pentagon's term for the improvements that it says the United States has made to the lands it has occupied. Especially in Europe, the United States attempted to collect from host countries the inflation-adjusted cost of buildings, roads, and airstrips as it returned military bases. As keepers of the purse strings, some Senators and Representatives wanted to see a positive number for the residual value of closing bases, even after the costs of the environmental damage were deducted. Another mechanism for keeping cleanup costs down was for the Defense Department to claim an "equitable division" of environmental responsibility, often on the basis that other countries' militaries also polluted U.S. bases before or during the U.S. tenancy.[22] Faced with a combination of Congressional pressure, legal claims, and bad press that threatened to restrict the United States' access to foreign bases, the military bureaucracy began to attempt a new policy.

In December 1993, William Perry, chief at the Pentagon, signed a new policy governing cleanup of overseas installations that were about to close. "The policy essentially chose to deal with environmental contamination within the context of subsequent residual value negotiations," wrote Colonel Richard Phelps, the Air Force's chief environmental lawyer in Europe, "limiting DOD funding of cleanups to those circumstances which impacted on operations, or which rose to the level of the human health risk based 'imminent and substantial danger.' "[23]

The policy clearly excluded cleanup of those bases that had already been closed in the Philippines and elsewhere. It also laid out guidelines for negotiations that were meant to provide "maximum compensation to the U.S." For example, one provision of the policy stated: "All host nation claims for damage will be challenged unless clearly substantiated."[24] But because the policy also limited cleanup to "known imminent and substantial dangers to human health and safety," and host countries had little access to information about such dangers, the policy placed all power in the hands of the military.

The lack of legislation and oversight for overseas base cleanup meant that funds would have to come from each base's operations and maintenance budget, where it competed with a host of other projects that were more traditionally military in nature. Much was left to the local commander's discretion, unless the matter began to affect diplomatic relations. And in those cases, it was powerful nations such as Germany and England, which had more leverage than other countries with the United States, that were likely to see a cleanup.[25] Whether the problem was lax environmental laws in poor nations or the United States' disregard for the claims of politically weaker countries, the result reinforced the idea that Europeans' lives mattered more than Panamanians' or Filipinos', and that Americans' lives mattered more than anyone else's.

The bias against cleanup at overseas bases conformed to a pattern of environmental racism in the treatment given to contaminated military facilities within the United States. The Defense Depot in the largely African American community of South Memphis operated a chemical-warfare dump in the heart of a residential area without ever informing its citizens. By contrast, when evidence showed that the active firing range on the Massachusetts Military Reservation, located on mostly White and economically privileged Cape Cod, was releasing heavy metals that might contaminate the water table, the Environmental Protection Agency (EPA) ordered both an end to the training and a full cleanup of the contamination. Although they struggle for such ends, the residents of South Memphis can only dream of such enforcement of environmental standards.[26]

The first skirmishes over base cleanup arose from Panamanians' desire for information about the facilities that they would inherit and the military's secrecy. When asked about the problem in early 1995, the Southern Command's chief official for base transfers, Colonel Richard O'Connor, threw up his hands and exclaimed, "We're guilty." O'Connor said there was a lot of suspicion, even of him, and added that he felt that the military branch commanders were hoping to delay the issue until their tour in Panama ended.[27]

Back in Washington, Dick McSeveney, an engineer and former marine who ran the Pentagon's treaty implementation office, designed the Installation Condition Report (ICR), the format for information to be given to Panama. The reports were supposed to summarize information about each facility's buildings and infrastructure and give an estimated "book value." "They were not designed as environmental reports," McSeveney told visiting Panamanians in 1995.[28] Typically four or five pages long, the reports were found sorely lacking by Panamanian officials.

The first major transfers occurred in September 1995, with the closure of Fort Davis and Fort Gulick, near Colón. Davis included warehouses, nearly four hundred units of family housing, an elementary school, a gymnasium and recreation center, dormitories, and retail stores sprawled over seven hundred acres, all slated to be overhauled into an industrial export zone. Fort Davis also encompassed more than three thousand acres of forest.[29]

The Fort Davis Installation Condition Report revealed that, at the installation's nursery school, the tap water, which unlike that in other Central American countries is normally safe to drink, had especially high levels of lead—up to 51 parts per billion, compared with the EPA's action level of 15 parts per billion. Even after water ran for ten to fifteen minutes, the lead level persisted at twice that needed to inflict IQ deficiencies on children and close to the amount that can cause permanent writing and speech disabilities. Nevertheless, the report concluded that "there is no known potable water supply system contamination."[30]

The Davis and Gulick ICRs also placed estimated book values on the buildings and other improvements, which might be used in negotiations with Panama over residual value and compensation for contamination. "It's not the U.S. government's intent to obtain any cash money," explained Nico de Greef of SouthCom. "It's there as a check to the consultation. If you are going to raise environmental claims that are obviously unreasonable, this will keep them in check. Like they say, 'You shouldn't look a gift horse in the mouth.'"[31] The discussion of residual value was a red herring. The treaties explicitly required that all non-removable property on the bases be transferred to Panama "without charge."[32]

Based on a list of Navy environmental documents obtained by the FOR, Panama requested eighteen Navy reports in mid-1995, including audits of the Navy's enormous fuel tank "farm" in Arraiján, which serviced military ships passing through the canal. The tank farm's thirty-one underground storage tanks had a capacity of more than a million barrels of diesel and kerosene and had a history of spills. In January 1995, one of the Arraiján tanks overflowed some 109,000 gallons of JP5 jet fuel, 70 percent of which was recovered. The rest—more than 30,000 gallons—ran off into the ground and wetlands by the canal.[33]

Colonel Donald Holzwarth, the U.S. Army South's chief environmental official and the man responsible for implementing the treaty's environmental provisions at that time, openly refused to release the requested documents about the tank farm, saying that they were internal and would not be useful to Panamanians. "I have always maintained that some documents beg a thousand questions and might lead someone down the wrong path," Holzwarth told me. "My guidance to [the Navy] is, Don't release something when it's inherently stupid [to release it]." He then admitted that he had no idea what was in the requested documents. "There is no cover-up," he said several times, though I had not suggested there was one.[34]

Ultimately, the Navy released the studies to the FOR under the Freedom of Information Act. The studies showed that the Navy had been cited for groundwater monitoring wells designed to detect fuel leaks from tanks but that did not work, and for locating a sludge pit adjacent to the eroding banks of the Velasquez River.[35] The Velasquez runs from Arraiján into the Panama Canal.

In response to the Pentagon's intransigence, more than fifty religious and peace figures called on President Clinton to address toxic contamination and fully share environmental documents on military bases being returned to Panama. The letter came on the eve of the meeting between Clinton and Pérez Balladares on September 6, 1995, that set base negotiations in motion. "Relations between the two countries will be mortgaged if future generations of Panamanians find their health and safety compromised by what we left behind," the letter said.[36]

The day after the presidents' meeting, the Panamanian delegation met with Defense Secretary William Perry and high-level military officials in Washington. At Pérez Balladares's request, the delegation gave a brief presentation about the firing ranges. According to someone who was present, after the meeting, General Barry McCaffrey, then chief of the Southern Command, which was using the ranges, took Foreign Minister Gabriel Lewis aside and asked him why Panama had raised the issue, which was clearly sensitive. Lewis said afterward that bringing up the firing ranges was as if two friends went out for a bicycle ride and the first thing one did was put a stick in the spokes of the other. After that, Panamanian negotiators did not raise the problem again during the base talks for two years.

Faced with a deepening public presumption of contamination, increased attention by the Panamanian media, and a newfound assertiveness by midlevel Panamanian officials, SouthCom went on a publicity offensive. Some of the ammunition closest at hand came from an initiative known as the Legacy Natural Resources Program.

The Legacy Program was established to fund conservation projects that were desirable but not necessarily required to comply with environmental laws. Congress appropriated $135 million in 1991–95 for such Legacy program projects as biological surveys, creation of nature trails, and preservation of military history. One Legacy Program project stretched the notion of conservation by supporting preservation of documents about the Air Force band.[37] The program's fundamental framework involved learning how to be better resource managers. Because the Defense Department had jurisdiction over some 25 million acres of land, it needed to be efficient. In a Legacy report on what they called the Pentagon's "earth resources," several engineers wrote: "The increased speed and lethality of modern weapons systems, along with better communications and the ability to see deep in the enemy's rear echelon, has resulted in the need for increased training space and, consequently, increased emphasis on resource management."[38] In other words, conservation was to be a function of military efficiency more than of environmental protection. In the words of a Virginia base commander speaking to a community meeting about contamination on the base, "We're in the business of protecting the nation, not the environment."[39]

In Panama, the Legacy project reportedly had been conceived by Air Force engineer James Cheevers, who was worried about the problems that military pilots were having with birds they encountered over Howard Air Force Base.[40] Through the Legacy Program, the Defense Department had commissioned a $500,000 study of flora and fauna on the bases in Panama, carried out by the Nature Conservancy and ANCON, the largest environmental group in Panama. "The primary goal of this project was to provide baseline data and management recommendations to allow installation managers to be good stewards, while carrying out the military mission," said Richard Warner of the Nature Conservancy. "Another benefit is the recreational and educational opportunity it provided military personnel and their families."[41]

Unsurprisingly, the study found rich biodiversity on military lands: more than eight hundred plant species and fifty-six animal species protected under Panamanian law. The environmental groups were never asked to look at toxics or dangers on military lands. Nevertheless, SouthCom literature and press releases began to use the survey to praise the U.S. military's "good stewardship" in Panama.[42]

Colonel Holzwarth laid out the military's environmental plan at a November 1995 meeting of the Joint Commission on the Environment. The Canal Treaties established the commission to monitor environmental impacts on treaty lands, but it had become practically inert since the invasion.[43] Now commissioners Gary Hartshorn, an independent-minded scientist with the World Wildlife Fund who had become the U.S. co-chair, and Panama's Ramiro Castrejon were actively seeking more information about potential contamination from the military. Holzwarth's briefing was a response.

"Environmental Awareness Campaign" and "Building Effective Relationships" read Holzwarth's slide presentation in large letters. The plan's "Proactive Public Affairs" strategy included producing brochures, hiring public-relations consultants, and distributing press releases "stressing environmental leadership." Cleanup would consist of addressing "any known imminent hazards 'as practicable.'" The Defense Department's plan for the bombing ranges amounted to describing "effective control measures" and offering advice on future land use.[44] That was it. The Panamanians present were livid.

Implicit in Holzwarth's presentation, and explicit in SouthCom directives at the time, was the assumption that the ranges would not be cleaned up at all. "Before 1998," an Army audit concluded, "U.S. Forces planned to clean up ranges using guidance from U.S. Southern Command, which basically was to transfer ranges as ranges." In other words, the lands would be cleared only to the extent needed to continue using them for military training. This plan, according to a later statement by the Army, "grew from specific Commander in Chief, U.S. Southern Command decisions made in 1995." The commander who made these decisions was General Barry McCaffrey, later the U.S. drug czar and a strong proponent of keeping several thousand U.S. troops in Panama after 1999.[45]

As a rationale for the no-cleanup policy, Army officers cited a provision in the Canal Treaties stipulating that "no change in the basic character and function of Military Areas of Coordination shall be made except by mutual consent" of the two countries. The argument was groundless, however, because the same treaty provision also allowed such a change in function "in accordance with Article IV" — the treaty provision for removing hazards to human health and safety.[46]

Back in Washington, the Pentagon released new guidance in October 1995 on cleanup for overseas base commanders that required, for closed bases, the negotiation of an explicit agreement for any cleanup occurring after the transfer.[47] And, because cleanup at many domestic bases took five, ten, even twenty years to complete, cleanup in Panama to similar standards would require action after the properties were transferred in 1999. But Washington had no such contingency in mind. "We do not contemplate any additional agreements to supplement the Treaty, nor do we believe that any are necessary to promote the interests of either government," the State Department's lead negotiator with Panama said in early 1996.[48]

The Pentagon's Panama version of the policy added one more provision, an interpretation of the treaty's requirement to do everything "practicable" to ensure "that every hazard to human life, health, and safety is removed" from the bases. Military planners decided that practicability should include the cost of the cleanup, the amount of time required, the impact on the environment, and the available technology, although the treaty and domestic environmental law included no such criteria for defining the term. The Pentagon added a redefinition of the word "remove" as found in the treaty: "Removing a hazard may take the form of containing, controlling, or physically removing [the danger]."[49]

As the problems in the Southern Command's environmental policy became known, Panamanian community and human rights groups became progressively more vocal in calling for a full cleanup. Vincentian and Jesuit religious communities issued statements demanding that the United States clean up the bases, while the Grassroots Human Rights Coalition of Panama (COPODEHUPA) and the Latin American Studies Center (CELA) publicly linked the problem with obtaining full sovereignty in the canal area. Panama had established the Interoceanic Region Authority (ARI) to oversee the transferred lands, and ARI invited some citizen groups to participate in an interagency environmental committee.

Two events in 1996 brought the issue into particular focus. On August 6, the United States transferred part of the Empire Range with an elaborate celebration of Panama's program to reforest the area. President Pérez Balladares and SouthCom chief General Wesley Clark even planted the symbolic first tree together on the range's soil in a prized photo opportunity. But within a month, CELA and COPODEHUPA revealed in a press conference that the 5,600 acre parcel was still loaded with unexploded mines, mortars, and other munitions. The lives of fifty thousand Panamanians near the range were endangered by the irresponsibility of the Panamanian and U.S. governments, said CELA's director Marco Gandásegui.

The Installation Condition Report on the property, delivered to Panama barely two weeks before the transfer, showed a demolition area and two "firing fans" for explosives launched into an impact area.

When mortars fell short, they landed in the firing fans on the parcel transferred to Panama. The report contained only three paragraphs about the use of explosives in the area but said that "some unexploded mortar rounds may still exist" and "excavation in this area should be avoided." The Panamanian government had not made this information public, but now every Panamanian newspaper ran stories on the "highly contaminated lands transferred to Panama," implicitly calling Panama to task along with the United States. The Southern Command denied the accusation, even though the press had quoted the military's own report.[50]

The same month, ARI finally released its master plan for the canal area, which called for "deferred use" of the impact areas and the preservation as "green areas" of other lands on the ranges. Panama had undertaken a national consultation process with political parties and organizations from a wide spectrum of civilian society to reach consensus on the future of U.S. military facilities in Panama and canal operations. A gathering on September 24–25 that brought together political parties, unions, women's groups, and peasant, indigenous peoples', and environmental organizations took a close look at the ARI master plan and unanimously endorsed it with minor changes. At the same time, the groups asked the Panamanian government to make sure the United States "proceeds to clean up and sanitize contaminated areas, as this action is indispensable for assigning acceptable uses to such areas in the General Plan."[51]

Panamanian managers saw clearly that military-base contamination was as much a domestic political thorn as a bilateral concern and appointed Rodrigo Noriega, a young environmental lawyer fresh from Yale University, to lead its discussions about base cleanup with the United States. One of Noriega's first tasks on the job was to join Panamanian police officials in an investigation of the death of a Panamanian found in July 1996 on the Piña firing range who had been killed accidentally by an explosive. The incident brought home again the human dimension of the problem.[52]

In February 1997, the military released a long-awaited study of the three active firing ranges that it operated in Panama. Panama had repeatedly asked for the study, whose draft version was ready ten months earlier. The report confirmed the existence of tens of thousands of unexploded grenades, mines, mortars, bombs, and other explosives on the three ranges and represented an advance in knowledge about both the problem of unexploded ordnance in Panama and potential solutions. According to the report's data, the Balboa West range alone had more than fifty thousand UXO items.[53]

Both the study and Pentagon officials asserted that the lands could not be cleaned up without destroying the area's environment, contributing to an erosion problem that already affects canal operations. This was because the most reliable techniques for detecting UXO require cutting or burning vegetation. And because large parts of the ranges were on steep terrain, erosion was a greater risk, and manual detection could be dangerous. As early as 1995, a SouthCom spokesman had articulated what would be the military's consistent position on the ranges. "Probably the best solution is to fence it all off," Colonel James Fetig told the *Miami Herald*. "That's all prime watershed for the canal, and they shouldn't mess with it anyway."[54] The range report thus conformed to a policy on U.S. cleanup responsibilities that had been set earlier.

I wrote comments about the range study in March and distributed them by electronic mail to activists as well as to a list of firing range cleanup companies that I had found on the Internet. The next day, I got a call from the study's technical author, Rick Stauber. "There were a lot of questionable practices [in that study]," Stauber told me. He had proposed a two-week series of field visits to the ranges to verify what the authors had learned from archives and interviews — a standard practice for range assessments — but the study sponsors in the Pentagon refused.

"There's a chemical weapons burial site in a place called Cerro Tigre," Stauber said and talked for another half-hour while I furiously took notes. Yet Cerro Tigre and many other sites in the former Canal Zone — some already transferred to Panama — were excluded from the scope of the study, which Stauber claimed violated Defense Department regulations. When he found that depleted uranium (DU) rounds had been tested in Panama, he was told not to pursue it. Evidence of UXO on areas outside the three firing ranges was also suppressed.

But what about the military's principal contention, that the ranges could not be fully cleaned up because finding all the unexploded ordnance would require cutting down the rain forest, contributing to siltation in the canal and deteriorating ecology for endangered species? Stauber said that he had suggested a method for detecting and removing unexploded ordnance that would allow for long-term protection of the forest. Small parcels of the range could be cleaned up each dry season, in a checkerboard pattern, then allowed to grow back for two or three years before work on an adjacent parcel began. This would prevent erosion, although it would take more time and money. The forested lands were second growth on the Empire and Balboa West Ranges, where such a method would not do away with a mature rain forest. But the military was not interested in Stauber's suggestion.

Stauber had lost his job because of his outspokenness. He spoke in a torrent and with encyclopedic authority about the explosives and their history in Panama, and about his DOD handlers. "I'd like to see those guys in jail," he said bitterly. "I have been personally involved in military [explosive ordnance disposal] operations for over seventeen years, and I have never seen an area that poses such a potential threat for a chemical accident as the various locations within Panama."[55]

After Stauber's call, I checked the draft version of the Panama range study, obtained through the Freedom of Information Act. The draft text clearly stated that the Army's Tropic Test Center (TTC) used a range in Panama "to test antitank mines and depleted uranium projectiles."[56] The final version of the report released to the Panamanian government said that "the ranges in Panama did not have a Nuclear Regulatory Commission license to fire depleted uranium."[57] It also deleted every single reference to "contamination," using instead the words "UXO concentration."

An upshot of the visible friction over military contamination was the interest of consultants and contractors in potential paid work to assess and clean up what the United States appeared unwilling to address. ARI hired Nick Morgan, an environmental engineer who had worked for the EPA and more recently for Greenpeace, to do a preliminary evaluation of conditions on the bases apart from the impact areas.

His report to ARI, delivered in August 1996, was guardedly optimistic. The bases in Panama did not house many of the industrial activities that had polluted European bases so thoroughly, and individual U.S. personnel were attempting to act responsibly, even in the absence of a responsible policy. The United States had built a first-class sewage disposal plant on Howard Air Force Base. Morgan recommended that Panama prioritize its environmental needs and directly request a comprehensive baseline environmental assessment for all the installations in Panama. ARI chief Ardito Barletta, worried about its implications for investment, suppressed the report for nearly a year.[58]

A turning point in Panama came during an informal cabinet meeting in May 1997, when the president and eight deputy ministers took a helicopter flight over the canal area, then heard a presentation by Rodrigo Noriega about the range study and possible options. Pérez Balladares gave a green light for diplomatic efforts to hold the United States environmentally accountable. Noriega had developed a proposed memorandum of understanding in which cleanup would be overseen by the Joint Commission on the Environment, whose mandate would be extended until 2005 and expanded to include environmental and canal agency officials from each government. Panama presented the proposal to the U.S. embassy in May. The tension was building.[59]

When the FOR publicly released information about depleted-uranium tests and the suspected chemical weapons dump on June 30, the press in Panama quickly picked up the story, and it created a media feeding frenzy. The U.S. embassy first said it was "very improbable" that the United States had used DU in Panama but had to back away from that statement after SouthCom confirmed that it had conducted storage tests (as opposed to firing tests, in which the rounds are actually shot) with depleted uranium.

The controversy closely coincided with a conference on base contamination sponsored by ARI, the Foreign Affairs Ministry, and the natural resources agency INRENARE in late July. The conference featured participation by high-level Panamanians and SouthCom and testimony by Stauber and Morgan, among others. In the days preceding the conference, Foreign Minister Arias and Mirei Endara, director of INRENARE, reportedly received calls from U.S. officials — including agencies that fund programs for reforestation — questioning Stauber's and Morgan's credentials and the aims of the conference.[60]

The same week, the Earthjustice Legal Defense Fund released a report on U.S. legal obligations to clean up the bases in Panama. One of the report's key findings was that, under U.S. and international law, the interpretation of whether cleanup is "practicable" must conform to the ordinary meaning of the word: "capable of being done, effected, or performed." In other words, the report said, "the United States must remove every hazard to human life, health, and safety before transferring a base unless doing so is technically impossible." What is "practicable" might come into play in choosing the remedy to be applied, but the United States could not use cost or time needed as criteria for deciding whether to conduct the cleanup or for the standard for cleanup.[61]

The Southern Command went into damage-control mode. For the ARI conference, it prepared a four-color booklet in English and Spanish titled "Depleted Uranium — The Facts," which emphasized the security precautions taken with the DU rounds brought to Panama in 1993, and denied any cover-up. But SouthCom did not address other underlying issues. First, Panama had never been notified about the storage tests with DU, demonstrating that Panamanians of all social stations had been kept outside the information loop. More important, the range study had largely suppressed a greater public-safety issue: chemical agents tested and abandoned on lands throughout the canal area. The Army's non-stockpile chemical weapons officer had told Stauber that a suspected chemical weapons dump was buried in the canal area, probably either on Cerro Tigre or in Chiva Chiva. The dump probably dated from World War II or the 1950s, when burial was the common method for disposing of chemical weapons. But compared with the toxicity of nonexplosive DU rounds, a cache of mustard gas bombs buried on unspecified lands already under Panamanian jurisdiction would pose a whole different order of danger.

The report the Army officer was peaking at while Stauber looked on was highly classified: the FOR's request to declassify the document under the Freedom of Information Act was denied after Army officials consulted the White House and reportedly were told that the document was not to leave the safe. The denial was an early indication of how sensitive U.S. officials were about the history of chemical weapons tests in Panama.

On June 9, three weeks before the story about depleted uranium broke, the U.S. Army's TTC had quietly submitted a formal proposal to stay in Panama after 1999 to continue testing weapons, soldiers, and equipment under tropical conditions. "The TTC currently conducts tests in Panama's forests, savannas and coastal areas with the goal of determining how tropic environments affect the integrity of materials and the performance and reliability of operating systems," TTC wrote in 1997.[62] In other words, the center's core mission was to study the rain forest's effect on war materiel, not the effect of war on the tropical environment, or even on the soldiers themselves. Besides tests of conventional munitions, TTC had tested nerve agent and DU without informing or obtaining permission from the Panamanian government.

The agency decreased from a staff of three hundred during its heyday in the 1960s to thirty-two in 1997. "The laboratory capabilities of the Tropic Test Center were world class in the late 1970s but were allowed to deteriorate . . . due to decreased emphasis on Tropic testing and conviction that the activity would have to be phased out or re-established in another country by 1999," the TTC wrote.[63]

The TTC's June 1997 proposal insisted that tests of explosives and live firing exercises in Panama were the center's "bread and butter income sources," accounting for 60 percent of its funding. The proposal called for continued use of parts of the Empire Range, Fort Sherman, Rodman Naval Station, offices and labs in East Corozal, and the Gamboa Test Area. The proposal also emphasized the scientific and academic components of the TTC's work, asking to be part of Panama's planned research and technology center, the City of Knowledge.[64]

But Panama's reactions to the TTC's uranium and chemical tests prompted the United States to exclude it at a critical moment from negotiations for a U.S. military presence after 1999. Panamanians in general are suspicious of scientific experiments, and the news of TTC weapons tests evoked those suspicions — and may have deepened them.[65] The TTC's hope was to be included in negotiations for the counterdrug base, but Army officials rejected the idea, according to a Panamanian negotiator. After the controversy over the TTC's use of DU erupted in early July, the Pentagon told the TTC that it was not to pursue formal discussions with Panama until after the other talks were concluded. The TTC, then, negotiated informally with Panama and for several months dated its communications with Panama July 21.[66]

For most of the rest of 1997, the TTC clandestinely negotiated with Panama to stay in the country and carry out military tests after 1999. The center conducted talks apparently without authorization from the U.S. government, and behind the back of the ARI, which had jurisdiction over the lands in question.[67] It was not until November 28 that the State Department authorized the TTC to hold formal talks with Panama under the condition that it "maintain a low profile in our discussions in order to avoid attention being diverted from larger issues such as the Multinational Counter-narcotics Center."[68]

The TTC tried to sweeten its overtures to Panama by claiming that its parent organization, the Army's Yuma Proving Ground in Arizona, had expertise and technical resources for environmental cleanup. But Yuma Proving Ground was not developing cleanup technology. Instead, the base provided a place for testing cleanup technology on lands it had contaminated.[69] A TTC delegation visited Panama in January 1998 to pursue negotiations, but Panama resisted making any commitment without a clear demilitarization of the agency. In this case, at least, the military's disingenuous claims resulted in suspicion, and the negotiations stalled.

The preliminary plan for the firing ranges that SouthCom released in January 1998 clearly fell within the limited mandate of the 1995 DOD policy. All work would be completed during the two dry seasons (January–April 1998 and 1999) that remained before the treaty expired. Out of more than 37,000 acres on the Empire, Balboa West, and Piña ranges, the military planned to clean up only 407 acres. Consistent with earlier SouthCom decisions and the agreement for the counterdrug center, which had been negotiated the previous month, the plan assumed continued military use of the range lands after 1999: "Land use changes would provide for unreasonable and impractical expectation of unrestricted land use."[70] Panama flatly rejected the proposed plan.[71] With no other plan in hand and the dry season under way, the Army began to implement it anyway.

By that time, the prolonged negotiations for the counterdrug center constrained all discussions of base cleanup. "We are all hostages to the [counterdrug center] negotiations," lamented one Foreign Affairs Ministry official close to the cleanup talks. Panama did not want to lobby Washington for post–1999 cleanup, he said, out of fear of the backlash it might create.[72]

Confronted with an emerging diplomatic problem, Ambassador Hughes sought an agreement somewhere between the extremes of doing only a surface sweep of accessible flat grasslands and compensating Panama with billions of dollars. " 'First, it's stop the bombing,' " Hughes recalled saying to Southern Command chief General Wilhelm. The military continued to use of some of the ranges until mid-1998, even after clearance had begun. "We have an obligation to clean up [in accordance with the treaty], so we need to stop using the ranges. We . . . finally got that agreed, but that was hard coming."[73]

Hughes convened interagency groups in both Washington and Panama to consider how to reach an agreement. The group in Panama was co-chaired by Hughes and Panama's foreign minister, and the group in Washington included a dozen agencies, including the Pentagon and the EPA. The State Department also sponsored a tour of U.S. ranges in

September 1997 for a group of Panamanians selected by the embassy to witness the problems faced by range cleanups in the United States.

Panamanian officials realized that they needed an agreement for cleanup of the ranges that extended beyond 1999. Cleanup of comparable ranges in the United States, such as Fort Ord in California and Kaho'olawe in Hawai'i, took ten or fifteen years. Panama's proposed memorandum of understanding for a binational cleanup center to function beyond 1999 had gone nowhere.

The range cleanup contracted by U.S. Army South and the Air Force —which had used the ranges—was mostly restricted to clearance of the surface in "accessible" areas, carried out by National Guard troops brought to Panama on two-week rotations. One soldier who participated in the operation on Piña and Balboa West said that some teams did not even have metal detectors. "For Piña the standing order that we had from the higher-ups was to pick up what was visible, and that was it," he reported. "They also said not to go into the jungle to look, just look on the trails. Each team was armed with trash bags, and told that if it looked clean, it must not have any UXO."[74]

Some areas, however, received special treatment. "We were only going to do a surface sweep," said Teresa Pohlman, an official with the Air Combat Command, but "Panama has been bumped up because of political considerations."[75] She was referring not to the demands for cleanup from Panamanians worried about community safety, but those of the Panama Canal Commission. Part of the Empire Range— about 4,800 acres—lay on land belonging to the Canal Commission that had been licensed to the Army on the condition that it be restored to the commission's satisfaction whenever the Army gave it back. The commission wanted some of the land cleaned up for use in a canal-widening project and asked the Army to remove explosives from the area.[76] At the commission's insistence, the Army Corps of Engineers contracted EOD Technology in 1997 to clean up 525 acres to a depth of one to four feet, to improve safety for workers in the area.[77] The Army resisted reimbursing the Canal Commission for the $1.7 million it spent on the cleanup, however, until a legal opinion from the Army General Counsel forced it to pay.[78]

The cleanup on the Empire Range focused on clearing areas closest to the canal, where widening of the waterway's Culebra Cut would require at least safe areas for operation. The other side of the ranges, where the military's own maps showed increased "encroachment" by

Panamanian farmers into the impact area, received considerably less attention (and funding). Furthermore, the Canal Commission was not satisfied with the Army's standard for "practicable" cleanup.

One of the Pentagon's ideas for the ranges was to deposit the many tons of soil that would be generated by the widening of the cut onto areas contaminated with explosives. Now the word "cover-up" did indeed come to mind. A Pentagon report revealed that the Army Corps of Engineers dumped tons of spoilage — soil — from a project to widen the canal onto two hundred acres in the Empire Range, effectively doing away with any jungle environment that existed on that land. The dumping of soil up to twenty meters deep on land that had been littered with unexploded ordnance threw into doubt the military's argument that it could not clean up without destroying the canal's watershed.[79]

During the same period, a rash of discoveries of explosives on lands already transferred to Panama served to heighten fears of what the United States would leave behind. In October 1997, after the transfer of Albrook air base, workers cutting brush for a path in a wooded area found what appeared to be a live grenade only fifteen meters from a residential area. When ARI and Foreign Ministry officials mentioned the incident to the civilian deputy of Colonel Michael DeBow, the U.S. officer in charge of environmental matters, the deputy reportedly told the Panamanians: "Whatever you find after the transfer is your problem."[80]

The following February, U.S. explosives experts discovered a bomb amid coral reefs on Iguana Island, on Panama's Pacific coast. Iguana Island was used by the United States during World War II and subsequently became a beach destination for tourists. Two months later, Panamanian police destroyed some thirty explosives that were found on the former Rio Hato air base, which was used by the United States as a firing range until 1969.

Consultants from the Wolf's Flat Ordnance Disposal Company, owned and operated by the indigenous Tsuu T'ina Nation of Alberta, Canada, surveyed a section of the Empire Range that reverted in 1996 and was being reforested. In May 1998, while seeking leftover munitions and training Panamanians to do the same, they found an antipersonnel mine in one of the range's maneuver areas. Army officers did not want to believe it and claimed that Wolf's Flat had planted the mine on the range. Relations between the military and Panama were deteriorating.[81]

That deterioration found acute expression in the communication between the men appointed by Panama and the United States to lead range-cleanup discussions. Lewis Amselem was a hard-nosed career official in the State Department used to Cold War politics, and the Panamanians found him abrasive. Fernando Manfredo Jr. had spent his working life on issues related to the canal, including a stint as the canal's chief administrator. U.S. officials viewed his appointment as a sign that Panama was taking a "political" approach to the problem. The joint working group they co-chaired, beginning in March 1998, was meant to work in parallel with the formal Joint Committee established by the treaty. But by July it was clear that the two sides had vastly different objectives and were speaking different languages. Manfredo proposed a memorandum of understanding for U.S.-funded cleanup of the ranges after 1999 and an environmental impact statement on measures to mitigate the ecological impact of detecting ordnance. Amselem called these " 'castle-in-the-air' proposals which go nowhere."[82]

It was also evident that Washington was unhappy with Panama's rejection of the counterdrug base and that its displeasure was bleeding into consideration of any post–1999 agreement to clean up the ranges. The State Department had the unpleasant task in July of informing Republicans in Congress that the deal for the counterdrug center had collapsed, and they could not have relished the idea of seeking money to clean up the mess of a military that would no longer be in Panama. The point man for this message was Amselem. He told Manfredo and the Joint Working Group on July 17 that they had "lost the best friend you have in the United States [in William Hughes]," and that there was an "anti-Panama feeling in Washington."[83]

Two weeks later, Colonel David Hunt communicated to Panama the military's position that any post–1999 agreement to clean up the ranges would necessarily mean a status-of-forces agreement for the presence of uniformed soldiers to do the cleanup. SouthCom was grasping at one last straw to keep a military presence in Panama: It could stay under the umbrella of an environmental operation.[84] Panama insisted that the cleanup could be done by civilian contractors, as it is on many U.S. ranges.

When Hughes left his post as U.S. ambassador in October 1998, no post–1999 agreement was in place. And without Hughes's interest, the United States simply stalled. When the Army presented its revised range-transfer plan to Panama in November 1998, it omitted the notion that the ranges' basic function or character could not be changed by the cleanup. But the result was largely the same: The United States would leave more than eight thousand acres adjacent to growing communities contaminated with tens of thousands of explosives. The Army would post signs and erect barriers on access roads but decided against putting fences around the explosive zones, because the jungle would reclaim them.[85]

The military's principal stated rationale for not doing more was environmental. If the Army had attempted to locate and remove all the ordnance to a depth of four feet (enough for light use) in two dry seasons, it would have had to clear-cut the forest, leading to an ecological catastrophe. But because it started the process late and would not consider a post–1999 cleanup agreement, it did not consider the checkerboard method of cleaning up parcel by parcel over an extended period. Panama pointed out that in Fort Ord, California, the Army was employing just such a method, including controlled burns, to detect ordnance on a large range. Foreign Minister Jorge Ritter formally asked the United States to fund an environmental impact study of such methods in Panama. Hughes responded that Panama was free to fund its own study.[86]

Panama's environmental agency, ANAM, did issue a statement on the impact of controlled burns. ANAM observed that, because the biomass of the ranges in Panama was greater than at Fort Ord, fires generated greater heat. It concluded that the method used at Fort Ord could be adapted to Panama, as long as parcels were limited to fifty-five acres, the affected agencies and communities were consulted, and a program of reforestation and species placement was instituted afterward.[87]

U.S. claims that further cleanup of the ranges was impracticable also were contradicted by a contractor who had been conducting the cleanup. Michael Short was project manager for explosives removal from ranges contracted by the Canal Commission in 1998 and 1999. Contrary to military assertions that ordnance removal from the jungle is too difficult or dangerous for workers, he said, "it is possible to safely clear UXO in the jungle. In fact, the jungle is easier due to the lack of kuna grass [a high, sharp grass common in Panama]."[88]

Panama experienced a similar cycle of frustration and confrontation on the problem of chemical weapons. San Jose Island was only part of the problem. Stauber's research indicated that the United States had buried chemical munitions at France Field in the 1930s, had established a disposal site in Chiva Chiva in the 1950s, and may have buried chemical weapons at other sites. In June 1997, the FOR requested portions of a 1993 document listing suspected overseas chemical munitions burial sites. The Freedom of Information Act request was for the section of the document that dealt with suspected sites in Panama. It was denied.[89]

The reasons given for denying the document on "suspected overseas burial sites" were instructive. The Army General Counsel's Office stated that the document "contains information concerning weapons systems and information of a foreign government, and the information could assist in the development or use of weapons of mass destruction."[90] In other words, the chemical agents abandoned in Panama may not have "dissipated" into a harmless state, or even into a militarily useless condition. If people with bad intentions obtained still usable chemical munitions from burial sites or other chemical dumps in Panama, they could cause havoc. But this was an equally compelling reason for the United States to inform Panama of the locations of chemical agents or munitions to forestall the possibility of accidents. The U.S. military had already disclosed information about the locations of other suspected burial sites, including in the United States.[91]

Panama repeatedly and formally requested documents from the United States on chemical weapons tests in Panama as early as August 1997.[92] But according to Foreign Ministry officials, the United States did not give Panama a single relevant document until July 1998, when the Army turned over copies of the four nerve agent test plans that had just been released to the FOR.[93] In all other cases, U.S. military officials responded with brief letters describing chemical warfare activities in general terms. In response to the ministry's August 1997 request, for example, Colonel DeBow wrote two paragraphs about tear gas and VX nerve agent tests.[94]

The Yuma Proving Ground had also contracted a former TTC project manager, Roy Blades, to search records for tests that the center had carried out in Panama involving explosives or hazardous chemicals.

The TTC's director said that the results were to be turned over to Panama. Blades was denied access to the archives of Aberdeen Proving Ground, but he still found reports on more than a hundred TTC tests in Panama that used dangerous materials. He sent his report to Yuma in September 1998, but the Army sat on it.[95]

Blades's research showed that twenty-seven nerve agent warheads were dumped in concrete-filled drums in the Pacific Ocean off Panama's coast. His report included a summary of a report on seventy-six tests of more than a dozen different high-explosive weapons fired from the air into the three canal area ranges during the Vietnam War. The report confirmed that the series left behind explosive duds from a variety of munitions, including five-hundred–pound bombs and extremely sensitive 40-millimeter grenades. Blades's report also recounted tests of gravel and anti-personnel mines, bombs for clearing helicopter landing areas in the jungle, and explosives for creating trenches and craters. From the 1960s to the 1990s, several missile systems were taken to Panama to test the effects of storage in the tropics, including the Pershing ballistic missile, Nike AJAX (the test included a simulated biological attack), Redeye, Lance, Hellfire, and Patriot missiles (they were not fired in Panama). One detonation test of anti-tank mines in 1987 started a fire that burned seventy acres on the Empire Range before the military's fire-control unit put it out.[96] The United States passed on none of this to Panama.

Instead, in response to Hughes's request to disclose documents, U.S. officials told Panama they would turn over a set of twenty-three compact disks with all the records of the TTC relating to tests in Panama. After what one Panamanian described as "practically an Odyssey," the awaited disks were given to Panama at the end of 1998. But nearly all the documents on the disks dealt with tests of nonhazardous materials, and most had nothing to do with Panama at all. And some documents had been deleted.[97]

Based on National Archives documents that he saw while working for a military contractor on a study of the active ranges, Stauber asserted that the United States had established a chemical burial site at France Field in the 1930s. The documents that Stauber found indicated that thirty-pound bombs that leaked mustard were involved, and that these munitions were both buried on land and dumped at sea. According to Stauber, the same documents stated that a storage magazine at France Field had been contaminated by leakage of mustard agent.[98]

In an implicit admission of this claim, the Department of Defense told ARI officials that toxic gases buried at France Field had dissipated. In 1979, when France Field was to transfer to Panama, military officials considered removing the material buried there but concluded that it was not dangerous, because its useful life was less than ten years.[99] The Pentagon's treaty implementation director Richard McSeveney said the same thing about chemical munitions: "They have a short shelf life."[100] U.S. Army South's Colonel Michael DeBow, then responsible for carrying out the military's base-cleanup programs in Panama, flatly told a Panamanian journalist that chemical munitions had not been used on the canal area firing ranges and that the Panamanian government should not be worried.[101]

U.S. Army South went further. Its original range plan had defined chemical munitions as only those that were not dangerous. In a section on definitions, the command stated: "Excluded from consideration are chemical warfare materials and chemical compounds which, through its [sic] chemical properties, produce hazards to human health, life or safety."[102]

TAKING IT TO THE HAGUE

Early in 1998, Panama moved to ratify the Chemical Weapons Convention (CWC). The convention requires that ratifying states declare whether they have abandoned chemical weapons in other countries without their consent. If the country where chemical weapons were abandoned ratifies the convention, the abandoning country is then also required to remove and destroy the weapons. The United States ratified the convention in 1997 but flatly stated in its May 1997 declaration that it had not abandoned chemical weapons in any other nation's territory.[103] Given the well-documented presence of chemical weapons remains on San Jose Island, the U.S. declaration was in clear violation of the convention. Chemical weapons buried before 1977 that remain buried and weapons dumped at sea before 1985 are exempt from the convention's provisions.

Panama's ratification of the CWC would allow it to exercise pressure in the Organization for the Prohibition of Chemical Weapons (OPCW) in the Hague, the implementing body established by the CWC, for the United States, Canada, and Great Britain to address any chemical munitions left behind. Panama formally deposited its ratification of the convention with the United Nations on October 7.

Hughes, meanwhile, met in August with the owners of San Jose Island, who were building tourist cabins there. He even visited the island, where he saw for himself the canisters and bombs that records showed had contained phosgene and other chemical agents. He then sent a request to Washington that a team of specialists be sent to the island to survey it for hazards.[104] Hughes and two different military officials said that the funds and explosives team were in place for the visit. According to one of the officers, Hughes made a verbal offer to Foreign Minister Ritter for a survey of San Jose.[105]

Meanwhile, on November 6, as required by the CWC Panama submitted its declaration to the Hague, in which Panama asserted that it had evidence that the United States had abandoned chemical weapons in San Jose. "That business of going to the Hague just torqued Washington something fierce," one of the U.S. officers said. Two days later, the CBS news program *Sixty Minutes* broadcast a report on the United States' toxic legacy in Panama, including footage from the San Jose Project showing goats being gassed and writhing to death. The program infuriated Defense Department officials.[106]

Then, according to two former senior military officers, lawyers in Washington took the issue out of the embassy's hands, an action facilitated by Hughes' departure from Panama in late October. The lawyers believed that the United States did not have a legal obligation under the CWC to do anything in Panama. Army Operations also objected to the survey, according to one officer, fearful of the liability it might create. After all, a survey team was likely to find bombs that invoked the CWC. The military "didn't want to expend the resources, and no amount of cajoling could change their minds," said one State Department official. State and the National Security Council backed up the Army. The team's visit to San Jose was canceled.[107]

As it was canceling the technical team's visit, the United States tried to divert OPCW officials in the Hague. When a Panamanian official met with the OPCW director general and the British representative to the OPCW in February 1999, both reported that U.S. representatives told them that Washington was dealing with the problem bilaterally with Panama. The United States said that "the OPCW's intervention wasn't necessary because they were addressing the issue bilaterally with Panama, which was not true," according to Daniel Delegado, Secretary General of the Foreign Affairs Ministry.[108] The U.S. response inhibited Panamanian action on chemical weapons until the very end of the PRD government in August 1999.

WITHDRAWAL

As the military evacuated more of its bases in Panama, new information emerged about heavy use of pesticides such as DDT and Chlordane on military installations. These chemicals were sprayed many years before in residential areas of the Canal Zone, often daily, to eliminate termites, even after they had been banned in the United States. A preliminary report commissioned by ARI found "plenty of indicators that demonstrate a significant human health hazard exists." The study, which took samples from Corozal and Clayton, concluded that "DDT, DDD, and DDE were all found in high quantities" on the two bases.[109] At the same time, a preliminary health study by University of Texas researchers of former Canal Zone residents found that many of them were worried about the effects of their past exposure to pesticides and other chemicals. Fifty-seven percent of the nearly four hundred people surveyed reported "frequent and heavy exposure to insecticides sprayed from trucks" while living in the Zone, and one in ten believed he or she had had illnesses or other problems as a result of the exposure.[110]

An employee of Lockheed-Martin, which was under contract to the Defense Department from 1996 to 1999 to haul toxic wastes out of Panama, reported receiving a broad range of wastes. "We were handling cyanides, asbestos, poisons, known carcinogens, herbicides, pesticides," said Alfredo Smith, a supervisor at the Lockheed warehouse on the Corozal base in Panama. "Some of this stuff had labels going back to the 1950s." Smith said that a Panamanian working under him began coughing up blood one day after handling an unmarked barrel filled with a chemical powder. Smith himself experienced headaches, rashes, and other problems and filed suit against Lockheed-Martin for lax safety procedures.[111]

Other former military areas also faced serious contamination problems. Water samples on the former Howard Air Force Base and at the Army's Fort Kobbe showed high levels of petroleum distillates.

"Howard is an ugly mess," said another consultant familiar with the bases' contamination.[112]

By this time, the United States was facing away from Panama, with diminishing interest in addressing contamination problems. According to a former senior military officer, in late 1998 the U.S. embassy received a letter from a retired canal worker who sought help with his pension. The man claimed to have helped bury hundreds of barrels of Agent Orange on the banks of the Chagres River in the mid-1970s. The Canal Commission, the worker said, was using Agent Orange as a defoliant or weed killer. When Southern Command officials visited him, he asked for help with his pension, and the military said no but did not investigate whether the claim was legitimate or ask the embassy to do so. The worker then refused to identify where the barrels were buried. "So those barrels might be out there," the officer said. "This guy might be telling the truth."[113]

Hughes's departure, Panamanian electoral distractions, and the treaty's clock shifted any possibility for a cleanup agreement back to Washington. In September 1998, Congress approved a ten-year, $100 million package to compensate Canada for the cleanup of former U.S. bases there. The package set an important precedent, especially because there was no legal cleanup obligation specific to Canada. In approving the measure, however, Congress required the Pentagon to consult with legislators before entering into negotiations to make ex gratia payments for other overseas base cleanup, unless it was part of a previous agreement.[114] Since the Pentagon maintained that it was fulfilling the Canal Treaty's cleanup provision, any negotiations that required additional funding would involve Congress from the beginning. The following March, twenty-five congressional representatives wrote to Defense Secretary William Cohen urging release of documents and greater cleanup efforts by the U.S. military at explosive and chemical weapons sites in Panama.[115]

In the wake of Panama's May 2 elections, which the incumbent PRD lost, the outgoing government assumed a more active approach, approving funds for the prestigious Washington law firm Arnold and Porter to conduct technical assessments and lobby for cleanup in Washington. But Panama's decision came too late to achieve any agreement before the canal was transferred and U.S. troops left Panama, which were watershed moments in the political psychology of U.S. attention to the isthmus. In early 1999, Secretary of State Madeleine

Albright, Pentagon chief William Cohen, and National Security Adviser Sandy Berger reportedly discussed Hughes's proposal to conduct range cleanup after the military left, but the Pentagon, according to Hughes, shot down the proposal.[116] Panama's lobbyists would have to reverse that decision. Under protest, Pérez Balladares accepted the transfer of the Piña Range on June 30, saying that more cleanup was needed.[117]

With an almost entirely new set of officials, the government of President Mireya Moscoso began the task of calling the United States to account for cleanup of the ranges and San Jose Island. Moscoso raised the problem of the ranges in a speech to the UN General Assembly in September 1999 and during a meeting with Bill Clinton the following month.[118] Arnold and Porter subcontracted a company that produced a photographic and narrative report on explosives visible in accessible areas on the ranges after the United States had transferred them. The United States did not budge, however, and even threw doubt on the veracity of Arnold and Porter's findings.[119]

On September 15, 2000, Panama's Foreign Minister José Miguel Alemán asked UN Secretary-General Kofi Annan to help mediate the dispute. "Panama cannot accept the demonstrated irresponsibility in this case by the United States," Alemán said, "especially because . . . we have sufficient technical evaluations to confirm for us that the cleanup of these areas is feasible, would not affect bio-diversity and would not damage the forests."[120]

In addition to the contract with Arnold and Porter, the outgoing government left Moscoso's incoming administration with another commitment related to cleanup. In July 1999, just weeks before the Empire Range was to be transferred to Panama, Panamanian police found a munition that they believed once contained sarin gas. It turned out that the munition was a white phosphorous round and did not contain sarin. But before that determination was made by the lab, outgoing foreign minister Ritter sent a letter to the OPCW stating that Panama had found a chemical munition and requesting that the OPCW make a technical inspection.[121] Ritter's note set in motion the machinery of the OPCW, which asked Panama for permission to visit and make a technical inspection.

This presented the incoming government with a dilemma. They had no photographs of chemical munitions containing live agent. And the OPCW was eager to carry out the requested inspection. So in early

2001, Panama paid for its own explosives-removal company, Geophex UXO, to carry out a survey of San Jose Island to gather evidence in preparation for the OPCW's technical inspection.[122] The OPCW inspection, which took place in July 2001, found four live mustard bombs of U.S. manufacture—three 500-pound and one 1,000-pound bombs—as well as more than one hundred other chemical munitions. "It is highly likely that a substantial number of dud munitions remain to be found on the island," the OPCW said.[123]

Foreign Minister Alemán confronted Secretary of State Colin Powell with the evidence in Washington on September 4, saying that it showed that the United States had violated the CWC's requirement to declare and destroy abandoned chemical weapons. He took the opportunity to press Washington to clean up firing ranges in the canal area. "If they were wrong with respect to the island of San Jose, they could be wrong with respect to the firing ranges," Alemán said. He also asked U.S. officials for information about chemical weapons that might have been left behind on former U.S. bases and ranges elsewhere in Panama. Around the same time, Panama amended its declaration to the OPCW, putting in motion a requirement that the United States address the chemical bombs on San Jose.

Panama quarantined San Jose Island until a more complete inspection for chemical weapons could be made. The State Department claimed that all chemical weapons had been expended or removed from the island before the United States left in 1948, but said it would study the report. After the attacks on the World Trade Center and the Pentagon on September 11, 2001, Panama postponed pressing its case.[124]

An OPCW team returned to San Jose Island in January 2002 to verify the technical team's findings. Secretary of State Powell said in March that the United States would try to "do what's right," but what he had in mind was limited. The State Department offered only to remove the seven chemical bombs confirmed by OPCW and train a team of Panamanians to destroy other bombs that may be found.[125] When the United States succeeded in ousting the Brazilian diplomat Jose Bustani from directorship of the OPCW in the following month, a crystal-clear message was sent to other nations: obeying Washington's will was more important than ridding the world of chemical weapons. Donald Mahley, the U.S. ambassador to the OPCW, reportedly told the organization's staff that "Latin Americans are . . . characterized by sheer incompetence," and then threatened to kill anyone who let his statements out of the room.[126] The comment demonstrated the Bush administration's contempt and cast a long shadow on Panama's efforts to hold the U.S. accountable for the chemical bombs it left behind in San Jose Island.

When the Pentagon agreed in 1977 to withdraw from Panama by the end of the century, it appeared to abandon the notion of perpetuity enshrined in the original Canal Treaties: that the United States would always control the Canal Zone. Canal defense would be handed over to Panama's own military, and the United States could rid itself of an aging utility. At the time, environmental issues were restricted to maintenance of the Smithsonian Institution's scientific-research facilities in Panama.

With the dismantling of Panama's defense forces in 1989, the U.S. military no longer had a counterpart in Panama, and the military bases and bombing ranges would be put to a civilian purpose. Instead of military officers who would control the lands after 1999, the United States' interlocutors were agencies that spoke a different language. The military responded by defining Panamanians' environmental responsibility in the canal area in such a way as to minimize its own liabilities.

Panamanians were at a disadvantage in the process. They had no representatives in Congress to secure funding to remove explosives and other hazards. They lacked information about what was actually on the bases and ranges and the methods available for cleaning it up. Nationalists were more focused on ensuring the U.S. military's departure than the cleanup, while the ARI's leadership wanted the contamination to be discussed quietly so potential investors would not be alarmed.

When Panama decided to make the issue a priority, the decision came too late to reach a cleanup agreement before the canal was transferred in December 1999. Panama would find itself in a situation similar to that of the Philippines, where years after two major U.S. bases closed, toxic wastes were generating health problems in adjacent communities. Nevertheless, Panamanians turned to the task of exercising full sovereignty over their territory and using the properties that had been occupied by the United States for nearly a century.

People gathered at several points in Panama City on the Friday morning of December 31, 1999. While the rest of the world focused on whether technologies would crash from the changing of digits, Panama prepared to receive the canal at noon. Marches came from downtown and from the National Institute, adjacent to the former Canal Zone, converging at the foot of the imposing canal administration building built atop an imperious hill. Panama's president, Mireya Moscoso, strode at the head of her contingent, waving a Panamanian flag and clearly content.

A crowd gathered at nearby Balboa High School, site of the 1964 conflict over the Panamanian flag that resulted in riots and, eventually, President Lyndon Johnson's agreement to renegotiate the canal treaty. In an emotional moment, the Panamanian flag was raised on the school's flagpole.

The formal canal transfer was taking place among U.S. and Panamanian officials high on the steps of the administration building, while the masses below watched the speeches on an enormous television screen that showed the minutes and seconds remaining. The symbolism of government at a remove from the people was lost on no one. It began to rain, hard. The crowd was bubbling. Precisely at noon, thousands of balloons were released into the sky, and the people down below — wet, happy — scaled the lawn toward the administration building and, with banners in hand, took over the site. The canal now belonged to Panama.

The Panama Canal and adjacent U.S. military bases were designed and maintained to serve U.S. interests. The growth and contraction of military sites in the Canal Zone and in Panama's interior, as well as the eventual dissolution of the Zone, reflected responses to and changes in these interests. The transfer of the canal to Panama in 1999 and the transfer of military bases between 1979 and 1999 changed the interests that the waterway and properties would serve; it also changed the resource base available to serve those interests. Although the U.S. agency that ran the canal could draw only on canal revenues for the cost of operations, maintenance, and modernization, the military bases could tap the United States' vast military budget for expenses that ranged from cutting lawns to undertaking major construction projects. Bases transferred to Panama that remained the property of the government drew on a much more limited budget for their upkeep and renovation.

What forces, then, determined what happened to the lands used by the U.S. military for nearly a century? If the United States left a vacuum, what filled it? What are the challenges faced by the alternatives to an imperialist military use of Panama's natural environment? And did the empire definitively depart from Panama? This chapter focuses on the new challenges Panama faced after the U.S. military's withdrawal.

By changing the functions of the properties once occupied by the U.S. military, the transfer opened opportunities for a transformation not only of the physical spaces, but also of their environmental and administrative organization. Under the pressures of rural–urban migration experienced by many cities, for example, Panama City had grown from 1960 to 1990 like an elongated sausage because the presence of the military in Canal Zone sites prevented what could have been a more organic, fan-shaped expansion. This exacerbated traffic congestion, as Panama built its road system to meet the elongated urban expansion. To the extent that the transferred properties served the Panamanian public sector, the process gave confidence to Panamanians that the U.S. departure was a good thing on balance.

However, the greater change may be the transfer of the Canal Zone from facilities planned and run by the state to an area subject to the forces of the national and international market and the interests of the private sector. The transfer infused both assets and liabilities into the economy at a time when countries throughout the hemisphere were divesting themselves of public assets and policy incentives for foreign investment and trade were growing, regardless of their social and environmental impacts.

Ecological and financial measures of uses given to the former bases tended to compete with each other. For some U.S. observers, the jungle's overgrowth on properties that had been transferred to Panama signified Panamanian mismanagement. U.S. journalists writing in 1993 about Fort Gulick, which once housed the U.S. School of the Americas, reported with horror that the fort "has trees growing on the roofs of the barracks," which were deteriorating with disuse. The jungle's reclamation of the hard-won advances of civilization became cause for lamentation about Panamanians' lack of enterprise.[1] In the Canal Zone's residential areas, meanwhile, the cut lawns that had typified the Zone's suburban feel became a marker for successful conversion to local use. When asked in the 1980s or 1990s how Panama would manage the canal after its transfer in 1999, a typical response was that Panamanians would not cut the grass properly.

The same evaluation pervaded some economic assessments of Panama's projected performance in using forest lands. In this view, jungle left undeveloped is not being exploited rationally. A 1996 study of the economic benefits from civilian uses of U.S. military bases bemoaned the fact that only one-third of the acreage of military bases to be transferred would have "efficient economic use" even twenty-five years after transfer. A closer look revealed that more than half of all of the acreage at Fort Sherman was jungle, which, according to the study, would be preserved for environmental and conservationist reasons.[2]

The transfer suggested questions about both Panama's and the United States' responses to the new arrangement. The first indications were that Panama, the Interoceanic Region Authority (ARI) and the new Panama Canal Authority—like the United States before it—would prioritize the interests of the international shipping industry over those of protecting Panama's tropical environment and marginalized communities. Panama's handling of the social and environmental dimensions of the plan to flood land to supply water for a third set of canal locks provided one test for this aspect of the transition.

For the United States, the military's departure forced U.S. businesses to compete on a more equal footing with companies based in other countries for access to the benefits from Panama's transit economy. When Panama acted to diversify the national origins of companies operating the canal's ports by contracting with a Hong Kong–based firm, those in the United States who had always opposed the canal transfer waged a fierce anti-China propaganda campaign. U.S. involvement in the war in neighboring Colombia also increased pressures by the United States to remilitarize Panama.

When the canal and the last U.S. military bases transferred to Panama at the end of 1999, Panamanians began to address issues long deferred during the U.S. presence. The new Canal Authority pushed forward a proposal to build a third set of locks, representing a dramatic and expensive expansion of the canal's capacity. The discovery in September 1999 of human remains buried on a former Panamanian military base ignited a drive to account for the crimes of the 1968–89 dictatorship, leading to the appointment of a Truth Commission that issued its report in April 2002.[3] Panamanians also began to address the ways in which racial discrimination had pervaded their society. Although discrimination based on race, gender, religion, and political opinion is outlawed in the country's constitution, Panama had no civil rights laws to regulate that ban, so that darker-skinned people have frequently faced discrimination in employment and services. Civil society organized in favor of an antidiscrimination law, which was enacted in 2002.[4]

Another issue was Panama's ecology. Despite passage of a 1998 law making environmental crimes punishable by fines of up to $10 million, the country still lacked effective action against contamination by polluters.[5] Like many nations, Panama was experiencing rapid urban growth with poor planning, leading to traffic jams that polluted the air and clogged the city. High oil consumption combined with the use of leaded gasoline (Panama was the last nation in Central America to prohibit it) had led to a severe lead contamination problem.[6] The construction of new toll highways made moving around easier for some, but it also helped choke drainage of waste in Panama Bay, which was beginning to stink, and it deforested urban park land. Unregulated mining threatened to contaminate water for many years in some areas.[7] Citizen environmental movements mobilized on such issues as prohibiting shipments of radioactive materials through the canal, but they were still weak in the face of the logic of short-term economic gain.

Compounding this, some lands transferred by the U.S. military were laden with explosives; they had become environmental sacrifice zones. In December 2000, the Panamanian Society of Architects warned that the site chosen to build a second bridge across the canal was at risk from unexploded ordnance left by the United States.[8] Less than two

Table 4. Panama: Numbers when the United States departed

Population: 2,856,000
Life expectancy: 74.45 years
Percentage of people living in cities: 56.2%
Political parties: 9
Monthly cost of living (1999): $224.72
Second worst distribution of income in Latin America, after Brazil
Unemployment in September 2000: 13.3%
   In August 1999: 11.8%
Percentage of people without potable water (1997): 11.1%
Percentage with dirt floors (1997): 13%
Literacy rate (1995): 90.8%
Gross national product (June 2000): $10.086 billion
Foreign debt (September 2000): $5.638 billion
Number of canal transits (fiscal year 2000): 12,303
Average time a ship waited to transit the canal (2000): 29.7 hours
   Wait time in 1999: 33 hours
Containers moved through ports in 1999: 772,324
   In 1995: 306,551
Percentage of land that was forested (1993): 44%
Percentage of electricity from hydropower (1998): 74%
Number of visitors to Panama (1999): 555,026
Hotel-occupancy rate (July–September 2000): 41.1%
   In 1998: 49.5%

(Ministerio de Economía y Finanzas, October 2000, [http://www.mef.gob.pa/informes/Documentos/Tercer%20Trimestre-2000.pdf]; Ministerio de Planificación y Política Económica [http://www.mippe.gob.pa/]; Instituto Panameño de Turismo [http://www.ipat.gob.pa/estadisticas/]; CIA factbook [http://www.cia.gov/cia/publications/factbook/geos/pm.html]; Autoridad del Canal de Panamá, fiscal year 2000 report [http://www.acp.gob.pa/].)

months later, a machine operator excavating in the area found a World War II–era 40-millimeter mortar caught in the teeth of his steam shovel. It was the eighth time since 1997 that explosives had been found outside the firing ranges on the western side of the canal.[9]

VISIONS FOR REUSE OF THE BASES

> Panama is unmatched in Latin America for the zeal with which state enterprises are being sold off. — Interoceanic Region Authority, 1998

The transfer of many properties between 1979 and 1999 established Panama's initial experiences in the reuse of canal lands.[10] In these and post–1999 experiences, there were four principal and often competing visions for how to use the military bases and the lands transferring to Panama under the Canal Treaties: a military vision; an environmental vision; a commercial or neoliberal vision; and a social vision.

The military vision presumed that, because the bases in U.S. hands served military purposes, those purposes should continue to be served after transfer to Panama, whether by a Panamanian force or through a continued arrangement with U.S. forces. This vision predominated in the early years of the Panama Canal Treaty, especially after Torrijos's death in 1981. The National Guard (Panamanian Defense Forces after 1983) was to be the benefactor of the U.S. military as defenders of the canal and, therefore, the guardian of the military bases. Because the future occupants would continue to be military, a radical change in the installations' functions was never foreseen.[11]

The environmental vision found its maximum expression in a 1993 proposal to create an interoceanic park system that would have stretched across the isthmus from the Pacific to the Atlantic. The 122,141 acre park system would have included military areas operated by the United States connected to one another by existing parks on land transferred to Panama by treaty in 1979. The project faced objections from the Canal Commission and the newly created ARI, which feared turning explosive firing ranges into parks, and was scrapped.[12]

The commercial or neoliberal vision has generally dominated Panamanian policy and actions for the reverted areas. The neoliberal vision's criteria for use can be described as:

—Turn over properties to the private market for development and use;

—Maintain state responsibility—and payment—for establishing basic infrastructure; and

—Maximize revenues rather than promote more equal distribution of income.

The social and civic uses of military bases have found expression in both planned development and in the spontaneous and popular invasion of lands by poor and middle-class families for use as housing. Many of the former Canal Zone buildings that the United States had used for administrative purposes were transferred when the treaties came into force in 1979 and assigned to the public sector, ranging from the courts and universities to executive branch agencies.[13]

One of Panama's interests was in compensating for the loss of national income represented by the U.S. military's expenditures. The Defense Department's spending on salaries, contracts, personal expenditures, and payment for services was drawn down gradually from 1992, when it amounted to up to $350 million, to $249 million in 1999, when the last soldiers left.[14] The Panamanian government sought to offset the loss of this income with increased revenues from the service sector: the ports, the international banking center, and tourism. The state's focus on high revenue producers came at the expense of investment in Panama's labor market. Those who had worked on the U.S. bases were left on their own, for example, with few if any incentives from the Panamanian government to establish their own businesses using the skills they had gained from their employment on the bases.

PARTICIPATION OR EXCLUSION?

The tensions between a participatory process for land use that benefits poor communities and one that reinforces social inequality were visible in diverse sectors. For example, the master plan for converting the bases approved by the Legislative Assembly in 1996 was explicit that "the market [is] the fundamental instrument for determining resource allocation."[15] On the other hand, the master plan was submitted for consideration by a widely representative gathering of Panamanian labor, women, church and business organizations; the government; and all political parties for three days in September 1996. They called for the plans to put "the human person at the center and objective of social and economic development of the interoceanic region, as well as the interests of the area's inhabitants and its ecology and environment." The plan incorporated that proviso and was approved by the Legislative Assembly and signed into law in July 1997. Although the final law included concerns for social justice and ecological protection in its first article, it did not incorporate any mechanism for ensuring that these concerns would be respected in the implementation of the plans.[16]

It was not surprising that a commercial vision dominated planning, given the training of Panama's leaders and the international context of economic policy. The Panamanians who largely shaped the process were Presidents Guillermo Endara and Ernesto Pérez Balladares, both from the banking community, and ARI administrator Nicolás Ardito Barletta (1995–99), who was trained at the University of Chicago, had been vice president of the World Bank for Latin America from 1978 to 1984, and was a protégé of the free-marketer George Shultz.[17] The emphasis on the market was reflected in the way Barletta described the authority's success in terms of dollars committed toward investment, not in jobs, quality of life, or other measures. Many of these promised dollars, it turned out, were not forthcoming.

The plans for tourism development are a case in point. Many of the tourism projects focused on generating revenue for the private sector. The Canopy Tower, a mountain-top radar site that was converted into a small hotel for bird-watchers, was the exception to the rule. More typical was the effort to turn Fort Amador on the canal's Pacific entrance into a hotel-and-casino complex, complete with a wharf for cruise ships, a professional golf course, a yacht club, and monorail transportation. Amador, which transferred to Panama in October 1996 and was to anchor Panama's tourism industry, faces emerald ocean waters on both sides of a causeway. Construction crews spent 1998 and 1999 installing new infrastructure — at Panama's expense — in preparation for the tourist complex.[18]

But most of the private investments in Amador trumpeted by Barletta were phantoms. The hotel-and-casino complex, dubbed Fantasy Island and the biggest-ticket item in the Amador plan, lacked financial backing, and the deposit placed on the project was only a small percentage of the $62 million that ARI invested in building and upgrading infrastructure in Amador and along the causeway. All but $20 million of the $507 million in promised investments in Amador were suspended because of lack of financing.[19]

By mid-2000, the hotel industry was feeling the negative effects of an oversupply of rooms, with an occupancy rate of 40 percent even during high season and falling to 33 percent in 2001, and of a wave of hotel sales, mergers, and government seizures for failure to pay taxes. The heaviest effects were felt in hotels that were not affiliated with international chains — that is, those that relied on local capital. The industry had not heeded the dictum that the country must promote attractions, not just hotels.[20]

The canal area's economy was not entirely dismal, however. The government's sale of public assets, including half of the electricity company, had generated a trust fund that amounted to $1.3 billion by the end of 1999.[21] The availability of funds allowed Panama to invest in a new light-rail system for Panama City and a second bridge across the canal, for which ground was broken in 2002.

HOUSING

An obvious social purpose that could be served by the thousands of buildings transferring to Panama under the treaties was filling the need for housing, identified in the early 1990s as an acute shortage. Panama's Housing Ministry rented out nearly three thousand housing units in areas that had been transferred in 1979, but when ARI assumed jurisdiction over the properties in 1993, it decided to sell the homes. Many renters subsequently objected to ARI's high assessments of the properties. The funds obtained through sales would establish a special fund to construct housing for low-income people. Initially, the master plan approved by the legislature mandated that the Special Housing Fund be administered by the Housing Ministry.[22] But the fund was transferred out of the Housing Ministry, which lacked budget support at the time to create public housing.[23]

Some lands transferred in 1979 were used by Panama's wealthy commercial class, while many poor communities that lacked housing and employment had little access to the properties — or even information. Others were pushed off the reverted lands, sometimes by force.[24] In Colón, the construction of a luxurious Arab Club on former military land provoked resentment among Colón's Black and poor communities.

Although government privatization marginalized many communities and nongovernmental organizations in decision making about how to use the former military properties, some indigenous Kuna communities and groups undertook impressive grassroots efforts. One community that successfully turned military property to social use was Kuna Nega, located near Panama City. "We came here with knowledge of our ancestors who once lived here," said Manuel Owens Cerezo, Kuna Nega's president, in 1995. The community was initiated by Kuna women living in miserable housing in the city, who sought out the land best suited for their needs. Then, with the help of a priest and the human rights group Service for Peace and Justice, they obtained aid from the Spanish government, assistance in the design of buildings, and a provisional title from Panama for forty-four acres. The community cleared part of the parcel in 1982 and built seventy-three homes, a sewing workshop for the creation of *molas* (the Kunas' traditional applique fabric art), a store to sell fried bread, a basketball court, a water-storage tank and generator, police and medical posts, and basic plumbing for the houses. The community faced major challenges, but the people of Kuna Nega were well organized for their collective welfare.[25]

An example of cooperation between Kuna and non-indigenous people is the squatter settlement in Loma Ková, Arraiján, on the west side of the canal from Panama City. The settlement began with Kuna families, especially women, who persevered without water or roads and stood up to dogs, tear gas, and other police harassment to remain on the land. The community won provisional titles to one hundred twenty-five lots and organized committees dedicated to education, health, garbage disposal, streets, water, women, work, and elections.[26]

ARI included another social use in the reverted areas — what the project's director, Juan David Morgan, called a "Quixotean dream." Run as a private nonprofit foundation, the City of Knowledge is a complex of university and private research institutions that inhabits 71 office buildings and 369 homes on 300 acres of the former Army headquarters on Fort Clayton, near Panama City. The "city" consists of a "technological park" and an academic area and hosts regional conferences on tourism, agriculture, and maritime services; university branches from Texas A&M and Florida State University; and pharmaceutical companies studying the medicinal properties of tropical plants.[27] In August 2001, UNICEF and Panama signed an agreement to move the fund's Latin American and Caribbean headquarters to the City of Knowledge, bringing hundreds of professionals. In addition, just a year after Panama received the base, the techno-park hosted forty-five companies that employed some seven hundred people.[28]

ENVIRONMENTAL TENSIONS

The master plan zoned national parks in the canal area and areas within the military bases that had remained forested — 113,263 acres in all — as "protected wooded areas." ARI also set in motion a project to reforest thirty-five hundred hectares on the western side of the canal. Some of the reforested lands would serve as a buffer to illicit entry into the explosive-impact areas still contaminated with unexploded munitions.[29]

In promoting the reforestation project, however, ARI set out a series of arguments framed by a cost-benefit analysis. It cited economic calculations of the value of a hectare of tropical forest — $826.32 — based largely on sustainable exploitation. The reforestation project sought to counterbalance some of the negative consequences resulting from the pressures of urban migration and development for profit. Nevertheless, it used the discourse of neoliberal economic policy to make its case.[30]

Some developers echoed this logic by making commodities of nature and its indigenous inhabitants. "One of our troubles is that we don't have something as marketable as a theme park, like Disney World," Herman Bern, promoter of the Gamboa Tropical Rainforest Resort, declared in 1998. "However, we have nature as our theme park. . . . We have several indigenous communities. We want to interact and work very closely with them, so that we can show their culture, their way of living. . . . We'll make a project that wealthy people will want to visit."[31]

Such discourse fed fears that areas set aside for conservation would be chipped away by development, regardless of how they were zoned. In December 1999, residents of the former Albrook air base were alarmed to see bulldozers cutting up a section of forested land that had been designated an "urban green area" in the master plan. ARI's plans had called for a road in the area to give access to a shopping mall then under construction. Although the so-called earth removal was suspended, the imbroglio raised questions about institutional abilities to protect forested areas from the saw and bulldozer.[32]

FLOODING THE POOR

Economically and environmentally, the canal comprises not only the waterway itself but also the facilities on its banks, including the former military bases — a complex of lands, waters, and activities that are tightly interwoven and interdependent. In that context, the fate of the canal — how it responds to the changing demands and opportunities of international maritime commerce — will deeply affect the environment, economy, and social reality of the watershed and communities around it.

In the 1950s and 1960s, the United States developed and eventually abandoned plans to construct a sea-level canal that would accommodate more and larger ships. The alternative modernization plan, adopted as a central recommendation in 1993 by the Tripartite Commission, a study commission established by the United States, Panama, and Japan, is to build a third set of locks that will allow passage of ships of 150,000 deadweight tons. (The maximum capacity of the current canal locks is 65,000 deadweight tons.) The Tripartite Commission estimated that a new set of locks would cost between $5.4 billion and $8.5 billion and take ten years to build. These factors would have an effect on canal tolls, Panama's revenues from the canal, and the country's debt load; they would also affect the watershed's ecology and residents displaced by newly flooded lands. When the canal was controlled by the United States, no government undertook the capital, political, and environmental costs of such a project.[33]

Operating a third set of locks will require dramatically more freshwater than passes through the current canal (55 million gallons per passage). Obtaining this water requires damming three rivers — the Indio, the Caño Sucio, and the Coclé del Norte — and expanding the legally defined canal watershed. According to the Panama Canal Authority, thirty-five thousand people would be affected by the flooding. Peasant groups in the area say the number of displaced will be much greater: more than a hundred thousand.[34]

In August 1999, the outgoing PRD government passed a measure to expand the watershed to include the areas needed for the new dams; it was signed into law the day before the new government came into office, with no consultation with the affected communities. Some members of these communities had been forced to move by earlier dam projects. "Our position is that if the development happens, it will be for the rich, and the poor will suffer more," said one peasant leader from the communities. The flooding may also cause ecological damage from floating aquatic life and the burning or decomposition of the forest's organic material, releasing carbon dioxide and methane, which contribute to the greenhouse effect.[35] Other critics raised straightforward fiscal questions about whether the canal expansion could even pay for itself, given the enormous cost and assumption of debt required.[36]

Opponents of the project — including religious, environmental and peasant groups — believe that the canal should be a means, not an end in itself, and they ask a fundamental question: Will Panama shape its own development by expanding the canal's vocation in the service of international maritime interests, or will it make decisions about development that serve Panama's people?

U.S. RESPONSES

> The Embassy is a natural point of contact for American businessmen and investors interested in Panama. It has become the first line of defense to serve the interests of American companies overseas.
> — U.S. Ambassador William Hughes, 1997

Two controversies at the time of the canal transfer illustrate how superpower politics continued to dog U.S. policy toward the isthmus: the outcry over the reputed Chinese control of ports, and the regional pressures generated by the war in Colombia.[37]

In contrast to when the bases were under U.S. management, Panama has an interest in diversifying its international commercial relationships, including in contracts for development of ports and other canal-area properties. "We need investment from Europe, the United States, and Asia, as well as Latin America," said Omar Jaén, an adviser to ARI. "It is important to not have a concentration in one group or country."[38]

As ships faced increased delays for passage through the canal and canal modernization was postponed during the 1990s, multimodal transportation assumed increased importance. Multimodal transportation combines the use of diverse means of moving cargo from one place to another, including maritime, rail, and, increasingly, aircraft transportation. The development of containers that can easily be moved by trucks and stacked on large ships, as well as on jets revolutionized the shipping industry and accelerated this process. It also meant that ports at both ends of the canal began to compete with the Panama Canal for certain kinds of cargo.[39]

With the implementation of the 1977 Canal Treaty, the two ports and the railroad were part of the package that transferred to Panama in October 1979 and came under the control of the National Port Authority. By most reports, the ports were run inefficiently, and the cost and time required to move containers led many shippers to use other ports in the region. Panamanian officials realized that private port developers with access to capital and technology could handle the ports more effectively. According to Hugo Torrijos, director of Panama's Port Authority in 1997, the state could move a container in three days for a cost of $600, whereas a private outfit could do it in only eight hours for $150. Between 1993 and 1995, Panama let concessions for two new ports.[40]

The port privatization strategy ran into a political snag in 1997, after Panama awarded concessions for the Balboa and Cristobal ports to Hutchison International, the largest port developer in the world. Panama initially planned to accept separate bids for the development of the two ports but suspended negotiations with companies that prequalified in September 1995, when Bechtel Enterprises, a multinational corporation based in San Francisco, proposed doing a study on the development of both ports and the railroad. Six months later, Bechtel submitted its proposal. Beginning in 2002, it would pay $2 million annually for all three projects, if it made a profit in previous years — an offer that even other U.S. companies described as "ludicrous." Panamanian officials were insulted. Ambassador Hughes and U.S. Commerce Secretary Ron Brown lobbied President Pérez Balladares on behalf of Bechtel's proposal, but Panama reimbursed Bechtel for the expenses of its study and reopened the process.[41]

Five companies participated in formal bidding in June 1996, four of them U.S. companies (in one case in consortium with a Danish shipper). The fifth company was Hutchison Ports Holdings, a Hong Kong conglomerate with ties to mainland China. The bids were a mix of proposals that addressed both ports, or only one, or just the rail-road, or all three. Companies submitted different kinds of information about what Panama would receive. Unable to compare the bids on an equal basis, Panama returned them. After a second round of bidding, word passed informally that one of the U.S. companies had won. Meanwhile, however, Hutchison approached Panamanian officials and said it would double its offer if the bidding were reopened. Pérez Balladares quickly announced a third round, and Hutchison executives flew back to Panama. Hughes protested, and one of the U.S. companies boycotted the process. In the end, Hutchison won the contract.[42]

Hughes penned a public letter accusing the Panamanians of a "lack of transparency" in the affair.[43] Panamanian officials dismissed the charges as sour grapes and pointed out that U.S. and Taiwanese companies had won other port concessions. "If one company offered $22 million and another only offered $10 million, I don't think anyone in the United States would be so stupid as not to choose the offer that was in the best interests of their country," said Labor Minister Mitchell Doens.[44]

"At first, there was no pressure from Bechtel," said Torrijos, who was the ports director at the time. But when it became clear that Hutchison had won the bidding, Bechtel called Torrijos and threatened him. When he told Bechtel it could have the contract if it paid the same as Hutchison, Torrijos said, the response was: "This is a joke. No one can pay that."[45] Meanwhile, one of the other losing U.S. companies pressed the Federal Maritime Commission to launch an investigation into whether the bidding process had unfairly affected U.S. shipping.[46]

In the end, Hutchison did not have to pay the full $22 million — at least, for the first six years. The contract gave Hutchison the use of land in the former Albrook Airbase to establish a container yard, although Panama had already ceded the same land to the Kansas City Railroad Company. To resolve the issue, Panama agreed to compensate Hutchison for the land by paying $60 million: $10 million a year taken from Hutchison's annual fee to Panama.[47]

The conflict did not go away. The *Washington Times* ran a front-page banner story in March 1997 alleging foul play in the port contract. The newspaper quoted one analyst as saying that, "in China, like in so many Asian countries, money buys influence."[48] The same day, a

House committee quizzed canal officials about Chinese involvement in the Hutchison contract. "I would certainly hate to see that special relationship [between Panama and the United States] threatened by the introduction of a third party which is . . . a former, and yet potential, foe of this country," said Democratic Representative Gene Taylor. "That was one of the two things, if I recall, that the opponents of the treaty were saying could happen, that a potential foe of our country could end up running the canal."[49] In Panama, an irritated President Pérez Balladares said that U.S. Democrats and Republicans had transferred to Panama their fight over mainland China and its financial involvement in the 1996 presidential campaign.[50] As recently as 2001, reporters asked Secretary of State Colin Powell to comment on alleged Chinese control of the canal.[51]

Why did the port concession provoke such acrimony among U.S. conservatives? One explanation is that this was a new version of the Monroe Doctrine. Returning to the status quo ante of Panama without military bases, the "first line of defense" of U.S. capital felt obliged to project phantom threats in order to protect U.S. economic interests. This time, it was not Europe that concerned the guardians of U.S. hegemony. The ports represent important sources of money; Manzanillo has surpassed the Port of Miami in tonnage.[52] With the withdrawal of U.S. troops, the United States returned to competing economically in Panama without what diplomats once called the "positive moral influence" of the military. China's economy emerged as a major —if not *the* major—competitor with U.S. production and export. In a world of accelerating globalization, some saw any hedging of the United States' privileged position in Latin America as a problem. Thus, the extreme Right in the United States launched a propaganda offensive declaring that Panama's port concessions to a competing player in the international market were a threat to U.S. security. It was immaterial to that offensive that Hutchison did not employ a single Chinese national in Panama. The companies operating the ports had no authority to pilot ships through the canal or to determine the place of warships in the queue, as Senator Trent Lott, the Republican Majority Leader mistakenly claimed.[53]

The projection of domestic anti-Chinese feeling onto Panama had a long history. During the Panama Canal's construction, U.S. officials sought laborers to replace West Indians, whom the White overseers considered congenitally lazy. They considered importing Chinese coolies, but the same exclusion laws that prohibited immigration of Chinese nationals to the United States made the proposal politically impossible.

MILITARY TEMPTATIONS

With the dismantling of the Panama Defense Forces in 1990, and the subsequent constitutional abolition of a national army in 1994, the remaining question appeared to be whether the U.S. military would continue to occupy and use some of the military bases and firing ranges. That question was not settled until 1998, when negotiations for the Multinational Counterdrug Center collapsed, and the two governments made a definitive decision for U.S. forces to leave Panama.

However, in light of the war in Colombia and escalating U.S. military involvement, the war's spillover into the Darién, and the need to demonstrate plans to defend the canal against potential dangers, Panama faced multiple pressures to militarize its security forces. In 1999 and 2000, the United States proposed a maritime intelligence agreement for surveillance of Panama's ports and a Visiting Forces Agreement, both of which would involve collaboration between Panamanian and U.S. security or military officials, but the Moscoso administration did not pursue the agreements.[54] A national security plan drafted in 1999 with advice from U.S. military officers incorporated uses by Panama's national police, navy, and presidential police for more than half a dozen facilities on the former U.S. bases.[55]

Units formed to protect Darién Province had grown to about twenty-five hundred men by early 2000 and were armed with mortars.[56] Later that year, Panama began building an airstrip capable of landing C-130 military-cargo aircraft in a remote Darién village with only two hundred inhabitants.[57] Meanwhile, between 2000 and 2002, as part of a dramatic increase in regional aid — itself a response to concerns about the escalating war in Colombia — Washington more than doubled police and military aid to Panama, to nearly $10 million. Sales of military equipment to Panama jumped during the same period, from $439,000 to $2.9 million.[58] Much of the equipment and training were explicitly military, despite Panama's constitutional prohibition of a national army.

The Pentagon continued to have access for military flights in and out of Panama by a private firm — based on a contract to transport cargo and passengers between Honduras and dirt strips in Colombia — on a daily basis. Not until an enterprising reporter discovered a request for proposals posted on the Internet did Panamanian civil society become aware that the Pentagon had been using Panama City's Tocumen Airport for "transportation services" in and out of Colombia, even after U.S. troops had left. Cargo included helicopter blades and hazardous materials, as well as passengers. The contract had been held since 1997 by Evergreen Helicopters, which played a clandestine role in the 1989 U.S. invasion. "Exposure to risk is higher than normal due to operations in/out of semi-prepared airstrips in remote locations," the Air Force's contract information noted.[59]

In February 2002, Panamanian and U.S. officials signed a "complementary arrangement" that streamlined the process for allowing U.S. Coast Guard troops to carry out anti-drug operations in Panamanian waters and for overflights in Panamanian airspace. Former President Jorge Illueca and others criticized the accord as a step toward allowing U.S. military forces back into the country.[60] The Coast Guard, widely known for its work in sea rescues, increasingly has conducted militarized anti-drug operations — for example, Coast Guard sharpshooters have fired from helicopters at boats suspected of carrying cocaine.[61] The debate over the "arrangement" was drowned out, however, by deepening corruption scandals within Moscoso's government and the Legislative Assembly.

LEGACIES

Panama has one of the most skewed distributions of income in Latin America.[62] The transfer of the military bases' infrastructure, valued by the World Bank at $4 billion, could eventually serve to narrow that gap, but early indications were that it did not. Neither did poor communities demonstrate much hope that they would benefit significantly from Panamanian control of canal operations.

The neoliberal framework as applied to redevelopment of the transferred properties risked the kind of loss Panama saw in Amador, in which the private sector promised much and produced little while the public paid for improvements in infrastructure that yielded few permanent jobs. Similarly, Panama's eagerness to maximize revenues from the port privatizations led to decisions that not only angered the advocates of U.S. companies in the embassy but led to planning problems that cut into the same revenues that Panama so dearly wanted.

A different policy for the transferred properties would unambiguously implement the master plan's imperative to put "the human person at the center and objective of social and economic development of the interoceanic region." This is unlikely to occur, however, unless Panamanians who oppose the neoliberal model develop and press for alternatives. Such alternatives may include state incentives for growth of small and locally owned businesses, which many economists have observed are more efficient generators of employment than investment in large multinationals.

Like such transfers elsewhere, the transfer to Panama of military bases under the terms of the Canal Treaties did not provide turnkey operations that users — public or private — could simply walk in to and use without adaptation. Despite perceptions among U.S. journalists and Panamanian elites that the bases represented a piñata of gifts to Panama, the bases in fact carried substantial liabilities that ranged from ongoing maintenance to the cleanup of toxics and explosives and renovation of infrastructure.

But possibly the greatest liability that Panama inherited in the canal area was the idea that the installations and the canal had to be run exactly as the United States had run them. Colonialism was not easily shaken.

7 ☆ CONTINUITY AND CHANGE IN THE MILITARY'S VISION

> When the North Americans threw out the sea-level canal of the French to adopt a lock canal, which at that time was undoubtedly more feasible, they proceeded to imprison the Chagres River to form the largest artificial lake in the world. . . .
>
> Goethals and his High Command decided to give battle to the Chagres. They had to surround it, force it to retreat, hunt it down, as if it were a jaguar, cornered by the machine hounds which the river-hunter engineers had set upon it. — Gil Blas Tejeira, Pueblos Perdidos, 1962

When Theodore Roosevelt, dressed in a white suit, posed in 1907 at the controls of a giant steam shovel as it cut huge swaths of earth from what would become the Panama Canal while West Indian workers looked on, he tapped ideas and established a mythology that would serve the U.S. canal enterprise for long afterward. During the nearly one hundred years of the American canal project, the dominant view of tropical nature and the jungle in Panama among the U.S. military and policymakers, conveyed graphically by Gil Blas Tejeira, was as an enemy or obstacle that had to be overcome and controlled to achieve the overriding U.S. goal of building and defending an interoceanic waterway.[1]

In Roosevelt's worldview, nature was a transforming agent for the civilized man. Through contact with the wild natural world, men were tested and became stronger. This required the preservation of wild reservations where White men could engage the natural world on its terms and come back to tell the tale. The canal regime he established in Panama required enormous amounts of human labor for construction, defense, training, and sanitation that would engage soldiers and workers directly and intimately with the natural world of the tropics. After Roosevelt's presidency ended in 1909, his successors did not promote his ideology of regeneration in the wild, and other purposes took precedence. But the encounter with the tropical Other remained integral to the U.S. mythology of the isthmus. As the centerpiece of that encounter, the canal project came to represent the taming of nature.

The military's institutional structure and evolution also shaped the encounter. Most military officers and enlisted men completed tours of a couple years in Panama and were gone. They were therefore more likely to bring to Panama images of the tropics and their people that were publicly propagated by leaders and media in the United States. If the values informing those images changed, as when the environmental movement challenged excavation using nuclear explosions, the military was sometimes forced to respond. Similarly, when the climate in the United States was especially hostile to African Americans, as it was in the early twentieth century and in the late 1980s, there was less to restrain the use of military power against dark-skinned Panamanians.

Before the United States occupied the Canal Zone, the U.S. military's relationship to the isthmus was primarily by water, through Navy frigates and their occasional landings of marines and sailors. Once the Zone was established, the Army took command of the garrison, and Army engineers assaulted the isthmian environment through construction of the canal, more than doubled the local population through importation of workers, and established a racially and environmentally privileged colony. Until 1928, when land expropriation came under the control of the State Department, the Army was expansionist and expropriated land at will outside the Zone.[2] The onset of World War II led to a new and even greater wave of land expropriations for U.S. military use, which was truncated by the nationalist protests in 1947 that threw out bases outside the Canal Zone.

The principal conventional job of the armed forces is to prepare for and fight wars. In Panama, however, the military was charged — and sometimes charged itself — with a wide variety of missions that were not only military in nature. The diverse nature of these missions and the different professions of the military men they brought to the isthmus led to various attitudes toward the tropics and toward the people who lived in Panama. The sanitary engineers of the canal-construction period aimed to beat back plant growth that could harbor mosquito larvae. Post–World War II commanders of the Jungle Warfare Training Center, however, sought to preserve the jungle as a realistic training ground, and treaty implementation officials trying to keep down the costs of range cleanup in the 1990s resisted expensive and time-consuming methods that involved cutting vegetation.

This mixed set of missions was a continuous source of conflicting responses to the U.S. military presence on the isthmus. When the military departed in the 1990s, its critics pointed to chemical weapons tests or to the destruction of El Chorrillo as its legacy in Panama. The military and its defenders, for their part, emphasized the benefits to Panama of the canal itself.

THE MILITARY'S MULTIPLE ROLES

We can distinguish seven kinds of missions carried out by the U.S. military in Panama: police interventions; engineering, especially associated with canal construction; tropical sanitation; canal defense, which often was interpreted liberally; troop training; tests of materiel for effects of the tropical climate; and intelligence and communication tasks.

Police functions, an early and frequent military mission, ranged from the gunboat interventions in street conflicts between 1856 and 1903 and supervision of elections during the canal construction era to tutelage of Panamanian police cadets in the wake of the 1989 invasion. The Good Neighbor policy of the 1930s substituted U.S. police interventions with the cultivation and growth of a Panamanian guard, and the National Security doctrine during the Cold War further supported the National Guard's growth up to and during the military regimes of 1968–89. The dismantling of the Panama Defense Forces during the 1989 invasion returned Panama to a condition akin to that of the pre–Good Neighbor period, with the isthmus dependent on Washington for local order. A brief U.S. intervention against an aborted police rebellion in December 1990 illustrated the relationship.

The police interventions primarily have been a urban undertaking, but the Panamanian urban environment is still viewed as an other in most accounts. The policing brought GIs from a foreign culture, whose image of Panama was shaped in the United States, into direct contact with Panamanians and made them the Panamanians' military and political superiors. Most of the soldiers also came from a culture different from Panama's, with little knowledge of its history. This sometimes resulted in cynicism about Panamanians' character and capabilities. Zone policeman Harry Francke complained about slow responses by

West Indian laborers to his questions and concluded, "Quick changes from negro to Spanish gangs demonstrated beyond all future question how much more native intelligence has the white man."[3]

A second mission involved engineering tasks that initially were associated with the lock canal but also included land and water surveys, road building, and civic action projects. These engineering missions included military control of road construction in the republic through the 1920s and the establishment in 1948 of the Inter-American Geodetic Survey, which fielded hundreds of military surveyors not only in Panama but throughout Latin America.[4] When the United States forged its plans for a nuclear-excavated canal in the 1960s, the engineers returned to Panama to test soils and hydrology and determine technical feasibility. The engineers' approach to the isthmus tended to focus on function, not motive or culture.

Third, the Army was responsible for medical protection and environmental sanitation of the Canal Zone against what one Army doctor called "a native population imbued with superstitious antagonism"[5] in a physical environment that its own engineers were turning topsy-turvy for the waterway. The elimination of yellow fever and reduction of malaria were an impressive feat, and they effectively made the canal possible. The Army's success against disease, and the treaty revisions in 1936 that removed sanitation of the terminal cities from the Army's prerogatives, ultimately reduced the role of General Gorgas's followers to research and responses to occasional outbreaks. But the story of White men's triumph over the vectors of disease in tropical Panama continued to hold potent symbolic value and to serve as a source of pride for the military and the U.S. project in general.

The military's central declared mission in Panama throughout the twentieth century was to defend the canal against potential aggressors. In the years before World War II, the United States showed little concern for potential threats to the canal from Panama itself, or even from Latin America. Instead, it was oriented toward more distant potential adversaries, such as Germany, England, and Japan. Even during World War II, military attitudes toward Panama focused on non-Panamanian foreigners, many of whom were deported to camps in the United States, and on the extent of Panamanian cooperation with U.S. desires for additional bases.

As a result, canal defense strategies invoked images of tropical people not as dangerous in themselves so much as incapable of thwarting more serious threats. "Action by the United States in Panama must be based on hard practical facts, rather than any fatuous illusions of fraternalism," wrote the Army War College commandant in 1940. "While Panama, to date, appears to cooperate . . . for the protection of the Canal Zone, a small country with the temperamental instability characteristic of mixed races is not too dependable."[6]

WORLD WAR II AND STRATEGIC CHANGES

The development of air power and radio and radar communications expanded the defensive and offensive reach of the military's mission in Panama, locating the isthmus as a hub for regional surveillance and for a string of bases as far as Ecuador and Guatemala that nominally served canal defense, especially during World War II.[7] "The development in size, range, speed, power and cruising radius of modern bombers makes it absolutely essential that we spread out our defense installations," wrote General David Stone, the garrison commander.[8] Air power also brought a desire to shield the canal from view from the air and, eventually, military coordination of civilian air-control traffickers. The air thus was added to water and land as a medium for potential combat and control.

Until the 1940s, Navy operations were limited to one ocean at a time and so depended heavily on the canal. Once the Navy fleet became large enough to cover contingencies in two oceans, the canal lost strategic value. The Cold War, however, supplanted canal defense against possible overseas enemies with the defense of national-security states against internal enemies. For this, the military would need to train the region's militaries and to study the tropics—map out its terrain and understand the effects of tropics on materiel. In Latin America, it would also need to develop a regional intelligence system. Panama became the regional hub for these missions.

A fifth set of missions, then, focused on training U.S. and Latin American troops for conflicts in the Pacific and Latin America, for which the bases in Panama were converted into a hemispheric site of mock and real encounters with the jungle and its inhabitants. The School of the Americas was the premier institution for training, but the Inter-American Air Force Academy trained even more Latin American soldiers (see table 5).

The largest training facility in Panama, however, revived Roosevelt's

Table 5. U.S. military training facilities in Panama, 1945–99

Training School	Years in Panama	Base in Panama	Number of Graduates
U.S. Army School of the Americas	1949–84	Fort Gulick	29,000
Inter-American Air Force Academy (IAAFA)	1945–89	Albrook Air Force Base	20,000+
Small Craft Instruction and Technical Team	1963–99	Rodman Naval Station	5,365
Inter-American Geodetic Survey Cartographic School	1952–60s	Fort Clayton	1,600 (1952–1964)
Jungle Warfare Training Center	1953–99	Fort Sherman	1,700 (1961); 9,145 (1967); 9,000 (1998)
Inter-American Police Academy	1962–64	Fort Davis	725

(Captain Gary L. Arnold, U.S. Air Force ["IMET in Latin America," *Military Review* (February 1987)]; "Escuela naval de EEUU graduará ultimos marinos" [*Critica en Linea*, http://epasal.epasa. com/critica/110698/boletin.html]; David Abel ["Farewell to Tarzan Training Ground," *Christian Science Monitor*, June 3, 1999].)

desire for redemption through contact with nature: the Jungle Warfare Training Center, founded in 1953 to keep "the art of jungle warfare alive" in the wake of the Korean conflict.[9] The center was based on nearly seventeen thousand acres on Fort Sherman and featured a grueling three-week course in jungle survival. Soldiers spent their first afternoon of training at the center's "prize possession, its zoo"; sessions holding the zoo's boa constrictor became a staple for visitors and photographers.[10] Most participants were U.S. soldiers, but Latin Americans also trained there. On the nearby Piña firing range, the Army built another jungle community—the "live-fire village" used for combat training for wars in Southeast Asia and Latin America. Such training served to test soldiers' masculinity against savage nature and toughen them for the task of fighting civilization's Asian and Latin American enemies.

Given the extraordinary jungle flora and fauna at the training courses in Panama, it is not hard to understand why many professional soldiers lamented the closure of the Sherman jungle training center in 1999. The Army cited budgetary reasons for not replacing the center, but more to the point was the military's institutional withdrawal from consciously engaging the tropics.

That withdrawal is evident in the fate of another set of missions in Panama: the testing of weapons and equipment under tropical conditions. The United States became interested in tropical testing of materiel in Panama in the late 1930s, an interest that expanded during chemical weapons tests on San Jose Island in 1943–47.[11] The military continued a host of uncoordinated tropical tests in the 1950s. U.S. involvement in and expansion of the war in Indochina renewed institutional interest in its presence in Panama, although more by analogy to another tropical region than by interest in Panama itself. As the United States acquired military commitments in multiple tropical areas, experience showed that the jungle was not an absolute barrier to combat forces, and U.S. armed forces sought ways to overcome the operational challenges of the jungle as a combat environment. The tactical problems ranged from poor mobility in thick vegetation and slippery soil and reduced accuracy of weapons to reduced human efficiency because of perspiration.[12] In the broad-scale U.S. counterinsurgency waged in Southeast Asia, the use of Agent Orange and other herbicides during the nine-year Operation Ranch Hand project sought to destroy the broadleaf plants that hid Vietnamese from U.S. eyes in the air and that fed purported supporters of the Vietcong (see figure 15).[13]

The Army's Tropic Test Center (TTC), founded in 1964, aimed to combine the "exciting experience" of the jungle with "objective measurement" by the scientific mind, the riotous vegetation of the tropics with intellectual rigor.[14] The TTC justified its activity on the fact that three-quarters of all wars in the world between 1959 and 1975 took place either partly or totally in the tropics, and Panama provided a rare area to test equipment: "There are very limited climatic analogs to the Canal Zone that are readily accessible to the United States."[15] But negotiations for the TTC's stay in Panama after 1999 were made secondary to the counterdrug center, and the TTC was absorbed by other commands when the military withdrew.

A final military use of Panama was as a center for intelligence gathering. After World War II, the isthmus was most important to the Army

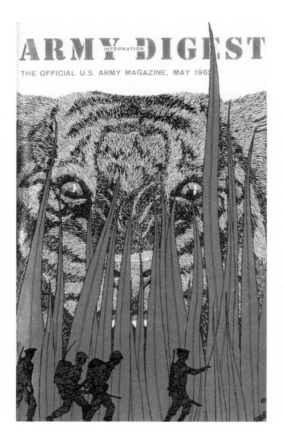

ARMY·DIGEST

INFORMATION

THE OFFICIAL U.S. ARMY MAGAZINE, MAY 1965

15. As this May 1965 cover of *Army Information Digest* shows, during the war in Southeast Asia, the Army viewed the tropics as a dangerous place. (*Army Information Digest*, May 1965.)

as "a good listening post and intelligence center for much of Latin America."[16] The School of the Americas and other regional training facilities served informally to gather intelligence on up-and-coming Latin American officers. The Navy's high-powered satellite on Galeta Island, built in 1952 and used for many years by the National Security Agency, reportedly transmitted pictures from the Malvinas that the United States passed on to the British officers during the war there.[17] And it was the capacity to obtain information by aircraft stationed at Howard air base that the United States most sought to keep during the 1995–98 negotiations for a continued military presence in Panama.

A minority view guiding U.S. actions in Panama saw the jungle and its myriad forms of life as an ally to the canal project. Beginning very early in the canal regime, conservationist ideas influenced the enterprise. The Canal Zone incorporated monuments to the jungle, which were both militarily convenient and of service to the scientific community, as well as the managed gardens of residential areas. Conservation in the Canal Zone was more utilitarian than pursued for its own sake, however.

Theodore Roosevelt was a naturalist who, during his presidency, established six national parks, sixteen national monuments, and fifty-three wildlife reserves.[18] A conflict raged at the time between two brands of conservationism: the movement led by John Muir, a spiritualist intent on maintaining the magnificence of ecologies unchanged by human hands, and National Forest Director Gifford Pinchot, who was pragmatic and political in his approach to the environment. Like Muir's movement, conservationist ideas rapidly became co-opted by the ideals of efficiency. Conservation by 1908 was defined as the use of "foresight and restraint in the exploitation of the physical sources of wealth as necessary for the perpetuity of civilization, and the welfare of present and future generations."[19] It was this concept of conservationism, in the service of the canal's long-term commercial and military goals, that would reign in the Canal Zone. The canal project's underlying goals typified the ideals of engineering efficiency by dramatically shortening the time and resources required for commerce and warships to pass from one ocean (or coast) to the other.[20]

The United States reiterated ideas of utilitarian conservation in the 1990s. By that time, both critics of the U.S. military and the military itself had internalized environmentalist discourse. The State Department's environmental concerns prioritized canal operations, reflected in U.S. Agency for International Development projects that emphasized preservation of forests in the canal watershed over reforestation in Panama's interior.[21] Preserving the forests in the canal area is critical to preventing erosion and siltation of the canal, which in turn keeps the canal's operations efficient and competitive.

Echoing proposals of a century before, Southern Command officials suggested in 1997 that U.S. soldiers train Latin American armies to protect forest reserves threatened by deforestation.[22] To market the deployment of the military for these missions, the Pentagon and State Department had to gloss over the tensions between the military's combat mission and the goal of preserving the environment and distort the SouthCom's environmental record at bases and firing ranges on the isthmus.[23] The firing ranges mined with explosives that the military had left behind in 1999, for example, became "protected areas" in which "the ecosystem will be preserved in its natural state."[24]

U.S. policymakers and environmentalists addressed these contradictions in part by focusing on Panama's contribution to deforestation, often attributed to poverty or ignorance of the forest's long-term value. U.S. military reports on Panamanian civilians' use of artillery-range lands for agriculture or hunting referred to "encroachment," a term that suggests — in addition to U.S. entitlement — the need to hold the line against ecological invaders and poachers. Some U.S. conservationists viewed Panamanian society as responsible for the blind and unbridled exploitation of tropical ecology and the U.S. military as responsible stewards of the land. "The U.S. military sites in Panama are just about the only part of the country around Panama City that hasn't be[en] destroyed," wrote one irate member of the Nature Conservancy in response to a report by the Earthjustice Legal Defense Fund on the U.S. military's environmental obligations in Panama. "All the rest of the area has been clear-cut and farmed."[25]

Another expatriate North American living in Panama wrote in 1997: "See what the Panamian [sic] people have done to their country — ecology is a mess thanks to them and they totally ignore World Wildlife and Sierra Club regarding destroying trees, burning of grass . . . and the hunt for turtles and their eggs for food and sex aphrodisiacs, just to name a few things."[26] Panamanians' disregard for environmental health was employed to justify military approaches to environmental crises.

The perception of environmental destruction outside the U.S.-run canal area was not groundless. In Panama's more populated interior provinces, cattle historically was the driving force for productive use of lands, usually established after slash-and-burn methods of farming had effectively worn out the tropical soils for agricultural crops. In 1800, close to 93 percent of the country is believed to have been covered with forest. By 1947, that proportion had dropped to 70 percent and by 1980 to 38–45 percent.[27] Indeed, deforestation is a growing problem in Panama and has ecological and economic repercussions that potentially reach far beyond its borders. The problem is growing most quickly in lands outside the area.

But the problem is linked to consumption in the Canal Zone itself. In an essay titled "Cattle and Ships: Culture, History and Sustainable Development in Panama," Guillermo Castro suggests that the growth in production in Panama's interior — especially of livestock — to supply the Canal Zone's population led to increased deforestation. The first significant growth in cattle production occurred during the canal-construction period to solve the problem of supplying an army of laborers. Later, the growth of cattle grazing in the interior, he wrote, "was connected to the Panamanian economy's ever increasing access to the enclave market, which was facilitated by the treaties of 1936 — rightly known as the 'meat and beer' treaty — 1954, and 1977." Castro believes that "the presence of an ecologically sustainable enclave has stimulated the tendency toward unsustainability that dominates the rest of Panama. Unsustainability . . . has built an ever tighter circle around the enclave of sustainability."[28]

CHANGE AND CONTINUITY

A range of factors influenced U.S. military attitudes toward Panama and the Canal Zone, some external and objective, others more attitudinal. They included:

— *Changing U.S. role.* The growth of the United States from a small colonial power to a global superpower increased its interest in Panama as an analog to other tropical regions; it also changed U.S. uses of its military presence in Panama. When the United States was engaged in war in the Pacific or Asia, it focused attention elsewhere and limited its interest in Panama's people and lands in themselves, except as a setting to prepare for war overseas.

— *Panamanian attitudes.* When Panamanians actively challenged the military's or the Canal Zone's hegemony, or when the interests of the two countries collided in other ways, U.S. officials were more likely to portray Panamanians as mongrel underlings or primitives who were less deserving than White U.S. citizens. When Panamanians were responsive to Washington's demands, U.S. representatives gave those Panamanians a wider berth.

— *Assumed perpetuity or end of the U.S. presence.* When the operating assumption was that the United States exercised sovereignty in perpetuity — or even for the foreseeable future, as on San Jose Island — little thought was given to potential Panamanian uses of lands once the United States departed. The rejection of the Filós–Hines Treaty in 1947 and, on a much larger scale, the ratification of the 1977 Canal Treaties planted the notion of conversion of the military's tropical holdings to Panamanian civilian use. In 1948 and in 1998, Panama's eagerness to receive land and the U.S. military's use of ranges until near the moment of departure made cleanup of explosives more limited.

— *Racial attitudes*. U.S. officials often assumed that Panamanians could not be relied on to act rationally and responsibly. Black Panamanians were "mostly ignorant and irresponsible, unable to meet the serious obligations of citizenship in a Republic," noted Embassy Officer Richard Marsh in 1910.[29] These expressions abated by the civil rights and Panamanian nationalist movements.

— *Assumption of superiority*. "U.S. military feeling is that control and operation of the Panama Canal is the United States' inherent right and is the most efficient and logical arrangement," said SouthCom in response to a request by the Interoceanic Canal Study Commission to survey public opinion in 1966. "The consensus is that the Canal could not properly operate without at least U.S. technical supervision."[30] According to this view, widely expressed throughout the twentieth century, Panamanians did not have the technical capacity, or even the potential, to run the canal adequately, in contrast to the rational apparatus of the U.S. Army.

— *Assumed identical interests*. Throughout the twentieth century, it was assumed that U.S. and Panamanian interests were identical and that U.S. policymakers defined what was rational and responsible for Panamanians. "If we are to have bases, there has to be recognition that it's based on mutual security interests," a White House official said to me in 1996 about the negotiations for a post-1999 U.S. military presence. In fact, Panama had entered into the negotiations primarily for economic and political reasons.

— *U.S. sacrifices*. A rationale for U.S. control in case of a dispute was that Panama had suffered very little for progress, whereas the United States had sacrificed a great deal. During the 1998 debate over cleaning up of firing ranges, U.S. Embassy Officer Lewis Amselem propounded this view:

> It was the United States and its armed forces that triumphed over the other great evil of our century, communism, at the cost of dozens of thousands of U.S. lives and uncountable millions of U.S. taxpayer dollars. I mention, in addition, that the same army also brought democracy to Panama, at the cost of 23 American lives. Panama has "paid" very little for the enormous economic, security and political benefits it has gained from its "special relationship" with the United States.[31]

The implication is that, if the United States has sacrificed more for good than other nations, then other nations are less deserving. Should the United States act to remediate fully the environmental damage done by its military activities, it will do so because of the country's good will, not from legal or moral obligation. The debate over this moral-political balance sheet, and what should be included in the debts on each side, continued after the U.S. departure in 1999.

WITHDRAWAL FROM THE JUNGLE

In the 1990s, the military's emphasis on technology increasingly took regional policy out of the human realm, especially in the area of intelligence. Taken on its face, the country's drug policy stemmed from problems associated with widespread addiction to narcotics in the United States. Because the discipline of engineering does not address motives so much as functions, it focused on the material mechanics of the drug production and consumption chain. The military developed remote technology that could "see" from great distances and more accurately than before, with less involvement of human pilots or operators and less chance of being seen. The technology under development included robots designed for urban assaults that climb stairs, work in teams, and map and navigate their surroundings; "micro-robots" that can go where human soldiers could not; and foliage-penetrating radar aboard unmanned aircraft.[32]

Because its definitions of the enemy range so widely, the drug war requires greater systems of control—and thus more far-reaching technology—to track potential trafficking suspects. For example, civilian air-traffic controllers are increasingly conscripted into surveillance and the confirmation of who is "friend" and who is "enemy." The methods for distinguishing between the two have been unreliable, as was demonstrated in April 2001, when a U.S. missionary and her daughter flying in a private plane were mistaken for traffickers, shot down, and killed.

The F-16s stationed at Howard Air Force Base in Panama aimed to identify markings on the sides of suspect aircraft over Peru and Colombia without ever being seen by the aircrafts' pilots. Planes with pilots who are never visible—to allies or to enemies—are symbolic of the corporate nature of contemporary military operations. Gone are the heroic human figures such as Goethals and Gorgas, who have been replaced by the novelty of technology and the race to outpace yesterday's machine.

In the 1990s, developing technology for military intelligence became a quest in itself. The stated motive for the new technology, apart from its presumed efficacy at finding things out, was to "let machines perform today's most hazardous missions," a Pentagon official told Congress, "thus minimizing casualties to the military's most important resource, its people."[33] But one of the effects of moving risk out of the human sphere into the world of technology is that soldiers are less likely to be changed through contact with nature and humans of other cultures. The renewal that Roosevelt sought by striking out on his ranch to hunt bear or by fighting Spaniards in Cuba will hardly come about from analyzing infrared images on monitors in an air-conditioned office in Key West.

The Pentagon's inclination to choose machines over people is palpable in the repeated rounds of base closures, which have been initiated by the military itself, not by fiscally minded congressional representatives. "Eliminating this excess capacity will . . . help ensure that the Department can sustain our high state of readiness and provide our troops with modern weapons," Defense Secretary William Cohen said when he announced the fourth major round of base closures in less than a decade in 1998. He then went on to detail how many Joint Strike Fighters, aircraft carriers, helicopters, and assault ships could be purchased if the military closed down the places where soldiers work.[34]

The U.S. departure from Panama occurred in a context in which U.S. policymakers and the public had become squeamish about "dirty" warfare but never questioned the United States' right to global preeminence. These contradictory desires have led to military action that appears antiseptic, executed from a distance — usually from the air — and that has changed other nations' behavior without showing U.S. television viewers their intestines and blood. Put another way, the United States has sought to exercise imperial control without confronting the messy aspects of that control.

In Panama, the United States maintains the prerogative under the 1977 Neutrality Treaty, which runs in perpetuity, to intervene in Panama if canal operations are in danger. The prerogative takes the United States, which now has no permanent installations on the isthmus, back to the status it held under the 1846 Bidlack Treaty. Then, as now, the

United States retained the right to intervene in Panama to protect operations in the transit area. During the fifty-five years that the Bidlack Treaty was in force, the United States intervened thirteen times. Moreover, the United States' departure from Panama in 1999 occurred just as the country was increasing its military involvement in neighboring Colombia. As the Panamanian sociologist Raúl Leis pointed out, "Much depends on the situation in Colombia. Panama will always be surrounded by the ghosts of military bases."[35]

The United States' relationship to the Panamanian isthmus will also depend on the evolution of its own self-image as a civilizing force and of its attitudes toward the tropics and dark-skinned people. Should the country's political leaders and media undertake a sustained and introspective examination of those attitudes and self-image, it will inevitably affect how the United States conducts its relationships with Panama, its people, and its environment.

AFTERWORD ☆ KNOWING OURSELVES

EXHORTATION TO READ A FRIENDLY TEXT

BY GUILLERMO CASTRO H.

Panama, like the rest of Latin America, has had a conflicted and often violent relationship with the United States since the early nineteenth century. As close as it has been, the relationship has also left a legacy — surprising only in appearance — of mutual ignorance on both sides. From that perspective, the need should be evident to know and make known the ways that the United States has seen Panama in the past in order to understand better both the function that vision has had in U.S. behavior in Panama, as well as the role it has played in forming and developing some of our own perceptions about Panama's past and future.

A substantial part of the U.S. vision is found in the interpretations articulated by U.S. authors of Panamanian reality and of the relationship between the two countries. Even if such writing — of good, bad, or weak quality — is very abundant, only a few works are available in Spanish and in Panama. These include *The Land Divided* by Gerstle Mack; *The Path between the Seas* by David McCullough; and *The People of Panama* by John and Mavis Biesanz. Even this limited number of books is characteristic in more than one sense. The first two works have the Panama Canal as their true protagonist and treat Panama only as a physical setting and part of the circumstance of that engineering project. The third was conceived as a manual for soldiers and officials stationed in the so-called Canal Zone in the early 1950s to know and deal with that external circumstance.

Only recently have we found a new current in this field, beginning with authors such as John Lindsay-Poland and the environmental historian Paul Sutter, whose essay on U.S. sanitation policy during the construction of the Panama Canal was published in Spanish in Panama by the journal *Tareas*. These writers seem to be characterized by a much more critical attitude toward their own society and by a greater concern for the political, military, economic, cultural, and environmental effects of the presence and activities of the United States on Panamanians, their country, and society.

An important part of the U.S. impact without doubt originates in the singular character of the United States enclave known as the "Canal Zone," around which the connections between the two countries were articulated between 1904 and 1914. The enclave of foreign capital has a long trajectory in the economic and political history of Latin America, especially in the first half of the twentieth century. These were essentially private monopolistic organizations that acquired control of a piece of territory with the aim of intensively exploiting a particular resource, generally minerals or tropical agricultural products, and made the most of the low cost of local labor and fiscal, legislative, and political advantages — including security and local control services — offered by the host state. This was the case of the banana enclaves in Central America and the Caribbean created by the United Fruit Company; the mining enclaves created in Chile and Peru by companies such as Anaconda Copper; and the oil enclaves in Mexico and Venezuela that were operated by U.S., British, and Dutch companies, to mention some of the better known examples.

The Canal Zone, nevertheless, differs from these examples in several ways. First, it was an enclave of state — not private — monopoly capital, whose administration and security depended directly on the executive power of the United States and on the Secretary of the Army, in particular. As far as we know, it was also the only enclave of this kind existing outside the United States. Second, the canal enclave's internal organization depended fundamentally on U.S. federal legislation, for its administration as well as for its labor and judicial regimes. Third, the security of the enclave depended always, in the first instance, on the U.S. military presence in Panama. And finally, the enclave operated outside any mechanism that would have determined the value of labor in the Panamanian economy, paying salaries established by U.S. legislation for public service that were much higher than their local equivalents, when such existed.

This, then, was how the enclave came to be the principal articulating power of the Panamanian economy, especially after the Arias–Roosevelt Treaty of 1936, which opened the Canal Zone economy to livestock, manufacturing, and service businesses operating in Panama.

The Zone then became the main factor for creating demand in the whole of Panama's economy. The backwardness of that economy itself contributed to the generation of extraordinary profits for the elites who sold their products to the military–industrial complex on the banks of the canal. Those elites benefited from monopolistic control of natural resources such as land, which was used extensively to raise cattle; from the low cost of labor; and, after the Remon–Eisenhower Treaty of 1955, from the salaries paid by the United States to Panamanians working in the Zone.

This articulating effect of the enclave further extended to other aspects of national life, in particular, to its politics and culture. In the context of the economy's extreme backwardness in the first half of the twentieth century, it was natural that the enclave would be perceived as the model of efficient management, especially by Panama's dominant social sectors, which in turn contributed to reinforcing cultural features characteristic of our society's oligarchic structure. Two examples have special relevance here.

The first refers to the racism of Panamanian culture, whose roots go back to the important role played by slavery and the slave trade from sixteenth-century Spanish colonialism to the abolition of that form of labor in the mid-nineteenth century. The enclave contributed to legitimating this cultural trait to the extent to which, as Lindsay-Poland's book illustrates, U.S. authorities used racial criteria for managing human resources over a long period, both during the construction of the canal and its later operation. The enclave also contributed to the legitimacy of the authoritarianism inherent in the royal culture forged in Panama beginning in the sixteenth century in the sense that its operational efficiency was associated with the vertical and authoritarian structure of its administration.

What is more, the canal enclave contributed to a model of relationships and mutual perceptions between Panama and the United States that was singularly perverse. Perhaps as in no other place in Latin America, the relationship between the two countries was forced to speak a language that was military and bureaucratic at its core. Unlike the case of Mexico, which also had a long and rich tradition of cultural relationships—as expressed in works such as *Insurgent Mexico* by John Reed—in Panama, the culture was of the barracks and the officer with colonial privileges. As in Cuba before the revolution, Panama had the culture of prostitution and bars, with the difference that there was no Hemingway among us who might leave an equivalent of *The Old Man and the Sea* as compensation.

So, Panama was perceived through the lens of the prejudices developed by Anglo-Saxon culture to justify and organize its colonial domination of the tropics, as seen in the writing by Gorgas and Goethals about Panama and as revealed in the unsuspected details of Lindsay-Poland's book. But it was also inevitable that, from our country, the United States would be perceived based on the worst aspects of imperial culture and behavior. With Panama on the dependent side of the relationship, the presence of the enclave also played an important role in the formation of perceptions of Panama by its dominant groups, its intellectuals, and even its popular sectors.

President Belisario Porras's statement in the 1920s that Panama existed by and for the canal is a clear example of this perception, which excludes a priori any possibility of true autonomous development for our country. That perception was perpetuated in turn by the vision of our internal social relationships proposed by Hernán Porras in his classic 1953 essay "The Historical Role of Human Groups in Panama," which also excludes any potential for transforming the structures of social and cultural domination established during the Spanish colonial period.

These elements throw into relief the importance of beginning a critical examination of the long-term cultural consequences left by nearly a century of the U.S. colonial presence in Panama. This examination is necessary to assume the full promise of having been able to overcome that presence politically by means of an unceasing struggle that began in the very moment of the colonial enclave's creation. We triumphed over the enclave, and we can be defeated by no one but ourselves in the struggle against its consequences.

Lindsay-Poland's work is an important contribution to this pending task. It demystifies the enclave's rationality, reveals its authoritarian and racist nature, and thus contributes to a critique of its legacy. He tells us of ill-known truths and badly understood realities and thus helps prevent useless hatreds between two peoples who share so much history. Panamanians must aspire to be universal if we want to survive as a people and as a nation in a globalized world, but we can achieve that only if we are authentic. On that path toward ourselves, John Lindsay-Poland has been and will be a welcome friend.

NOTES

Introduction

1 See Velma Newton, *The Silver Men: West Indian Labour Migration to Panama, 1850–1914* (Kingston: University of the West Indies, 1984); Michael Conniff, *Black Labor on a White Canal: Panama, 1904–1981* (Pittsburgh: University of Pittsburgh Press, 1985); John Biesanz, "Race Relations in the Canal Zone," *Phylon* 11 (1950): 23–30; George Westerman, "School Segregation on the Panama Canal Zone," *Phylon* 15 (1954): 276–87.

   The words *White, Black, Latino,* and *Indigenous* are used in this book in two ways. First, they signify actual groups of people with different ethnicity and skin color. But since race is at least in part socially constructed, they also refer to *perceptions* of social groups, often with the charged assumptions that are prevalent in racist societies.

2 For further discussion of nature and civilization in U.S–Latin American relations, see Fredrick Pike, *The United States and Latin America: Myths and Stereotypes of Civilization and Nature* (Austin: University of Texas Press, 1992), and George Black, *The Good Neighbor: How the United States Wrote the History of Central America and the Caribbean* (New York: Pantheon, 1988).

3 The exception to this was in 1907, after pneumonia had killed hundreds of West Indians and the Canal Commission was forced to recruit thousands of new European laborers: Newton, *Silver Men,* 133, 154; Joseph Bucklin Bishop, *The Panama Gateway* (New York: Charles Scribner's Sons, 1913), 300–1. See also Conniff, *Black Labor.*

4 Marie Gorgas and Burton J. Hendrick, *William Crawford Gorgas: His Life and Work* (New York: Doubleday, Page and Company), 140.

5 Elting E. Morison, ed., *The Letters of Theodore Roosevelt,* vol. 4, 1007–8; Stephen J. Randall, *Colombia and the United States: Hegemony and Interdependence* (Athens: University of Georgia Press, 1992), 85.

6 William Franklin Sands, *Our Jungle Diplomacy* (Chapel Hill: University of North Carolina Press, 1944), 31.

7 Alfred Charles Richard Jr., *The Panama Canal in American National Consciousness, 1870–1990* (New York: Garland Publishing, 1990), 151, 191, 299.

8 David McCullough, *The Path between the Seas* (New York: Simon and Schuster, 1977), 511; Mark Sullivan, *Our Times: 1900–1925* (New York: Charles Scribner's Sons, 1926), 466. In a reprise of this arrangement, between 1979 and 1999 U.S. law required that the undersecretary of the Army be appointed chairman of the Panama Canal Commission's Board of Directors and that the other four U.S. members of the board, who together with the chair formed a majority, vote with him: Public Law 96–70, 96th Cong., 1st sess. (19xx), sec. 1102(a).

9 Jack Vaughan, conversation with author, January 27, 1999.

Chapter 1

1 "The Colombian Revolution near Panama," *Harper's Weekly*, August 23, 1902, 1157. W. C. Gorgas, "The Conquest of the Tropics for the White Race," *Journal of the American Medical Association* 52 (June 19, 1909): 1969.

2 For further discussion of these stereotypes, see John J. Johnson, *Latin America in Caricature* (Austin: University of Texas Press, 1980), and Michael J. Hunt, *Ideology and U.S. Foreign Policy* (New Haven, Conn.: Yale University Press, 1987), 58–68.

3 Alec Pérez-Venero, *Before the Five Frontiers: Panama from 1821 to 1903* (New York: AMS Press, 1978), 14, 26, 32–33.

4 Alfredo Figueroa Navarro, *Dominio y sociedad en el Panamá Colombiano, 1821–1903* (Panamá: Impresora Panama, 1978), 8.

5 Hernan Porras, *Papel histórico de los grupos humanos en Panamá* (Panamá: Editorial Portobelo, 1998), 60–61.

6 Stanley Heckadon Moreno, "La Colonizacion campesina de bosques tropicales en Panamá," in *Colonización y destrucción de bosques en Panamá*, ed. Stanley Heckadon Moreno and Alberto McKay (Panamá: Asociación Panameña de Antropología, 1984), 21.

7 Omar Jaén Suárez, *Población del istmo de Panamá del siglo XVI al siglo XX* (Panama: n.p., 1978), 301–4.

8 Ibid., 25.

9 John Haskell Kemble, *The Panama Route, 1848–1869* (Berkeley: University of California Press, 1943), 178.

10 Joseph Schott, *Rails across Panama: The Story of the Building of the Panama Railroad, 1849–1855* (New York: Bobbs-Merrill, 1967), 173; David McCullough, *The Path between the Seas* (New York: Simon and Schuster, 1977), 37.

11 McCullough, *Path*, 33–38.

12 John and Mavis Biesanz, *The People of Panama* (New York: Columbia University Press, 1955), 37.

13 Aims McGuinness, "In the Path of Empire: Race, Patriotism, and U.S. Military Intervention in Panama during the California Gold Rush, 1848–1860," paper presented at the Congress of the Latin American Studies Association, Miami, Florida, March 2000.

14 Pérez-Venero, *Five Frontiers*, 98–103.

15 *Use by the United States of Military Force in the Internal Affairs of Colombia*, 58th Cong., 2d session, Sen. Doc. 143, 4–5.

16 Ibid., 5–7, 90–93.

17 Roy P. Basler, ed., *The Collected Works of Abraham Lincoln* (New Brunswick, N.J.: Rutgers University Press, 1953), 4:561–62, 5:370–75; Carlos Cuestas Gómez, *Soldados americanos en Chiriquí* (Panamá: n.p., 1990), 77–78.

18 Celestino Andrés Araúz and Patricia Pizzurno, "El intervencionismo foráneo en el istmo de Panamá (1858–1902) (II)," *El Panamá América*, supp., January 4, 1998.

19 Kenneth J. Hagan, *American Gunboat Diplomacy and the Old Navy, 1877–1889* (Westport, Conn: Greenwood Press, 1973), 153–55.

20 "Some Panama Outrages," *New York Times*, April 4, 1885.

21 Thomas Bayard to Ricardo Becerra, March 27, 1885, U.S. Department of State, *Foreign Relations of the United States 1885*, 239.

22 Hagan, *Gunboat Diplomacy*, 172–74; Pérez-Venero, *Five Frontiers*, 113–15; "Panama Now in Danger," *New York Times*, April 29, 1885.

23 "Outrages by Insurgents," *New York Times*, April 18, 1885.

24 "Position of the American Forces," *New York Herald*, April 25, 1885; "Aspinwall Laid Waste," *New York Times*, April 2, 1885.

25 Hagan, *Gunboat Diplomacy*, 172–77.

26 Pérez-Venero, *Five Frontiers*, 114–15, 126n. Gil Blas Tejeira, *Pueblos perdidos* (1962; reprint Panamá: Editorial Universitaria, 1995), who writes that his novel "respected the fundamental historical facts, taken from authentic documents," offers a sympathetic portrayal of Prestan as a passionate man representing Colón's Black community who was hated by foreign Whites for his skin color and by Colombian conservatives for his rebellion against their corrupt rule.

27 Jack Shulimson, "U.S. Marines in Panama, 1885," in Lieutenant-Colonel Merrill L Bartlett, USMC, *Assault from the Sea: Essays on the History of Amphibious Warfare* (Annapolis, Md.: Naval Institute Press, 1983), 112; Hagan, *Gunboat Diplomacy*, 181–82.

28 "Americans on the Isthmus," *New York Herald*, May 10, 1885; "Position of the American Forces," *New York Herald*, April 29, 1885.

29 "Position of the American Forces."

30 "The Occupation of Panama," *New York Tribune*, May 8, 1885.

31 Ibid.

32 "Position of the American Forces," *New York Herald*, April 29, 1885; "Not a Junketing Tour," *New York Times*, May 17, 1885. A note that immediately follows this article describes the near-lynching of a Black man in Baltimore for an attack on a policeman's wife. The *Times* recounts the Black man's alleged attack on the woman as if it were a fact, then acknowledges that there was "some doubt as to his being the man."

33 *New York Herald*, May 10, 1885.

34 *New York Tribune*, May 8, 1885.

35 Ibid.

36 Shulimson, "U.S. Marines," 116–17.

37 Thomas D. Schoonover, *The United States in Central America, 1860–1911: Episodes of Social Imperialism and Imperial Rivalry in the World System* (Durham, N.C.: Duke University Press, 1991), 77–79.

38 Ronald Takaki, *Iron Cages: Race and Culture in Nineteenth Century America* (New York: Oxford University Press, 1990), 269.

39 Alfred Thayer Mahan, *Armaments and Arbitration* (New York: Harper and Brothers, 1912), 160–63.

40 Ibid. See also Takaki's brilliant analysis in *Iron Cages*, 266–77.

41 Thomas G. Dyer, *Theodore Roosevelt and the Idea of Race* (Baton Rouge: Louisiana State University Press, 1980), 140.

42 Pérez-Venero, *Five Frontiers*, 138–44, 151–52 (emphasis added). Individual North American mercenaries also played a role in the war, although it is unclear how important that role was. A U.S. veteran artilleryman of the Spanish–American War directed the Conservatives' defenses of Panama City during the Liberals' assault in July 1900. Another U.S. veteran from the war in Cuba joined the Colombian army as late as October 1902: see Ibid., 133–34, and "The War in Colombia," *New York Times*, October 15, 1902.

43 Omar Jaén Suárez, *Hombres y ecología en Panamá* (Panamá: Smithsonian Tropical Research Institute, 1981), 78–79.

44 *Harper's Weekly*, August 23, 1902.

45 Humberto Ricord, *Panamá en la guerra de los mil días* (Panamá: n.p., 1989), 304–5.

46 Spooner amendment, in *U.S. Statutes at Large* 32 (1902): 482.

47 Richard L. Lael, *Arrogant Diplomacy: U.S. Policy toward Colombia, 1903–1922* (Wilmington, Del.: Scholarly Resources, 1987), 5.

48 E. Taylor Parks, *Colombia and the United States, 1765–1934* (Durham, N.C.: Duke University Press, 1935), 387–91.

49 Schoonover presents a persuasive account using new documentary evidence in *United States in Central America*, 97–110.

50 See Walter LaFeber, *The Panama Canal: The Crisis in Historical Perspective* (New York: Oxford University Press, 1989), 27–31.

51 James D. Richardson, *A Compilation of the Messages and Papers of the Presidents*, vol. 9 (Washington: Bureau of National Literature and Art, 1910), 6922–23.

52 Constitution of the Republic of Panama, 58th Cong., 2d sess., 1904, Sen. Doc. 208, 22.

53 McCullough, *Path*, 547–49.

54 Jaén Suárez, *Hombres y ecología*, 126; Bonifacio Pereira Jimenez, *Biografía del río Chagres* (Panamá: Imprenta Nacional, 1960), 78–84.

55 William C. Gorgas, "The Part Sanitation Is Playing in the Construction of the Panama Canal," *Journal of the American Medical Association* 53 (August 21, 1909): 597–99. I am grateful to Paul Sutter for sharing his paper, "Pulling the Teeth of the Tropics," and helping to shape my thinking about the role of tropical medicine in Panama. A Spanish version of his paper has been published in the Panamanian journal *Tareas*.

56 Hugh Gordon Miller, *The Isthmian Highway* (New York: Macmillan, 1929), 13.

57 Gorgas and Hendrick, *Gorgas*, 33, 155, 313.

58 Ibid., 66–68, 86.

59 Joseph A. LePrince and A. J. Orenstein, *Mosquito Control in Panama* (New York: Knickerbocker Press, 1916), 195–96.

60 Lieutenant-Colonel Charles F. Mason, "Sanitation in the Panama Canal Zone," in George W. Goethals, *The Panama Canal: An Engineering Treatise* (New York: McGraw-Hill, 1916), 98.

61 Gorgas and Hendrick, *Gorgas*, 227.

62 Malcolm Watson, *Rural Sanitation in the Tropics, Being Notes and Observations in the Malay Archipelago, Panama and Other Lands* (London: John Murray, 1915), 138–39.

63 Lieutenant-Colonel James Stevens Simmons, *Malaria in Panama* (Baltimore, Md.: Johns Hopkins Press, 1939), 121.

64 *Annual Reports of the Isthmian Canal Commission*, –1914 (Washington, D.C.: Government Printing Office, 1907–14).

65 Velma Newton, *The Silver Men: West Indian Labour Migration to Panama, 1850–1914* (Kingston, Jamaica: University of the West Indies, 1984), 145–52; Mason, "Sanitation," in Goethals, *Engineering Treatise*, 110–11.

66 Simmons, *Malaria in Panama*, 122, 136.

67 A. Grenfell Price, *White Settlers in the Tropics* (New York: American Geographical Society, 1939), 150, 163.

68 E. R. Stitt, *The Diagnostics and Treatment of Tropical Diseases* (Philadelphia: Blakiston's Son and Company, 1929), 860. Stitt was later a director of the Gorgas Memorial Institute.

69 W. M. James, "The Past and Future of the Medical Association of the Isthmian Canal Zone," *Proceedings of the Medical Association of the Isthmian Canal Zone* 6 (1914): 55–64.

70 Herbert C. Clark, "The Tropics and the White Man," *American Journal of Tropical Medicine* 29 (May 1949): 308.

71 *Annual Report of the Isthmian Canal Commission, 1913* (Washington, D.C.: Government Printing Office, 1913), 532–33.

72 Walter G. Baetz, "Syphilis in Colored Canal Laborers," *Proceedings of the Medical Association of the Isthmian Canal Zone* 7 (1914): 18.

73 Herbert C. Clark, "Some Anthropometric Data Collected from Local Autopsy Records," *Proceedings of the Medical Association of the Isthmian Canal Zone* 14 (1921): 21–35.

74 Joseph Bucklin Bishop, *Goethals: Genius of the Panama Canal* (New York: Harper and Brothers, 1930), 4.

75 Frederic J. Haskin, *The Panama Canal* (New York: Doubleday, 1913), 154, 162–63.

76 Ira E. Bennett, *History of the Panama Canal, Its Construction and Builders* (Washington, D.C.: Historical Publishing, 1915), 163.

77 Newton, *Silver Men*, 133–34.

78 William C. Gorgas, *Sanitation in Panama* (New York: D. Appleton and Company, 1915), 287–88. See also Gorgas and Hendrick, *Gorgas*, 258–63.

79 Gorgas, *Sanitation in Panama*, 288–89. For proposals to address overpopulation in the United States with new colonization of Latin America, see the statement by Henry Wellcome, U.S. House Committee on Foreign Affairs, *Gorgas Memorial Laboratory*, 70th Cong., 1st sess., January 20, 1928, 32–33, and R. Ashton, "Some Lessons in Sanitation from the Panama Canal Zone," *Trans. Mining and Geo. Inst. of India* 7 (1912–13), as cited in A. Grenfell Price, *White Settlers in the Tropics* (New York: American Geographical Society, 1939), 4.

80 Weston Chamberlain, *Twenty-five Years of American Medical Activity on the Isthmus of Panama, 1904–1929* (Mount Hope, Canal Zone: Panama Canal Press, 1929), 9.

81 Dalferes Curry, "Annual Oration," *Kentucky Medical Journal* 20 (November 1922): 739–46.

82 W. E. Deeks and W. M. James, *A Report on Hemoglobinuric Fever in the Canal Zone* (n.p.: Canal Zone: Isthmian Canal Commission Press, 1911), 12.

83 Dr. George W. Crile, statement in U.S. House Committee on Foreign Affairs, *Gorgas Memorial Laboratory*, 29.

84 Willard H. Wright, *Forty Years of Tropical Medicine Research* (Washington, D.C.: n.p., 1970), 19. In 1948, after an outbreak of yellow fever,

Clark also hunted and killed hundreds of monkeys to study reservoirs of the disease: *Annual Report of Gorgas Memorial Laboratory, 1950,* 82d Cong., 1st sess., House doc. 10, 1–6, and *Annual Report of Gorgas Memorial Laboratory, 1949,* 82d Cong., 2d sess., House doc. 398, 5–14. Of the monkeys, 203 were howler monkeys (including 22 pregnant howlers), which in 1966 and 1973 came under the purview of Panamanian wildlife-protection laws and the U.S. Endangered Species Act: Nature Conservancy and ANCON, *Rapid Ecological Assessment of the Lands in Panama Managed by the U.S. Department of Defense* (Panama, 1994), 16.

85   *Annual Report, 1948,* 15–19; *Annual Report, 1949,* 4–5.

86   Clark, "Tropics and the White Man," 303–309.

87   Andrew Balfour, "Personal Hygiene," in W. Byam and R. G. Archibald, *The Practice of Medicine in the Tropics* (London: Henry Frowde and Hodder and Stoughton, 1921), 7–10.

88   Simmons, *Malaria in Panama,* 216–18.

89   In 1911, canal defense was taken over by the Army's Tenth Infantry, which set up a post called Camp Otis, although a regiment of marines stayed in Panama until 1914. In that year, the Army more than doubled its force in Panama and did so again the following year, so that the number of troops on the isthmus increased more than tenfold — from 797 to 8,111 — between 1913 and 1917, the year that the Panama Canal Department was organized. The garrison averaged 7,400 troops from 1918 to 1934: see Simmons, *Malaria,* 218–21, 230–31.

90   William D. McCain, *The United States and the Republic of Panama* (New York: Russell and Russell, 1965), 48–60.

91   James Howe, *A People Who Would Not Kneel: Panama, the United States, and the San Blas Kuna* (Washington, D.C.: Smithsonian Institution Press, 1998), 76.

92   At home, the Senate had approved a constitutional amendment six months before prohibiting the sale of alcohol that became the Eighteenth Amendment in January 1919: John Major, *Prize Possession: The United States and the Panama Canal, 1903–1979* (London: Cambridge University Press, 1993), 139.

93   Ibid., 140.

94   Cuestas Gómez, *Soldados americanos,* 232–33. Many details of the occupation are reviewed in chapters 3, 5, and 8.

95   César Samudio, *El Canal de Panamá, 1903–1955* (Panamá: n.p., 1992), 108–10.

96   McCain, *United States and Panama,* 89.

97   Alexander Cuevas, "El Movimiento inquilinario de 1925," in *Panamá, dependencia y liberación,* ed. Ricuarte Soler (San José, Costa Rica: Editorial Universitaria Centroamericana, 1975), 31–75.

98 Ibid., 73; Samudio, *El Canal*, 112. U.S. Chargé Dana Munro reported that one of the Panamanians died falling from a balcony and did not mention the other two deaths: see FRUS, *Foreign Relations of the United States 1925*, 2:665.

99 "Saw a Rebellion Started in Panama," *New York Times*, October 19, 1925. See also "Panama," *Current History*, December 1925, 412–13; "American Soldiers Guard Panama City," *New York Times*, October 13, 1925.

100 Major, *Prize Possession*, 152.

101 Lowell Thomas, *Old Gimlet Eye: The Adventures of Smedley D. Butler* (New York: Farrar and Rinehart, 1933), 127–28.

102 Ivan Musicant, *The Banana Wars* (New York: Macmillan, 1990), 144–56.

103 Colonel James H. Alexander, "Roots of Deployment — Vera Cruz, 1914," in Bartlett, *Assault from the Sea*, 133–41.

104 Musicant, *Banana Wars*, 291.

105 For the role of U.S. bases in Panama in Central Intelligence Agency operations against Guatemala's Arbenz government in 1954, see Kate Doyle, "The Art of the Coup: A Paper Trail of Covert Actions in Guatemala," *NACLA Report on the Americas* 31 (September–October 1997): 37; Nick Cullather, *Secret History: The CIA's Classified Account of Its Operations in Guatemala, 1952–54* (Stanford, Calif.: Stanford University Press, 1999), 32–33, 53.

Chapter 2

1 Otto Probst, interview by the author, San Jose Island, July 24, 1998.

2 Stetson Conn, Rose C. Engelman, and Byron Fairchild, *The Western Hemisphere: Guarding the United States and Its Outposts* (Washington, D.C.: Office of the Chief of Military History, 1964), 302, 326.

3 Major, *Prize Possession*, 299–300, 305.

4 Conn et al., *Western Hemisphere*, 414; U.S. Army Caribbean Defense Command, *History of the Panama Canal Department* (Canal Zone: n.p., 1946), vol. 2, 61. Raúl Leis, *Comando Sur: Poder hostil* (Panama: Centro de Estudios y Acción Social Panameño, 1985,) 41, gives the figure of sixty-eight thousand troops stationed in Panama in 1943.

5 Don Eddy, "Panama . . . Our No. 1 Danger Spot," *American Magazine*, November 1941, 20.

6 "Thoughts in the Jungle," *Time*, September 28, 1942, 64.

7 Brenda Conrad, "Panama Threat," *Woman's Home Companion*, March 1941, 13–15, 88–103; April 1941, 22–24, 88–105; May 1941, 24–25,

97–113; June 1941, 26, 70–78, 83; July 1941, 26–27, 82–85; August 1941, 28, 42, 50–51, 57.

8 Robert Harris and Jeremy Paxman, *A Higher Form of Killing: The Secret Story of Chemical and Biological Warfare* (New York: Hill and Wang, 1982), 26.

9 Edward B. Clark, "As Chemical Warfare Chieftain," *Chemical Warfare Bulletin* 27 (July 1941): 84–88.

10 Ibid., 88–89.

11 Leo Brophy, Wyndham D. Miles, and Rexmond C. Cochrane, *The Chemical Warfare Service: From Laboratory to Field* (Washington, D.C.: Department of the Army, 1959), 227.

12 "Chemical Annex to the Panama Canal Defense Project," December 1, 1940, 7, 17, Panama Canal Department decimal file 1915–45, RG 338, National Archives (hereafter, PCD 1915–45).

13 W. C. Rucker, "Cyanogen Chlorid Fumigation at Canal Zone Ports," *Nation's Health* 6 (1924): 387–89.

14 Major-General Preston Brown to Army Adjutant General, March 13, 1931, RG 175, National Archives, Washington, D.C. (hereafter, NA).

15 Acting Chief of Staff Colonel Wallace C. Philoon, "Chemical Annex to Panama Canal Defense Project," PCD 1915–1945.

16 Brophy, et al., *Chemical Warfare Service*, 263, 265, 375.

17 The bases were Camp Paraiso, Fort Clayton, Corozal Post, Albrook Field, Howard Field, Rio Hato, France Field, and Fort Gulick. The magazines ranged in size from eight feet by twelve feet at Camp Paraiso, Clayton, Albrook, Gulick, and Rio Hato, to a thirty feet by forty-five feet at France Field, which included bombs: see Lieutenant-General Daniel Van Voorhis to Adjutant General, August 1, 1941, PCD 1915–45.

18 "Camouflage Problems in the Canal Zone: Report on a Survey of Camouflage Requirements in the Canal Zone Made on March 25–April 8, [1941]," PCD 1915–45; Lieutenant-Colonel S. C. Godfrey, "Cerro Tigre Drainage Project," August 21, 1936, RG 98, NA.

19 Jack Cadenhead to Eric Jackson, letter, November 1997; Jack Cadenhead, telephone interview by the author, May 24, 1998.

20 Lieutenant-Commander L. E. Daly to Chief, Research Division, Bureau of Medicine and Surgery, February 21, 1944, and March 5, 1944, released by Naval Research Laboratory to Nathan Schnurman under Freedom of Information Act (FOIA).

21 E. J. Kahn Jr., "The Army Life," *New Yorker*, March 11, 1944, 74.

22 Major, *Prize Possession*, 307.

23 Karen Freeman, "The Unfought Chemical War," *Bulletin of Atomic Scientists*, December 1991, 31.

24 U.S. Army Signal Corps, *The San Jose Project*, videocassette, c. 1945, RG 111, National Archives.

25 Hongmei Deng and Peter O'Meara Evans, "Social and Environmental Aspects of Abandoned Chemical Weapons in China," *Nonproliferation Review*, spring–summer 1997, 101–2.

26 David Pugliese, "Panama: Bombs on the Beach," *Bulletin of the Atomic Scientists* 58 (July–August 2002), 57.

27 Robert D. McLeod Jr., "In the Wake of the Golden Galleon," *Armed Forces Chemical Journal* 9 (March–April 1955): 36–39.

28 "A Historical Record of the San Jose Project," c. 1945, PCD 1915–45.

29 Captain Jay S. Stockhardt, "San Jose Project," *Armed Forces Chemical Journal* 2 (January 1948): 32. Note the wide discrepancy in dates for this story.

30 Brophy and Fisher, *Chemical Warfare Service*, 136.

31 Herasto Reyes, "Contaminaciones militares en Panamá: El Caso de la Isla de San José," *La Prensa* (Panama; hereafter referred to as LP), July 3, 1997.

32 Headquarters, San Jose Project, "General Order Number 11," July 6, 1944, report on San Jose Project, PCD 1915–45.

33 U.S. Department of State, *Foreign Relations of the United States, 1947*, 8:923.

34 Stockhardt, "San Jose Project"; "Operating Trails through Jungle with Flame Throwers," PCD 1915–45.

35 Eugene Reid, telephone interview by the author, September 16, 1997.

36 Harris and Paxman, *Higher Form of Killing*, 64–67, 137–38.

37 Brigadier-General Jerome Waters to Commander, Caribbean Defense Command, December 31, 1945, PCD 1915–45. Representative Mike Mansfield also noted, in a report on Panama's rejection of a 1947 base agreement that included San Jose, that the project tested "new types of toxic chemicals and gases as well as those captured from the German Army": Congressional Research Service, *Background Documents Relating to the Panama Canal* (Washington, D.C.: Government Printing Office, 1977), 978.

38 Office of Chemical Officer, Panama Canal Department, to Lieutenant-Colonel J. C. Prentice, Office of Chief of Chemical Corps, December 10, 1946, PCD 1915–45.

39 Signal Corps, *San Jose Project*; "Metes and Bounds of the Parcels of Land Needed to Meet the Requirements Set Forth in: 'A Long Term Strategic Plan for the Defense of the Panama Canal, 1946,'" 1946, PCD 1915–45.

40 Herasto Reyes, "La siembra de la contaminación," LP, July 29, 1997. The Signal Corps film says the goats were shipped from New Orleans.

41 Signal Corps, *San Jose Project*.

42 Colonel John R. Wood, "Work of the CC Medical Division," *Armed Forces Chemical Journal* 2 (January 1948): 7.

43 Marion B. Sulzberger, "Protection and Treatment of the Skin Exposed to Blister Gases," in *Advances in Military Medicine*, ed. E. C. Andrus et al. (Boston: Little, Brown, 1948), 591.

44 Constance M. Pechura and David Rall, eds., *Veterans at Risk: The Health Effects of Mustard Gas and Lewisite* (Washington, D.C.: National Academy Press, 1993), 1. A full history of chemical weapons tests using humans as subjects has yet to be written. Additional sources include *Cold War Era Human Subject Experimentation*, Subcommittee on Legislation and National Security, House Committee on Government Operations, September 28, 1994; and Freeman, "Unfought Chemical War."

45 Pechura and Rall, *Veterans at Risk*, 3.

46 John W. Dower, *War without Mercy: Race and Power in the Pacific War* (New York: Pantheon, 1986), 39–40.

47 Harris and Paxman, *Higher Form of Killing*, 118.

48 "Notes on Conference Held at Office of the Chief, Chemical Warfare Service," March 4, 1944, RG 175, NA.

49 Untitled history of San Jose Project, n.d. (after 1952), 30, from the records of Henry Heitman.

50 Minutes of the Meeting of Advisory Committee on Effectiveness of Gas Warfare Materiel in Tropics, May 17, 1944, RG 175, NA.

51 Lieutenant-Colonel E. C. de Hostos, Report to PCD Intelligence Office, November 2, 1918, PCD 1915–45.

52 Jorge Rodríguez Beruff, *Política militar y dominación: Puerto Rico en el contexto latinoamericano* (Rio Piedras, Puerto Rico: Ediciones Huracán, 1988), 158; Ernest Reimer, telephone interview by the author, September 3, 1997; *History of the PCD*, vol. 3, chronology, unnumbered page. Pechura and Rall, *Veterans at Risk*, 376, reports that the 27th Chemical Contamination Company (Puerto Rican) was involved in field tests in 1944.

53 Major-General Ray E. Porter to General Willis Crittenberger, September 21, 1946, ABC file, RG 165, NA.

54 Report on San Jose Project, PCD 1915–45, 4, 12.

55 Secretary of Defense William Cohen to Representative José Serrano, "San Jose Project Report No. 24 Summary," letter, April 7, 1998.

56 Brophy and Fisher, *Chemical Warfare Service*, 38–39.

57 Bob Robinson, "'45 Army Tests in CZ Leaves Vet Disabled," *Richmond Times–Dispatch*, October 23, 1978; "Veteran Finally Learns Mustard Gas Was Tested on Him," *Richmond Times–Dispatch*, November 16, 1978.

58 Reyes, "Siembra."

59 Lieutenant-Colonel Joseph Escude, Chemical Warfare Service, to San Jose

Project Division, December 21, 1945; Lowell A. Elliott to Brigadier-General Egbert F. Bullene, September 19, 1945, from the records of Henry Heitman.

60 William R. Brankowitz, *Chemical Weapons Movement History Compilation*, Report SAPEO-CDE-IS-870 (Aberdeen Proving Ground, Md.: Program Manager for Chemical Demilitarization, 1987).

61 Captain Henry M. Cook, San Jose Project, "Annual Report on Medical Department Activities," January 18, 1948, PCD 1915–45.

62 Richard Downes, "Parameters for Security Agreements in Panama: Lessons from the 1947 U.S–Panama Defense Sites Controversy," in *El Canal de Panamá en el siglo XXI* (Panamá: Universidad de Panamá, 1998), 237–38. See also David Acosta, *Influencia decisiva de la opinión pública en el rechazo del convenio Filós — Hines de 1947* (Panamá: Impresora de la Nación, 1983), 33; and Thomas L. Pearcy, *We Answer Only to God: Politics and the Military in Panama, 1903–1947* (Albuquerque: University of New Mexico Press, 1998).

63 G. A. Lincoln, memorandum, December 11, 1946, ABC file, RG 319, NA.

64 Secretary of State George C. Marshall to Foreign Minister Ricardo J. Alfaro, October 8, 1947, *Foreign Relations of the United States, 1947*, 8:921. The chemical tests on San Jose were still secret at that time.

65 General Willis Crittenberger, "Negotiations between the Republic of Panama and the United States of America for a Defense Site Agreement, 1946–1947," RG 319, Army General and Special Staff, Plans and Operations Divisions, NA, as cited in Pearcy, *We Answer Only to God*, 153.

66 Guillermo Sánchez Borbon, "Aquel 12 de diciembre," LP, December 12, 1997. The number of wounded is cited in José Montano, "El CMA y el rechazo al convenio de bases militares Filós–Hines," *El Panamá América*, December 12, 1997.

67 Downes, "Parameters for Agreements," 244–45.

68 Spruille Braden, *Diplomats and Demagogues* (New York: Arlington House, 1971), 351–55.

69 Captain Jay S. Stockhardt and First Lieutenant Stephen D. Noyes, "The San Jose Project Moves," *Armed Forces Chemical Journal* 3 (January 1949): 53–54.

70 Reid, interview.

71 Rick Stauber, telephone interview by the author, June 26, 1998. Colonel Edmund W. Libby, former U.S. Army Project Manager for Non-Stock-piled Chemical Materiel, gave a dud rate for "bulk high-explosive and chemical-loaded artillery rounds [of] between 5 to 10 percent": Libby, communication with author, July 23, 1998.

72 "San Jose Project Post Diary, 1947," San Jose Project files, NA.

73 "San Jose Project Post Diary, 1 January–31 December 1948," in San Jose Project files.

74 Lieutenant-Colonel Grant S. Green Jr. to Jeffrey Farrow, December 19, 1979, Carter Presidential Library, Atlanta, Ga.

75 Pugliese, "Bombs on the Beach," 59.

76 Stockhardt and Noyes, "San Jose Project Moves," 54.

77 Rick Stauber, interview by the author, August 1997.

78 "San Jose Project Post Diary, 1948," San Jose Project files.

79 Ibid.; Colonel Paul R. Smith, Chemical Corps, "Status of Close-out Operations," July 13, 1950, RG 175, NA.

80 "Preparándonos para enfrentar el problema," *El Panamá América*, January 10, 1995.

81 Green to Farrow; Glenn Tupper to author, letter, June 22, 1998.

82 Brankowitz, *Chemical Weapons Compilation*.

83 "Chemical Corps Tropical Test Team, Fort Clayton, Canal Zone," Dugway Proving Ground, January 25, 1956, 33, obtained by the author through FOIA.

84 Ibid., 9, 11, 13 (emphasis added).

85 Ibid., 11.

86 Brankowitz, *Chemical Weapons Compilation*.

87 Roy E. Blades Jr., "Report Bibliography on U.S. Army Tropic Test Center and Other Department of Defense Activities concerning Ammunition, Biological, Chemical, Demolition, Fuzes, Munitions, and Missile Weapons Systems Test Projects Conducted in the Panama Canal Zone, Republic of Panama," n.d., released to the author by the U.S. Army Developmental Test Command under FOIA.

88 Dugway Proving Ground, "Environmental Test Branch Test Plan 36," September 25, 1958, obtained by the author through FOIA.

89 Joseph Oppedisano, telephone interview by the author, September 6, 1999; brief supporting Oppedisano's appeal to Board of Veterans Appeals, September 21, 1992.

90 U.S. Army Test and Evaluation Command, Dugway Proving Ground, "Chemical Corps Participation in Project Swamp Fox I," November 1962, 6, obtained through FOIA.

91 U.S. Army Test and Evaluation Command, Dugway Proving Ground, "Environmental Field Test: Food Testing and Screening Kit, Chemical Agents, ABC–M3," December 1962, 12, 21–23, obtained through FOIA.

92 U.S. Army Tropic Test Center, *Materiel Testing in the Tropics*, 6th ed. (Panama: 1979), I-5.

93 Colonel Pedro Florcruz, telephone interviews by the author, November 22 and December 28, 2000; "Locations and Coordinates of Tropic Test Center Test Sites," n.d., obtained through FOIA.

94 Dugway Proving Ground Test Plan 704, "Surveillance Test (Environmental) of Mine, Gas Persistent, VX, 2-Gallon, ABC-M23" (USATECOM Project No. 5-3-9504-1); Dugway Proving Ground Test Plan 719, "Surveillance Test (Environmental) of Projectile, Gas Persistent, VX, 155 mm, M121A1" (USATECOM Project No. 5-4-9503-1); Dugway Proving Ground Test Plan 723, "Surveillance Test (Environmental) of Rocket, Gas Persistent, VX, 155 mm, M55" (USATECOM Project No. 5-4-9502-1); and Dugway Proving Ground Test Plan 586, "Surveillance Test (Environmental) of Rocket, Gas, Nonpersistent, GB, 115 mm, M55 (USATECOM Project No. 5-4-9501-01)," February 1964, all obtained through FOIA. The United States discontinued production of VX agent, as well as the M55 rocket, in 1968. Sarin production ceased in 1957, but it remained in the U.S. stockpile through the 1990s: Stockholm International Peace Research Institute, *Chemical Disarmament: New Weapons for Old* (New York: Humanities Press, 1975), 81.

95 Military planners in 1978 projected that, if the United States used chemical weapons, there was a 10 percent chance that they would be employed in the tropics. They estimated a 75 percent "probability of employment" for temperate climates, 10 percent for desert, and 5 percent for arctic: Dugway Proving Ground, "Test Operation Procedure for Development Test II of XM30 Protective Mask" (AD 553903), c. 1981, 44.

96 Richard Dow to author, letter, November 10, 2000; idem, telephone interview by the author, November 15, 2000; Dugway Proving Ground Test Plan 704, 18.

97 Dugway Proving Ground Test Plan 704; James McLaughlin, interview by the author, Wilmington, Del., September 5, 2001; Florcruz, interview.

98 The planning document for the test indicates that the VX mines were to be detonated, three at a time: "During each cycle, three mines (VX or simulant-filled) will be subjected to a firing test to determine the functionability of mines and components. The procedure will be as follows: a. The mine (with full complement of firing components) will be electrically fired through the side burster, using an M1 activator and an adapter." Despite the reference to simulant, the materials list for this test does not include any simulant. Some warheads may have been shipped to test sites with simulant as a control on the experiment (Ibid., 11).

99 But a March 1968 interim report on the test stated that, during every cycle, the detonation of the VX mines was "Satisfactory" but "at the Desert, Tropic and Temperate Test Sites, the VX agent was drained from the mines prior to detonation tests due to the lack of suitable test areas." See Doris R. Zylstra and First Lieutenant John W. Raibikis, Dugway Proving Ground, "Surveillance (Environmental) Test of Mine, Gas Per-

sistent, VX, 2-Gal, M23, Interim Report" (March 1968), 8, 13, obtained through FOIA.

100 McLaughlin, interview.

101 PRC Environmental Management, Inc., "Unexploded Ordnance Assessment of U.S. Military Ranges in Panama: Empire, Balboa West and Piña Ranges," January 1997, 25.

102 The Army's history of the movement of chemical weapons documents one return shipment from Panama to the United States of bottles of nerve agent in January 1968: Brankowitz, *Chemical Weapons Compilation*.

103 Dugway Proving Ground Test Plan 586, 9; McLaughlin, interview. A Tropic Test Center employee in the 1980s confirmed that San Lorenzo was an established test site for firing into the ocean: Arnold Talbott, telephone interview by the author, January 7, 2001.

104 Richard Dow to author, letter, November 11, 2000.

105 John Ronco to author, letters, July 18 and July 23, 2001.

106 Florcruz, interview; McLaughlin, interview.

107 McLaughlin, interview. In Colón, tear gas used by U.S. troops during the riots led to the death of six-month-old Maritza Avila Alabarca (Eric Jackson, "Martyr Days," unpub. ms., 1998).

108 Roy E. Blades Jr., telephone interview by the author, December 11, 2000.

109 Idem, "Report Bibliography."

110 Public Law 121, 91st Cong., 1st sess. (November 19, 1969), 210.

111 Erimsky Sucre, telephone interview by the author, August 1998.

112 C. J. Peters and Mark Olshaker, *Virus Hunter: Thirty Years of Battling Hot Viruses around the World* (New York: Anchor, 1997), 65–71.

113 Harris and Paxman, *Higher Form of Killing*, 170–71.

114 *Annual Report of the Gorgas Memorial Laboratory, 1965*, 1; *Annual Report of the Gorgas Memorial Laboratory, 1968*, 4–5. See also M. A. Grayson and Pedro Galindo, "Epidemiologic Studies of VEE in Almirante, Panama," *American Journal of Epidemiology* 88 (1973): 80–96.

115 "Venezuelan Equine Encephalitis: Report of an Outbreak Associated with Jungle Exposure," report produced for Walter Reed Army Institute of Research, November 1984.

116 Drew Fetherston and John Cummings, "CIA Linked to Infecting of Cuban Swine," *Star-Ledger* (Newark, N.J.), January 9, 1977.

117 Alexander Cockburn, "From Pearls . . .," *The Nation*, March 9, 1998, 9.

118 Veteran who requested anonymity, written communications to and telephone interviews by the author, June 1999.

119 Tod Robberson, "U.S. Tested Agent Orange in Panama, Accounts Say," *Dallas Morning News*, August 20, 1999; idem, "Bases May Have Used Agent Orange, Ex-Officer Says," August 24, 1999; October 11, 1999.

120 Robberson, "Bases May Have Used Agent Orange."

121 Dick Maggrett, "Report: Army Secretly Tested Agent Orange in Panama, VA Compensating One Widow," *Stars and Stripes*, September 12, 1999.

122 A 1985 project conducted by the Tropic Test Center tested the "AH–64 Chemical Biological (CB) Protective Mask": R. H. McIntosh et al., "Development Test II (Prototype qualification test — government (Tropic Environmental Phase) of AH–64 Chemical Biological (CB) Protective Mask," May–December 1985, obtained through FOIA; Captain Jerzell L. Black, "NBC Stakes in Panama," *CML*, *Army Chemical Review*, September 1987, 32–35.

123 Colonel Michael DeBow, cochairman, Environmental Subcommittee, Joint Committee, to Licenciado Ramiro Castrejón, cochairman, Environmental Subcommittee, Dirección Ejecutiva para Asuntos del Tratado, letter, August 18, 1997.

124 Graham Stullenbarger, "Proposal for Tropic Test Center Membership in the City of Knowledge," July 21, 1997, B2.

Chapter 3

1 Glenn T. Seaborg, *Stemming the Tide: Arms Control in the Johnson Years* (Lexington, Mass.: Lexington Books, 1987), 347.

2 Joint Committee on Atomic Energy, *Peaceful Applications of Nuclear Explosives — Plowshare*, 89th Cong., 1st sess. (January 5, 1965), 25.

3 *Report of the Atlantic–Pacific Interoceanic Canal Study Commission* (Washington, D.C.: Government Printing Office, 1970), 9.

4 David McCullough, *The Path between the Seas* (New York: Simon and Schuster, 1977), 481–88.

5 John Major, *Prize Possession: The United States and the Panama Canal, 1903–1979* (London: Cambridge University Press, 1993), 284–85, 305–6.

6 E. A. Martell, "Plowing a Nuclear Furrow," *Environment*, April 1969, 4; Joint Chiefs of Staff to Admiral Radford, memorandum, October 23, 1956, fiche 1980–365B, Declassified Documents Reference System, Arlington, Va. (hereafter, DDRS).

7 Trevor Findlay, *Nuclear Dynamite: The Peace Nuclear Explosions Fiasco* (Sydney: Brassey's Australia, 1990), 4–9; "Proceedings of the Third Plowshare Symposium," in Joint Committee, *Peaceful Applications*,

January 5, 1965, 62; Glenn T. Seaborg, *The Atomic Energy Commission under Nixon* (New York: St. Martin's Press, 1993), 11–12.

8 Harold Brown to author, letter, October 2, 2000; Luke J. Vortman to author, letter, June 5, 2000; Luke J. Vortman, telephone interview by the author, May 29, 2000; *Panama Canal Improvement Plans — 1959, Long Range Study: Preliminary Study, Plan VI* (San Francisco: Parsons, Brinckerhoff, Hall, and MacDonald, 1959), 2; *Industrial Uses of Nuclear Explosives*, UCRL-5253 (Berkeley: University of California Radiation Laboratory, 1958) 5–6, 42–72.

9 *Industrial Uses*; Milo Nordyke, ms. provided to the author, Livermore, Calif., 2000. More than forty years later, Vortman could not remember the origin of the idea (Luke Vortman, telephone interview by the author, May 29, 2000).

10 See Robert A. Divine, *Blowing on the Wind: The Nuclear Test Ban Debate, 1954–1960* (New York: Oxford University Press, 1978), 188–92.

11 Joint Committee, *Peaceful Applications*, 62.

12 Nordyke, ms.

13 Project Chariot, like the nuclear canal, was to take place on lands used and inhabited by indigenous people.

14 *Panama Canal Improvement Plans — 1959*, 1–2; Vortman letter; Milo Nordyke, interview by the author, Livermore, Calif., May 22, 2000.

15 John W. Finney, "A Second Canal?" *New Republic*, March 28, 1964, 21–24.

16 William E. Price to Roy Rubottom, June 17, 1959, "1959, Panama," Records of Assistant Secretary of State for Inter-American Affairs, subject files 1957–59, RG 59, NA.

17 Proposed statement by the president is in "1959 Panama"; Roy Rubottom to Douglas Dillon, May 21, 1960, fiche 1984-167, DDRS.

18 Acting Secretary of State Douglas Dillon to Secretary of the Army Wilber M. Brucker, July 18, 1959, "Panama, 1959, Canal Studies," Records of the Bureau of Inter-American Affairs, subject files relating to Panama 1958–59, RG 59, NA (hereafter, Panama 1958–59). The same month, Gerald Johnson of Livermore and John Kelly, who directed the Atomic Energy Commission's Peaceful Nuclear Explosives branch, briefed Governor General William Potter and other Canal Company officers in Panama: Lieutenant Governor John D. McElheny, "Memorandum for Record," July 24, 1959, in Panama 1958–59.

19 House Foreign Affairs Committee, Report on United States Relations with Panama, 86th Cong., 2d sess. (August 31, 1960).

20 Atlantic–Pacific Interoceanic Canal Study Commission, *Plan for Study of Engineering Feasibility of Alternate Sea–Level Canal Routes Connecting the Atlantic and Pacific Oceans: Appendix 12, Prior Studies and Reports,*

September 1965, 5, "Technical Reports relating to Research Projects, 1963–1971," *Records of the Nuclear Cratering Group*, RG 77, NA, Pacific Region.

21 Finney, "A Second Canal?" 23.

22 *Panama Canal Improvement Plans — 1959*, 2.

23 Roy Rubottom to Christian Herter, May 11, 1960, fiche 1984-185, DDRS; Roy Rubottom to Montgomery, June 28, 1960, fiche 1985-10, DDRS. Eisenhower was especially interested in the Mexican Tehuantepec route and considered publicly announcing U.S. interest in it, but he was dissuaded by political and technical considerations. Secretary of State Christian Herter feared the impact on Panamanian relations and on nuclear-test–ban policy: Herter to Eisenhower, July 27, 1960, fiche 1982-132, DDRS.

24 House Committee on Merchant Marine and Fisheries, "Report on a Long–Range Program for Isthmian Canal Transits," 86th Cong., 2d sess., 1960 (H. Rept. 1960), 7, 41.

25 "National Security Council 6026," December 29, 1960, fiche 1984-77, DDRS; Major, *Prize Possession*, 334; "NSC Minutes of Meeting," January 5, 1961, fiche 1991-190, DDRS.

26 "National Security Action Memorandum No. 152," April 30, 1962, fiche 1981-505A, DDRS; Lieutenant-Colonel Bernard C. Hughes, *History of the U.S. Army Engineer Nuclear Cratering Group* (Livermore, Calif.: Lawrence Radiation Laboratory, 1969), 1–2.

27 Wilber M. Brucker to Douglas Dillon, August 7, 1959, Panama 1958–59; Findlay, *Nuclear Dynamite*, 26.

28 Robert J. Fleming Jr. to Herbert C. Bonner, February 8, 1963, "Estimates for Sea-Level Canal — File No. 1," Correspondence relating to studies on a new nuclear-excavated canal, 1952–71, RG 185, NA (hereafter, Correspondence 1952–71).

29 Colonel M. C. Harrison, engineering director, Panama Canal Commission, to Lieutenant-Colonel Ernest Graves Jr., director, Nuclear Cratering Group, Lawrence Radiation Laboratory, January 28, 1963, "Estimates for Sea-Level Canal — File No. 1"; Ernest Graves to "Bill," March 18, 1962, "General Information on Nuclear Excavation, 12/61–12/63," Correspondence 1952–71.

30 Robert H. Thalgott, Atomic Energy Commission, to Colonel M. C. Harrison, Panama Canal Company, August 1, 1963, Correspondence 1952–71.

31 Department of State, "Treaty Banning Nuclear Weapon Tests in the Atmosphere, in Outer Space and Under Water," August 5, 1963, TIAS no. 5433, *United States Treaties and Other International Agreements*, vol. 14, pt. 2, 1317; Major, *Prize Possession*, 334–35.

32 Seaborg, *Stemming the Tide*, 317–21.

33 Governor Robert J. Fleming Jr. to Panama Canal Company engineering and construction director, December 18, 1963, "Revised Canal Requirements Study, 2/62–12/63," Correspondence 1952–71.

34 "Memorandum of Conference with President," January 13, 1964, fiche 1994-200, DDRS.

35 William J. Jorden, *Panama Odyssey* (Austin: University of Texas Press, 1984), 87–92.

36 Ibid., 101–2.

37 John Sheffey to "Helen," July 18, 1969, "Chron File (May thru Sep 1969) #7," chronological files, Records of the Atlantic–Pacific Interoceanic Canal Study Commission, RG 220, NA (hereafter, APICSC).

38 Colonel Alex G. Sutton, "IOCS Memorandum FD-84," May 15, 1969, study files, APICSC.

39 "Plan for Study of Engineering Feasibility of Alternate Sea-Level Canal Routes Connecting the Atlantic and Pacific Oceans, Appendix 11, Agreements Required with Host Countries," September 1965, Technical Reports Relating to Research Projects 1963–1971, Records of the Nuclear Cratering Group, RG 77, NA Pacific Region (hereafter, NCG/NA).

40 James H. Stratton, "Sea-Level Canal: How and Where," *Foreign Affairs* 43 (April 1965): 513–18.

41 Atlantic–Pacific Interoceanic Canal Study Commission, "A Plan for Study of Engineering Feasibility of Alternate Sea-Level Canal Routes Connecting the Atlantic and Pacific Oceans, Appendix 6: Detailed Plan for Data Collection," September 1965, NCG/NA.

42 Stephen V. Kaye and Paul S. Rohwer, "Dose-Estimation Studies Related to Proposed Construction of an Atlantic–Pacific Interoceanic Canal with Nuclear Explosives: Phase III," December 1970 (Oak Ridge National Laboratory), from the archives of Lawrence Livermore National Laboratory, U.S. Dept. of Energy (hereafter, LLNL/DOE).

43 G. Corry McDonald, "Nuclear Electrical Power for Canal Construction," *Mechanical Engineering* 88 (August 1966): 22–28.

44 U.S. Army Engineer Reactors Group, *An Introduction to the Army Nuclear Power Program* (1970, from the Army Corps of Engineers archives, Fort Belvoir, Va.), 39; Panama Canal Company, *Annual Report for Fiscal Year Ended June 30, 1969* (Washington, D.C.: Government Printing Office, 1969), 15–16; Lósimo Wong, "Posibilidad de un canal panameño," *Tareas*, no. 22–23 (1970), 15. See also H. S. Effron, "Power Wherever She Goes," *Soldiers* (December 1972), 42–46.

45 "With the exception of recent alluvial and shore-line deposits, rock units encountered throughout the traverse are competent types and will stand on relatively steep excavation slopes": Isthmian Canal Studies memoran-

dum 186, "Geologic Explorations, Caledonia Bay Route 10, Geology and Topography," February 1947, Records of the Washington Office 1904–74, Isthmian Canal Studies, RG 185, NA.

46 *Panama Canal Improvement Plans — 1959*, 17.

47 Lieutenant-Colonel W. R. Wray to Lieutenant-Colonel Ernest Graves Jr., director, Nuclear Cratering Group, Lawrence Radiation Laboratory, October 18, 1963, "General Planning Information, 10/60–12/63," Correspondence 1952–71. The Army's reconnaissance work was authorized by a secret exchange of diplomatic notes in June 1963.

48 Ibid., March 16, 1964, "Sea Level Canal Studies, 9/13/63–8/9/66," Correspondence 1952–71.

49 J. Cress et al., U.S. Army Engineer Nuclear Cratering Group, "Project Pre-Gondola III, Phase I Summary Report," April 1970, Plowshare report PNE-1114, NCG/NA.

50 "Analysis of Array Concepts for Nuclear Excavation of the Chucunaque Valley Shales, Route 17 (Preliminary Report)," Inter-Oceanic Canal Studies memorandum, January 22, 1968, 1–2, 4–11, NCG/NA. See also Luke J. Vortman, "Ten Years of High Explosive Cratering Research at Sandia Laboratory," *Nuclear Applications and Technology* 7 (September 1969): 286–87.

51 Atlantic–Pacific Interoceanic Canal Study Commission, *Interoceanic Canal Studies 1970* (Washington, D.C.: Government Printing Office, 1970), 123.

52 Jack W. Reed, "Acoustic Wave Effects Preliminary Report," June 19, 1967, and J. W. Reed, "Airblast Safety Evaluations for Routes 17A and 25E," February 1970, Air Blast Working Group Reports, APICSC.

53 Jack Reed, telephone interview by the author, June 2, 2000.

54 Lawrence Radiation Laboratory, *Isthmian Canal Studies, Annex III, Appendix 1: Nuclear Excavation Plan*, Livermore, Calif. (September 1964), 40.

55 Glenn C. Werth, Lawrence Livermore National Laboratory, to James E. Reeves, Atomic Energy Commission Nevada Operating Office, January 19, 1966, in LLNL/DOE.

56 John A. Blume Associates, "Preliminary Estimate of Structural Effects from Nuclear Excavation on Routes 17 and 25," July 1967, NVO-99-17, Study Files, APICSC.

57 Dean V. Power to James E. Reeves, September 15, 1966, in LLNL/DOE; "Status Report: Ground Shock Technical Working Group," May 11, 1967, in LLNL/DOE.

58 Ibid.; Ground Shock Technical Working Group, Interoceanic Canal Feasibility Studies, "Technical Recommendation," 7 July 1967, in LLNL/DOE.

59 Public Information Study Group, "Questionnaire for Panama," January 1967, 1, Working Study Files, APICSC.

60 John S. Kelly to AEC Commissioners, June 7, 1967, in LLNL/DOE.

61 Ibid. In 2001, Eleta did not remember suggesting a nuclear shot in the Darién province and asserted that he had discouraged the United States from pursuing a sea-level canal away from the current canal route (Fernando Eleta, interview by the author, January 30, 2001, Panama City). Panama's technical director for canal studies, Simón Quiros Guardia, however, said that he supported a nuclear explosion in situ in Darién to determine its effectiveness, and that "Eleta was in agreement. . . . He believed that nuclear explosions in Panama would show the world and Panama that it could be done with security" (Simón Quiros Guardia, interview by the author, February 1, 2001, Panama City).

62 "Se Habla en el congreso de ruptura," *La Estrella de Panamá*, May 5, 1966; "Radiactividad en el aire superficial en varios puntos de EU," *La Estrella de Panamá*, May 21, 1966; "Lluvia radiactiva en India a causa de explosión China" *El Panamá América*, May 30, 1966.

63 "Panamá podría sufrir contaminación por la explosión nuclear francesa, expresa la Comisión Legislativa," *La Estrella de Panamá*, May 20, 1966; Rufus Smith to U.S. State Department, March 9, 1965, fiche 1981-218B, DDRS; "En Nuestra historia no hay nada," *La Estrella de Panamá*, May 8, 1966.

64 "Explosiones atómicas en el Darién," *El Panamá América*, April 21, 1966.

65 "Questionnaire for Panama," APICSC.

66 John Sheffey to Interoceanic Canal Study Commissioners, March 15 1966, "Chron File #1 (July '65–March '66)," chronological file, APICSC.

67 Jorden, *Odyssey*, 114–16. The text of the treaties is in *Congressional Record*, July 17, 21, and 27, 1967.

68 Colonel Alex G. Sutton, "IOCS Memorandum FD-84," May 15, 1969, Study Files, APICSC.

69 "Darién Indians Protest U.S. 'Invasion,'" *Panama American*, March 22, 1966.

70 "La Lecciión de Yapilikiña," *La Prensa*, April 27, 1966; "El Canciller aseguró que los estudios no afectan a Indios," *La Estrella de Panamá*, March 20, 1966.

71 "Press Analysis," April 10, 1966, Working Study Files, APICSC.

72 Cable, n.a., May 17, 1966, Working Study Files, APICSC.

73 Atlantic–Interoceanic Canal Study Commission to President Richard Nixon, December 1, 1970, Reports, APICSC. This was the classified re-

port; the public report's language was equally conclusive: cf. *Interoceanic Canal Studies 1970*, 106.

74   Seaborg, *Commission under Nixon*, 26; Findlay, *Nuclear Dynamite*, 225.

75   Luke Vortman, telephone interview by author, May 29, 2000.

76   Harold Brown to author, letter, October 2, 2000.

77   Robert C. Pendleton et al., "Differential Accumulation of I-131 from Local Fallout in People and Milk," in *Joint Hearing before the Senate Labor Committee, Subcommittee on Oversight and Investigations, Health Effects of Low-Level Radiation*, April 19, 1979, 96th Cong., 1st sess., 2336–64; Bruce A. Bolt, *Nuclear Explosions and Earthquakes: The Parted Veil* (San Francisco: W. H. Freeman, 1976), 92.

78   John Gofman, telephone interview by the author, May 11, 2000.

79   T. M. Tami and W. C. Day, "Predicted Exposure Rates within the Nuclear Crater and Lip Area," May 1969, Nuclear Cratering Group Technical Memorandum 69-7, NCG/NA.

80   Seaborg, *Commission under Nixon*, 127–28; John Gofman, interview by the author, San Francisco, May 13, 2000.

81   Richard S. Lewis, *The Nuclear Power Rebellion: Citizens vs. the Atomic Industrial Establishment* (New York: Viking Press, 1972), 207–20; Seaborg, *Commission under Nixon*, 23.

82   Eleta, interview.

83   Eleta, interview, and Quiros Guardia, interview. The treaty left the door partially ajar for nuclear excavation in Article 18, which allows Latin American nations to "carry out explosions of nuclear devices for peaceful purposes — including explosions which involve devices similar to those used in nuclear weapons," provided they do so in accordance with Articles 1 and 5, which prohibit "any device which is capable of releasing nuclear energy in an uncontrolled manner and which has a group of characteristics that are appropriate for use for warlike purposes" (Findlay, *Nuclear Dynamite*, 105).

84   Nuclear Cratering Group, "Military Engineering with Nuclear Explosives," June 1966, NCG/NA.

85   National Defense Study Group, "Final Report on the Effect of Construction of an Atlantic–Pacific Interoceanic Sea Level Canal on the National Defense of the United States," June 1970, 6-7, Study Files, APICSC.

86   Findlay, *Nuclear Dynamite*, 100–105.

87   Seaborg, *Commission under Nixon*, 15–17.

88   Gofman, telephone interview.

89   David Perlman, "Engineers Toss Ideas for A-blasts," *San Francisco Chronicle*, May 16, 1959.

90   Carl R. Gerber et al., *Plowshare* (Oak Ridge, Tenn.: Atomic Energy Commission, 1966), 1–2.

91 Lieutenant-Colonel Bernard C. Hughes, "Preliminary Assessment of Nuclear Crater Slope Stability as Related to the Interoceanic Canal Studies," April 12, 1968, NCG/NA.

92 Colonel Alex G. Sutton Jr., "Final Report, Management and General Support," IOCS Memorandum FD-84, annex F, 53, Working Study File, APICSC.

93 Herter to Eisenhower, July 27, 1960, fiche 1981-132, DDRS.

94 Spurgeon Keeney to McGeorge Bundy, 17 November 1965, tab E, fiche 1979-220A, DDRS.

95 Ralph Sanders, *Project Plowshare: The Development of the Peaceful Uses of Nuclear Explosions* (Washington, D.C.: Public Affairs Press, 1962), v–vi.

96 Walter Fade, "The Sea–Level Canal," paper presented to the Canal Zone Post of the American Society of Military Engineers, Canal Zone, Panama, December 1964, 11.

97 Reed argued that the negative effects from conventional excavation of a canal would be worse than those for nuclear excavation. "I think they came up with a value of something like five cancer fatalities [from radioactive fallout] around the world," Reed said. "I consider that pretty trivial. In contrast . . . moving that much dirt by conventional earth moving methods would kill 165 truck drivers" (Reed, interview).

Chapter 4

1 Edward H. Williams, M.D., "Negro Cocaine 'Fiends' are a New Southern Menace," *New York Times*, February 8, 1914; as quoted in Mark Cook and Jeff Cohen, "How Television Sold the Panama Invasion," *Extra!* January–February 1990.

2 Hamilton Wright, "Report on the International Opium Commission," Senate Doc. 377, 61st Cong., 2d sess. (1910), 50–51.

3 "This Drug Endangered Nation," *Literary Digest*, March 28, 1914, 687.

4 E. M. Green, "Psychoses among Negroes: A Comparative Study," *Journal of Nervous and Mental Disease* 41 (1914): 697–708. For the American Medical Association's contribution to the hysteria, see *Journal of the American Medical Association* 34 (June 23, 1900): 1637, and ibid., 36 (February 2, 1901): 330.

5 Williams, "Negro Cocaine 'Fiends' "; David F. Musto, *The American Disease: Origins of Narcotic Control*, 3d ed. (New York: Oxford University Press, 1999), 7–9.

6 Ibid., 298.

7 "U.S. Army School of the Americas," *Military Review* (April 1970), 89;

Captain Gary L. Arnold, U.S. Air Force, "IMET in Latin America," *Military Review* (February 1987), 40.

8 U.S. General Accounting Office, *School of the Americas: U.S. Military Training for Latin American Countries* (Letter Report, 08/22/96, GAO/NSIAD-96-178); and list of Panamanian School of the Americas graduates obtained through FOIA, available from ⟨http://www.soaw.org⟩.

9 Arnold, "IMET," 40; Inter-American Air Force Academy Web site, ⟨http://www.lackland.af.mil/iaafa/english/index.htm⟩. During the 1960s, training included air counterinsurgency operations: see Willard F. Barber and C. Neale Ronning, *Internal Security and Military Power* (Columbus: Ohio State University Press, 1966), 163.

10 After moving to Washington, the Inter-American Police Academy was credited with training Latin American police in terrorist activities such as demolition and torture: Michael McClintock, *Instruments of Statecraft: U.S. Guerrilla Warfare, Counterinsurgency, Counter-terrorism, 1940–1990* (New York: Pantheon, 1992), 190.

11 Major-Gen. W. Yarborough, "Address to Armed Forces Chemical Association," *Armed Forces Chemical Journal* 18 (December 1964): 5–11. Yarborough had distinguished himself as commander of the Army's Special Warfare Center the year before and in 1962 had recommended the deployment of clandestine teams in Colombia, backed by the United States, to "execute paramilitary, sabotage and/or terrorist activities against known community proponents": McClintock, *Instruments*, 222.

12 General Robert W. Porter, "Look South to Latin America," *Military Review* 48 (June 1968): 83.

13 Arnold, "IMET," 33.

14 Major Charles J. Bauer, "USARCARIB's Biggest Little School," *Army Information Digest* (October 1962), 26.

15 Robert White to Secretary of State Cyrus Vance, October 11, 1978, National Security Archives Web site, ⟨http://www.gwu.edu/~nsarchiv⟩.

16 Based on documents obtained under FOIA by School of the Americas Watch, Web site, ⟨http://www.derechos.org/soaw⟩ in 2000. During the same period, 313 Panamanian soldiers were trained at the school.

17 After several weeks, Noriega had to cancel the agreement and refund the money that the CIA had paid him for the privilege (Duane R. Clarridge, *A Spy for All Seasons: My Life in the CIA* [New York: Scribner, 1997], 236–38).

18 Frederick Kempe, *Divorcing the Dictator: America's Bungled Affair with Noriega* (New York: G. P. Putnam's Sons, 1990), 157–60.

19 National Action/Research on the Military Industrial Complex, *Invasion: A Guide to the U.S. Military Presence in Central America* (Philadelphia:

American Friends Service Committee, 1985), 14–15. See also Leis, *Comando Sur*, 51–53, 93–100.

20 John Dinges, *Our Man in Panama: The Shrewd Rise and Brutal Fall of Manuel Noriega* (New York: Random House, 1991), 148–49.

21 Tom Barry, *Panama: A Country Guide* (Albuquerque, N.M.: Interhemispheric Resource Center, 1990), 113, 137n.

22 U.S. Department of Defense, secret memorandum to Zbigniew Brzezinsky, Special Assistant for National Security, 14 October 1977, Carter Presidential Library, Atlanta, Ga.

23 Brittmarie Janson Pérez, *Golpes y tratados* (Panamá: Instituto de Estudios Políticos e Internacionales, 1997), 63; Seymour M. Hersh, "Our Man in Panama," *Life*, March 1990, 81–86.

24 Kempe, *Divorcing the Dictator*, 58.

25 Hersh, "Our Man in Panama," 81–86.

26 Ibid., 88; Kempe, *Divorcing the Dictator*, 26, 162; Dinges, *Our Man in Panama*, ix.

27 Murray Waas, "Made for Each Other," *Village Voice*, February 6, 1990, 31–32.

28 Lawrence A. Yates, "Joint Task Force Panama: Just Cause—Before and After," *Military Review* 71 (October 1991): 63.

29 Lally Weymouth, "Panama—The May '88 Option," *Washington Post*, December 31, 1989, C1.

30 Musto, *American Disease*, 277–79.

31 Craig Reinarman and Harry G. Levine, *Crack in America: Demon Drugs and Social Justice* (Berkeley: University of California Press, 1997), 20.

32 Jerry Adler et al., "Hour by Hour Crack," *Newsweek*, 28 November 1988, 64–75.

33 Tom Morganthau and Mark Miller, "Getting Tough on Cocaine," *Newsweek*, November 28, 1988, 76–79.

34 Troy Duster, "Pattern, Purpose, and Race in the Drug War," in Reinarman and Levine, *Crack*, 263–64.

35 Micah Fink, "Don't Forget the Hype: Media, Drugs, and Public Opinion," *Extra!* September 1992; Donna M. Hartman and Andrew Golub, "The Social Construction of the Crack Epidemic in the Print Media," *Journal of Psychoactive Drugs* 31 (October–December 1999): 423–31.

36 John Weeks and Phil Gunson, *Panama: Made in the USA* (London: Latin America Bureau, 1991), 83–86.

37 Reinarman and Levine, *Crack*, 22–23.

38 Ibid., 22–24.

39 Bob Woodward, *The Commanders* (New York: Simon and Schuster, 1991), 129.

40 Ibid., 162.

41 Colonel John D. Waghelstein, "A Latin American Insurgency Status Report," *Military Review* 67 (February 1987): 46–47.

42 *Clear and Present Dangers: The U.S. Military and the War on Drugs in the Andes* (Washington, D.C.: Washington Office on Latin America, 1991), 37.

43 Ronald H. Cole, *Operation Just Cause: The Planning and Execution of Joint Operations in Panama, February 1988–January 1990* (Washington, D.C.: Office of the Chairman of the Joint Chiefs of Staff, 1995), 14.

44 Woodward, *Commanders*, 133–34; John T. Fishel, *The Fog of Peace: Planning and Executing the Restoration of Panama* (Carlisle Barracks, Pa.: Strategic Studies Institute, 1992), 21.

45 Committee of Santa Fe, *A Strategy for Latin America in the Nineties*, n.p., 1988, 34. The Committee of Santa Fe was composed of radically conservative thinkers who assembled a policy blueprint, first for the incoming Reagan administration, then for what would be the Bush administration in 1988.

46 Sen. Cong. Res. 14, *Congressional Record*, September 5, 1996, S9982-S9983. Legislation enacting the Canal Treaties in 1979 also urged negotiations for post–1999 military bases, but with no political rationale: Public Law 70, 96th Cong., 1st sess. (September 27, 1979), 459.

47 Cook and Cohen, "Television."

48 Major Joseph A. Goetzke, memorandum reproduced in Investigations Subcommittee of House Armed Services Committee, *The Invasion of Panama: How Many Innocent Bystanders Perished?* 102d Cong., 2d sess. (July 7, 1992), 204.

49 "U.S. Praises Church," *Los Angeles Times*, December 30, 1989.

50 Panama's Chamber of Commerce estimated direct losses between $670 million and $1.17 billion: Roberto N. Méndez, *¿Liberación . . . o crimen de guerra?* (Panamá: CELA, 1994), 219.

51 Michael R. Gordon, "Inquiry into Stealth's Performance in Panama Is Ordered by Cheney," *New York Times*, April 11, 1990.

52 Weeks and Gunson, *Panama*, 4–9.

53 Richard Boudreaux, "U.S. Army and Local Civilians Try to Revive a Pillaged Seaport," *Los Angeles Times*, December 31, 1989.

54 Cook and Cohen, "Television."

55 Marc Cooper, "The Press and the Panama Invasion," *The Nation*, June 18, 1990, 852.

56 William Branigin, "Fifty Kilos of Cocaine Turn Out to Be Tamales," *Washington Post*, January 23, 1990.

57 Fishel, *Fog of Peace*, vii–viii, 38.

58 Katherine Ellison, "Noriega's Papers at Heart of Dispute," *San Jose Mercury News*, July 23, 1990.

59 CODEHUCA Report, January 27, 1990, as cited in Independent Commission of Inquiry on the U.S. Invasion of Panama, *The U.S. Invasion of Panama: The Truth behind Operation "Just Cause"* (Boston: South End Press, 1991), 49.

60 David Noble, *KQED Forum*, radio broadcast, San Francisco, December 19, 1996.

61 Miguel Antonio Bernal, "Panama: Modernization without Democracy?" speech, Lehigh University, Bethlehem, Pa., March 25, 1998.

62 Marc Cooper, "Same as It Ever Was," *Village Voice*, May 28, 1991, 34.

63 *Drug Control: Heavy Investment in Military Surveillance Is Not Paying Off*, GAO-NSIAD-93-220 (Washington, D.C.: General Accounting Office, 1993), 3.

64 *Clear and Present Dangers*, 37.

65 Peter Reuter, Gordon Crawford, and Jonathan Cave, *Sealing the Borders: The Effect of Increased Military Participation in Drug Interdiction* (Santa Monica, Calif.: RAND Corporation, 1988), xi–xiv.

66 Patrick E. Tyler, "Seven Hypothetical Conflicts Foreseen by the Pentagon," *New York Times*, February 17, 1992.

67 Peter Zirnite, *Reluctant Recruits: The U.S. Military and the War on Drugs* (Washington, D.C.: Washington Office on Latin America, 1997), 29.

68 *Drug Control: Long-Standing Problems Hinder U.S. International Efforts*, GAO-NSIAD-97-75 (Washington, D.C.: Government Printing Office, 1997). Maria Fernandez, interview by the author, Washington, D.C., February 25, 1997.

69 Colonel David Hunt, interview by the author, Panama City, July 30, 1997.

70 "Deben mantenerse bases militares de EE.UU," LP, December 25, 1991; "Pulso de la nación," LP, May 16, 1995.

71 "Panama Turnabout: Yankee, Don't Go Home," *Washington Post*, October 16, 1995.

72 Elaine M. Grossman, "Southern Command Chief Proposes Keeping over 5,000 Forces in Panama," *Inside the Pentagon*, August 17, 1995, 1.

73 Gina Marie Hatheway, "Report to Senate Foreign Relations Committee," February 13, 1997, 9.

74 Bradley Graham, "Panama May Ask U.S. to Delay Military Pullout," *San Francisco Chronicle*, September 4, 1995.

75 William J. Hughes, interview by the author, Ocean City, N.J., June 12, 2000.

76 Hatheway, "Report," 10–17.

77 Ibid., 20.

78　National Security Council official, interview by the author, December 4, 1996.

79　Hatheway, "Report," 17.

80　Carlos Vargas and Juan Manuel Díaz, "Gobierno panameño cuestiona manifestaciones de R. Gelbard," *El Panamá América*, April 9, 1996.

81　José Otero, "Dinero lavado entra a Panamá por bancos de EU," LP, April 11, 1996.

82　John Lindsay-Poland, "Talks Begin to Keep U.S. Bases in Panama," *Panamá Update*, fall 1995, 1.

83　Wilfredo Jordán Serrano, " 'Me trago mis palabras,' " LP, June 22, 1996.

84　Idem, "Barletta favorece conversión de Howard en centro antidrogas," LP, July 12, 1996.

85　Fernando Manfredo Jr. to author, letter, January 27, 1997.

86　Major Thadd Buzan, telephone interview by the author, September 11, 1995.

87　"Declaration by the Conference on the Analysis and Discussion of the General Land Use Plan and Regional Plan of the Interoceanic Authority," Panama, n.p., September 24, 1996.

88　Graham Stullenbarger, telephone interview by the author, June 23, 1998.

89　Jorge Ritter, interview by the author, Panama City, February 1, 2001.

90　Hughes, interview.

91　U.S. military officer, interview by the author, Washington, D.C., June 17, 2000.

92　Ricardo Alberto Arias, interview by the author, Panama City, July 28, 1998; unclassified Pentagon document, January 1998.

93　"Illusions of a War against Cocaine," editorial, *New York Times*, January 24, 1998.

94　U.S. military officer, interview by the author, Panama City, January 31, 2001.

95　Jeanette Becerra Acosta, "Panamá concede 'excesivas responsabilidades' a Washington en el CMLN: México," *El Excelsior*, January 27, 1998.

96　Unclassified Pentagon document, January 1998.

97　The State Department also attempted to negotiate agreements with Costa Rica and Peru but failed. See Coletta Youngers, "The U.S. 'War on Drugs' Rages On," *Enlace*, July 1998.

98　House Committee on International Relations, *Post–1999 U.S. Security and Counter-Drug Interests in Panama*, 106th Cong., 1st sess. (July 29, 1999), 11.

99　Jack Vaughan, telephone interview by the author, January 27, 1999.

100　U.S. military official, interview by the author, Panama City, July 25, 1998.

101 U.S. military officer, interview by the author, Washington, D.C., June 17, 2000.

102 U.S. Senate Committee on Foreign Relations, *The Panama Canal and United States Interests*, 105th Cong., 2d sess. (June 16, 1998), 2.

Chapter 5

1 U.S. Southern Command Public Affairs Directorate, "U.S. Forces Good Stewardship of the Environment and Its Installations in Panama," handout, August 1, 1996, 1; *Sixty Minutes*, CBS News, November 8, 1998; Ibid.

2 Andrés Romero, interviews by the author, Huile, Panama, August 11, 1996, and August 1, 1997.

3 Colonel David Hunt, "Executive Summary: 1999 Range Clearance Activities," May 3, 1999, in Jorge Eduardo Ritter et al., *Memoria cronológica: El Proceso de saneamiento de las bases militares y otras areas utilizadas por los Estados Unidos en la República de Panamá, Panama: 1999*.

4 Harry A. Francke, *Zone Policeman 88* (New York: Century Company, 1913), 105.

5 *Unexploded Ordnance Assessment of U.S. Military Ranges in Panama: Empire, Balboa West and Piña Ranges*, prepared for Department of Defense Panama Canal Treaty Implementation Plan Agency, January 1997 (hereafter, *UXO Assessment*), 30–36.

6 The Nature Conservancy and ANCON, *Ecological Survey of the U.S. Department of Defense Lands in Panama, Phase IV: Fort Sherman, Piña Range and Naval Security Group Activity, Galeta Island* (Panama, 1995), 31.

7 Juan Luis Batista, "Quince mil hectáreas de Zozobra," LP, July 28, 1997.

8 Dirección de Información e Investigación Policial, Policía Nacional, "Informe general estadístico de artefactos explosivos encontrados y efectos causados a nivel nacional, en la República de Panamá," mimeograph, September 4, 1997.

9 Bob Askew, June 29, 1997, and Thomas Carey, July 1, 1997, Zonelink newsgroup, ⟨www.lostparadise.com⟩.

10 Helmut Stoeberl, sworn statement, February 1989, obtained by the author from the U.S. Army South through FOIA.

11 *UXO Assessment*, A-6.

12 Batista, "Quince mil hectáreas de aozobra."

13 "Panama Canal Treaty: Implementation of Article IV," September 7, 1977, TIAS no. 10032, *United States Treaties and Other International*

Agreements, vol. 33, pt. 1: 313–14; "Panama Canal Treaty," September 7, 1977, TIAS no. 10029, *United States Treaties and Other International Agreements*, vol. 33, pt. 1: 58.

14   Kathleen H. Hicks and Stephen Daggett, "Department of Defense Environmental Programs: Background and Issues for Congress," Congressional Research Service, March 6, 1996.

15   Richard A. Wegman and Harold G. Bailey Jr., "The Challenge of Cleaning Up Military Wastes When U.S. Bases Are Closed," *Ecology Law Quarterly* 21 (1994): 924.

16   Seth Shulman, *The Threat at Home: Confronting the Toxic Legacy of the U.S. Military* (Boston: Beacon Press, 1992), 109–12.

17   Michael Satchell, "The Mess We've Left Behind," *U.S. News and World Report*, November 30, 1992, 30.

18   *Hazardous Waste: Management Problems Continue at Overseas Military Bases*, GAO/NSIAD-91-231 (Washington, D.C.: U.S. General Accounting Office, 1991), 46–47.

19   House Armed Services Committee, Defense Environmental Restoration Panel, *Department of Defense Environmental Programs*, 102d Cong., 1st sess. (April 17, 1991), 102.

20   Satchell, "The Mess We've Left," 30.

21   "Military Base Closures: U.S. Financial Obligations in the Philippines," GAO/NSIAD-92-51 (Washington, D.C.: U.S. General Accounting Office, 1992), 3.

22   Congress urged the Defense Department to seek an "equitable division" in the 1993 Defense Authorization Act: Public Law 102-484, sec. 1301(e)(2)(A). That year the House bill actually called for saddling host nations with the entire cost of cleanup: H.R. Conference Report 966, 102d Congress, 2d sess. (1992), 683.

23   Lieutenant-Colonel Richard A. Phelps, Headquarters, U.S. Air Forces in Europe, "Environmental Law for Department of Defense Installations Overseas," Web site, ⟨http://128.174.5.51/denix/Public/Library/Overseas/overseas.html⟩ (1997).

24   Secretary of Defense message, "DoD Policy and Procedures for the Realignment of Overseas Sites," December 14, 1993, sec. 5.C.(3).

25   Wegman and Bailey, "Challenge of Cleaning Up," 940–41.

26   Doris Bradshaw, "Memphis: The Aftermath of Militarism and Army Racism," *Touching Bases*, winter 1999–2000, 6–7; Wendy Williams, "Toxins on the Firing Range," *Scientific American*, June 2000.

27   Colonel Richard O'Connor, interview by the author, Panama City, January 1995.

28   Richard McSeveney, interview with author, Washington, D.C., November 1995.

29 Center for Treaty Implementation, "Department of Defense Property Transfer 1995 to 1999," Panama, 1995.

30 U.S. Army Garrison–Panama, "Installation Condition Report: Fort Davis Military Reservation," February 2, 1995; J. Martin Wagner and Neil A. F. Popovic, "Environmental Injustice on U.S. Bases in Panama: International Law and the Right to Land Free from Contamination and Explosives," *Virginia Journal of International Law* 38 (spring 1998): 415–16.

31 Nico de Greef, telephone interview by the author, June 26, 1995.

32 "Panama Canal Treaty," September 7, 1977, art. XIII, sec. 2.

33 *Tropic Times*, January 27, 1995, as cited in Sayda de Grimaldo, "La reversión de bienes y el desafío ambiental: Reflexiones finales," *Bases militares: Seguridad ambiental y desarollo nacional* (Panamá: Autoridad de la Región Interoceánica, 1995), 103; Lider Sucre, Panama Audobon Society, to author, letter, June 29, 1994.

34 Sayda de Grimaldo to author, letter, September 4, 1995; Colonel Donald Holzwarth, telephone interview by the author, October 10, 1995.

35 Atlantic Division, Naval Facilities Engineering Command, *Environmental Compliance Evaluation*, 1992, "Recommendations," sec. 11.

36 Joan Brown Campbell et al. to President Bill Clinton, letter, September 4, 1995.

37 L. Peter Boice, untitled presentation at the Legacy Resource Management Program East Coast Regional Workshop, Norfolk, Va., September 11–14, 1994; and *1996 DoD Budget: Potential Reductions to Operation and Maintenance Programs*, GAO/NSIAD-95-200BR (Washington, D.C.: General Accounting Office, 1995), 20; *Fiscal Year 1991 Defense Appropriations Act*, Public Law 101-511.

38 David M. Patrick, Maureen K. Corcoran, Paul E. Albertson, Lawson M. Smith, U.S. Army Corps of Engineers, "Earth Resources Stewardship at Department of Defense Installations," Legacy Resource Management Program Technical Report GL-94-9, March 1994, fig. 2.

39 Shulman, *Threat at Home*, 13.

40 *Gulf Defender*, June 17, 1994, as cited in de Grimaldo, "Reversión de bienes," 101–2. The U.S. Senate referred to this purpose of some Legacy-funded projects when reporting on the program in 1996: "Assessing bird migratory patterns so that operational flights may avoid high bird volume transit areas at certain times of the year enhances the safety of flight operations for all the services." Defense Authorization bill, FY 1997, sec. 323.

41 Richard Warner, The Nature Conservancy, presentation at the Legacy Resource Management Program East Coast Regional Workshop, Norfolk, Va., September 11–14, 1994.

42 "Protección del medio ambiente es prioridad del Comando Sur," *La Estrella de Panamá*, February 17, 1995.

43 "Responses to Resolutions of Joint Commission on the Environment of the Panama Canal," Views of the United States Technical Secretary, mimeograph, June 1996, 9.

44 Colonel Donald R. Holzwarth, "U.S. Southern Command Panama Canal Treaty Environmental Strategy," briefing to the Joint Commission on the Environment, Panama November 14, 1995.

45 U.S. Army Audit Agency, *Lessons Learned—Panama Canal Treaty Implementation*, June 26, 2000, 9, 12; U.S. Army Audit Agency, *Closeout Plans--Republic of Panama*, August 24, 1998, 54.

46 "Agreement in Implementation of Article IV of the Panama Canal Treaty," annex B, para. 3(d).

47 John White, "Environmental Remediation Policy for DoD Activities Overseas," memorandum for secretaries of the military departments, October 18, 1995, sec. 2.b.(4).

48 Ambassador Michael Skol to Jo Becker, Fellowship of Reconciliation, letter, November 27, 1995.

49 Brigadier-General Joseph G. Garrett III, "Policy Guidance for the Transfer of DoD Installations to the Government of Panama," November 2, 1995, sec. 4.b.

50 U.S. Army–South, "Installation Condition Report: Empire Range–Military Area of Coordination, Parcel 1 (4,100 acres), Parcel 2 (1,056 acres), Parcel 3 (451 acres)," July 11, 1996; Latin American Studies Center (CELA) press release, September 3, 1996. See also stories on September 4, 1996, in *Critica Libre*, *El Siglo*, *La Prensa*, *La Estrella de Panamá*, *El Universal*, and *El Panamá América*.

51 "Declaration on General Land Use Plan," September 24, 1996.

52 Ingeniero Juan Antonio Stagg to temporary minister of foreign affairs, memorandum, July 18, 1996.

53 *UXO Assessment*, 5, 75.

54 Tim Johnson, "Old U.S. Bombs Create Fields of Fear for Panamanians," *Miami Herald*, February 23, 1995.

55 Rick Stauber to Mike Keffe and Thomas Girman, memorandum, November 2, 1995, 16.

56 *UXO Assessment*, draft version, April 1996, 25.

57 *UXO Assessment*, 24–25.

58 Nicholas Morgan, *Panama Reverted Areas Project: Hazardous Site Evaluation* (Panama: Intercarib, S.A./Nathan Associates, 1996).

59 "Memorandum," 1997, n.a., copy obtained by author; telephone interviews with Foreign Affairs Ministry officials, May 1997.

60 ARI official, interview with the author, Panama City, July 26, 1997.

61 Wagner and Popovic, "Environmental Injustice," 460–62.

62 "Proposal for Tropic Test Center Continued Presence in Republic of Panama," June 9, 1997, 3–4.

63 Tropic Test Center, "Proposal for Tropic Test Center Membership in the City of Knowledge," July 21, 1997, 23; "Vision 21: The Plan for 21st Century, Laboratories and Test and Evaluation Centers of the Department of Defense," Report to the President and Congress, available in 1998 from: ⟨http://www.dtic.mil/labman/vision21/index.html⟩.

64 "Proposal for Tropic Test Center," June 9, 1997, 3.

65 A majority of Panamanians interviewed in 2001 were opposed to some scientific experiments and skeptical about their benefits. Eighty percent believed that scientists can be "dangerous": Secretaría Nacional de Ciencia, Tecnología e Innovación, *Indicadores de percepción social de la ciencia y la tecnología en Panamá, 2001* (Panamá, 2001), 62.

66 Panamanian officials, interviews by the author, Panama City, October 1997; successive TTC proposals.

67 Panamanian official, interviews; TTC proposals.

68 Graham Stullenbarger, acting director, Tropic Test Center, e-mail to Panamanian official, December 1, 1997.

69 "Proposal for Tropic Test Center," July 21, 1997; Lenny Siegel, member of Defense Science Board Task Force on Unexploded Ordnance, telephone interview by the author, November 1997.

70 *USARSO's Range Closure Plan: Empire and Piña Ranges*, 23 January 1998, 7, 9–11. Under the counterdrug-center deal, Panama's National Police would license use of the ranges to foreign forces for unspecified training activities.

71 Foreign Minister Ricardo Arias to William Hughes, March 23, 1998, *Memoria cronológica*.

72 Foreign Ministry official, personal communication, February 1998.

73 William J. Hughes, interview by the author, June 12, 2000.

74 Eric Jackson, "Americans Major Players on Both Sides of Cleanup Dispute," *Panama News*, October 26, 1999.

75 U.S. Army Audit Agency, *Lessons Learned*, 22–24; *Closeout Plans*, 19–21; Teresa Pohlman, telephone interview by the author, 1998.

76 *Closeout Plans*, 19–20.

77 Michael Short, EOD Technology, telephone interview by the author, June 29, 1999; Lieutenant-Colonel Reynold Hoover, interview by the author, Panama City, March 22, 1999.

78 *Closeout Plans*, 20–21.

79 Short, interview; Naval Explosive Ordnance Disposal Technology Division, *Unexploded Ordnance Site Investigation of U.S. Military Ranges in Panama: Empire, Balboa West and Piña Ranges*, Washington, D.C., 1998, 60.

80 Sayda de Grimaldo, interview by the author, Panama City, October 1997.

81 *Memoria cronológica*, 65.

82 Lewis Amselem to Fernando Manfredo Jr., July 20, 1998, in *Memoria cronológica*, n.p.

83 Manfredo's account of the meeting (see ibid).

84 *Memoria cronológica*, 80; U.S. military official, interview by the author, July 1998.

85 U.S. Army South et al., *Range Transfer Report: Empire, Balboa West & Piña Ranges*, October 29, 1998; Hoover, interview.

86 Foreign Minister Jorge Ritter to U.S. Ambassador William Hughes, October 1, 1998, in *Memoria cronológica*, n.p., 101.

87 Carlos Melgarejo to Fernando Manfredo Jr., January 15, 1999, *Memoria cronológica*, n.p.

88 Michael Short, "UXO and the Panama Canal," presentation at UXO Forum, Atlanta, Ga., May 25–27, 1999.

89 Fellowship of Reconciliation to U.S. Army, letter, April 25, 1997; denial letter from U.S. Army Chemical and Biological Defense Command, May 13, 1997; appeal of denial by Fellowship of Reconciliation, July 19, 1997.

90 Lawrence M. Baskir, principal deputy general counsel, Department of the Army, to author, letter, May 20, 1998.

91 For example, one publicly available report included a thirteen-page chapter on Water Island, located in St. Thomas and the site of the San Jose Project after it left Panama. The report listed suspected burial sites and included a map of the sites: U.S. Army Program Manager for Chemical Demilitarization, "Survey and Analysis Report, Second Edition," December 1996, pp. vi-1–vi-13.

92 Ramiro Castrejón, cochairman, Environmental Subcommittee, DEPAT, to Colonel Michael DeBow, cochairman, Environmental Subcommittee, U.S. Army South, letter, August 1, 1997 (CCj-388-97).

93 Rodrigo Noriega, director of international affairs, Ministry of Foreign Affairs, to author, note, June 8, 1998; Ramiro Castrejón, telephone interview by the author, June 1998; Fernando Manfredo Jr. to author, communication, July 20, 1998.

94 Colonel Michael DeBow to Licenciado Ramiro Castrejón, August 18, 1997.

95 Roy Blades, telephone interviews by the author, June 24 and November 23, 1998; Graham Stullenbarger, Tropic Test Center, telephone interview by the author, September 8, 1998. The Fellowship of Reconciliation submitted a FOIA request for the report in November 1998, and the Army released the report in May 2002.

96 Blades, "Report Bibliography."

97 Panamanian official to author, letter, January 4, 1999; abstracts of TTC

compact disks; Arnoldo Cano, ARI, to Daniel Delgado, February 19, 1999.

98 Rick Stauber to author, letter, July 18, 1998; "EU enterró municiones," *El Panamá América*, April 13, 1998.

99 ARI press release, May 3, 1998.

100 Richard McSeveney, interview by the author, Alexandria, Va., April 24, 1998.

101 Rafael Pérez Jaramillo, "¿Panamá: Laboratorio de armas químicas?" *El Panamá América*, April 19, 1998.

102 *USARSO's Range Closure Plan*, 1.

103 U.S. Arms Control and Disarmament Agency, "Primary Declaration Identification for the Submission of Initial Declarations in accordance with Articles III, VI and the Verification Annex," May 29, 1997.

104 Hughes, interview.

105 U.S. military officer to author, letter, February 13, 2001.

106 U.S. military officer, interview by the author, January 31, 2001; *Lessons Learned*, 15.

107 U.S. military officer, interview by the author, June 17, 2000; U.S. military officer to author, letter, February 13, 2001; State Department official, telephone interview by the author, February 12, 2001.

108 Panama Foreign Ministry, Organization for the Prohibition of Chemical Weapons (OPCW) desk officer, written communication, February 10, 1999; Daniel Delgado, interview by the author, Panama City, February 1, 2001.

109 "Exposure Scenario Characterization for Human Health Risk Assessment due to Pesticide Contamination in the Canal Area," September 2, 1999.

110 "Panama Canal Zone Residents Environmental and Health Survey," *Canal Record*, June 2000; Deborah del Junco to author, communication, March 2, 2001.

111 Tod Robberson, "Former Panama Residents Nagged by Health Worries," *Dallas Morning News*, October 11, 1999.

112 *Panama News*, January 7, 2000; consultant to author, e-mail, January 28, 2000.

113 Officer interview, Panama City, January 31, 2001, Panama.

114 National Defense Authorization Act for Fiscal Year 1999, sec. 321.

115 Sam Farr et al. to William Cohen, letter, March 12, 1999.

116 Hughes, interview.

117 President Ernesto Pérez Balladares, speech, *Memoria cronológica*, n.p., June 30, 1999.

118 Hermes Sucre Serrano, "EU y Panamá tienen que encarar el compromiso de descontaminar bases," *La Prensa* (Panama), September 25, 1999;

Betty Brannan Jaén, "Moscoso planteó a Clinton temas vitales," *La Prensa* (Panama), October 20, 1999.

119 Henry Raymont, "Grupos bilaterales tratarán agenda presentada por Moscoso," *El Panamá América*, January 20, 2000.

120 Foreign Minister José Miguel Alemán to U.N. Secretary-General Kofi Annan, letter, September 15, 2000; Panamanian official, telephone interview by the author, December 6, 2000.

121 Rafael Pérez Jaramillo, "Amenaza química sigue en papel," *El Panamá América*, September 4, 2000.

122 Foreign Ministry official, interview with author, 29 January 2001.

123 OPCW Technical Assistance Visit, final report, August 14, 2001, 13–14.

124 Andrew Bounds, "Panama Accuses U.S. over Chemical Weapons," *Financial Times* (London), September 7, 2001.

125 Betty Brannan Jaén, "EU busca separar al director de OPAQ," LP, April 5, 2002; Pugliese, "Bombs on the Beach," 60.

126 George Monbiot, "Diplomacy US style," *The Guardian* (London), April 23, 2002.

Chapter 6

1 *Washington Post*, July 27, 1993, August 8, 1993.

2 Marco A. Fernandez B. and José Galán Ponce, *Evaluación Económica del Retiro de las Bases Militares* (Panama: n.p., 1996), i, 39.

3 Comisión de la Verdad, "Informe final," Panama City, April 18, 2002.

4 "Informe especial," Defensoría del Pueblo Web page, ⟨http://www.defensoriadelpueblo.gob.pa⟩ (2000); Pro-Dignidad, "Informe ejecutivo de la Ley 47," Panama, March 2002.

5 Carlos A. Cordero, "Asamblea aprueba ley de ambiente," *El Panamá América*, June 10, 1998.

6 Energy Information Agency, "Central America: Environmental Issues," Web site, ⟨http://www.eia.doe.gov/emeu/cabs/centamenv.html⟩ (September 2000).

7 Abdiel Zárate, "Cerro Quema: La Contaminación amenaza," LP, October 11, 1997.

8 Yuriela Sagel, "SPIA considera peligrosa ruta de nuevo puente sobre el canal," *El Panamá América*, December 7, 2000.

9 "Hallan bala antiaérea en Pedro Miguel," LP, February 24, 2001.

10 Interoceanic Region Authority (ARI), "Facts and Figures," mimeograph, December 1998, 2.

11 Jesús Q. Alemancia and Raúl Leis, *Reversión canalera: Informe de un*

desafío (Panama: Centro de Estudios y Acción Social Panameño, 1995), 16–17.

12 Ibid., 63–65; Rosario Arias Peña, "Conversión civil de las bases militares," *Servicio Paz y Justicia–Panamá*, 1995, 34.

13 Arias Peña, "Conversión civil," 31–35.

14 The amount cited for what the military spent in Panama was widely manipulated for political reasons and therefore inconsistent. A December 1993 SouthCom briefing estimated Department of Defense expenditures in Panama for Fiscal Year 1992 at $255 million. In 1995, when the United States and Panama began discussions for a post–1999 military presence, SouthCom was emphasizing the economic impact of the withdrawal. Then, SouthCom figures for 1994 showed an increase in expenditures to $341.7 million: U.S. Southern Command briefing, December 1993; Marco A. Fernández and José Galán Ponce, *Evaluación económica del retiro de las bases militares* (Panama: n.p., 1996), 55, citing SouthCom's Center for Treaty Implementation.

15 Intercarib S.A./Nathan Associates, *Plan general de uso, conservación y desarollo del area del canal, informe final: Programa de acciones* (Panama: n.p., 1997) (hereafter, *Plan General*), 4. See also Charlotte Elton, "Sustainable Development and the Integration of the Canal Area," in Orlando Perez, ed., *Post–Invasion Panama: The Challenges of Democratization in the New World Order* (Lanham, Md.: Lexington Books, 2000), 57–68.

16 "Declaration of Coronado III (Panama 2000)," n.p., September 1996; "Ley No. 21," *Gaceta Oficial*, July 3, 1997.

17 Stephen Kinzer, "The Winner in Panama," *New York Times*, May 18, 1984.

18 "Plan estratégico para el desarollo turístico de Fuerte Amador: Informe final" (Panama: EDSA, 1996), 4–9.

19 LP, February 24, 2000; Omar Wong Wood, "ARI podria perder 62 millones de balboas," *El Universal*, February 21, 2000.

20 "Venta y cierre de hoteles por la crisis del turismo," *El Panamá América*, July 22, 2000; hotel data are available on the IPAT Web site, ⟨http://www.ipat.gob.pa⟩, and on Ministerio de Economía y Finanzas, "Informe Económica Annual 2001," Web site, ⟨http://www.mhyt.gob.pa⟩.

21 Consejo Económico para América Latina, "Balance preliminar de las economías de América Latina y el Caribe, 1999," Web site, ⟨http://www.eclac.org/espanol/Publicaciones/ba199/panama.htm⟩.

22 *Plan General*, 205.

23 Miguel Cardenas, Panamanian Housing Ministry, telephone interview by the author, February 25, 2000.

24 Silvio Hernández, "Housing Shortage Reaches Crisis Point," Inter-Press Service, August 11, 1995.

25 Members of Kuna Nega, interviews by the author, Chiva Chiva, Panama, May 1995.

26 Members of Loma Ková, interviews by the author, Arraiján, Panama, May 1995.

27 "La Ciudad del Saber quedará en Clayton," *El Panamá América*, March 19, 1998; Hermes Sucre Serrano, "Trasladan Ciudad del Saber a Clayton," LP, November 20, 1999; Jorge Arosemena, telephone interview by the author, March 29, 1999.

28 José Miguel Alemán, "La UNICEF en Panamá," LP, August 12, 2001; Gabriela de Rodríguez Nin, interview by the author, Panama City, January 29, 2001.

29 *Plan General*, 37, 39.

30 Orlando Acosta and Carlos Gómez, "La Cuenca del canal y la valorización del bosque tropical," *UNTAC Boletín Trimestral*, no. 3, ARI, March 1995, 1; Carlos Gómez, "La Reforestación en las areas revertidas," *UNTAC Boletín Trimestral*, no. 5, ARI, March 1996, 1.

31 Herman Bern, "Benefits to the Hotel Industry of the Development of Ecotourism," presentation, Panama City, February 1998.

32 Emily Zhukov, "Albrook Hill under Attack," *Panama News*, January 18, 2000 and *Plan General*, map 4.1.

33 Esteban Martínez Lasso, "Alternativas al canal de Panamá," in *El Canal de Panamá en el siglo XXI* (Panamá: Universidad de Panamá et al., 1998), 163–86; José Eulogio Torres A., *Los Grandes desafíos que plantea la reversión del canal* (Panamá: Imprenta Universitaria, 1999), 97–129.

34 Pastoral Social Cáritas–Panamá, *La Carta* 67 (November 2000).

35 *La "Otra" cuenca del canal: Oportunidad o amenaza?* (Panama: CEASPA, 2000), 32, 84.

36 See Eduard Niesten and John Reid, "Economic Considerations on the Panama Canal Watershed Expansion," Web site, ⟨http://www.conservation-strategy.org/Panama_eng.pdf⟩ (June 2001).

37 "EU apuesta por Panamá, pero con transparencia," LP, April 4, 1997.

38 Omar Jaén, interview by the author, Panama City, March 1999.

39 The so-called land bridge across the United States, by which cargo moves between the Atlantic and Pacific oceans in rail or truck containers, also has become a competitor with the canal.

40 Gina Marie Hatheway, Senate Committee on Foreign Relations, staff report on Panamanian ports, May 14, 1997 (hereafter, Hatheway report), 8–11.

41 Ibid., 11–14.

42 Ibid., 15–20.

43 "EU apuesta por Panamá."

44 LP, May 18, 1997.

45 "Sin Novedad en los puertos, dice Torrijos," LP, March 23, 1997.

46 Hatheway report, 34.

47 Michele Labrut, "Panama Will Pay Compensation to Ports Administrator," *Journal of Commerce*, August 25, 1997.

48 *Washington Times*, March 19, 1997.

49 House Committee on National Security, Special Oversight Panel on Merchant Marine, *Annual Authorization of the Panama Canal Commission*, March 19, 1997, 56–57.

50 Rolando Rodríguez and Vilma Figueroa, "Republicanos y demócratas trasladan su pugna a Panamá," LP, April 13, 1997.

51 Associated Press, "Powell Not Worried about Canal," February 6, 2001.

52 *Panama News*, October 2000

53 Rowan Scarborough, "China Company Grabs Power over Panama Canal," *Washington Times*, August 5, 1999.

54 "Memorándum de acuerdo entre el Ministerio de Gobierno y Justicia y la República de Panamá y la Agencia de Inteligencia de Defensa de los Estados Unidos de América para el acopio combinado e intercambio de información e inteligencia marítima," *El Siglo*, November 25, 1999; Rafael Pérez Jaramillo, "Acuerdo de fuerzas visitantes incluiría maniobras antidrogas," *El Panamá América*, July 25, 2000.

55 Not all the proposed uses were implemented: Manuel Domínguez, "La Policía no será 'remilitarizada,'" LP, December 3, 1999; Yuriela Sagel, "Violencia externa amenaza Panamá," *El Panamá América*, December 3, 1999.

56 Jahiro Polo, "Plan de seguridad es víctima de tensiones," LP, February 19, 2000.

57 Jean Marcel Chéry, "Pueblo de 200 personas tendrá pista más grande de Darién," *El Panamá América*, December 5, 2000.

58 Center for International Policy, "Just the Facts 2001–2002," Web site, ⟨www.ciponline.org/facts.htm⟩.

59 Eric Jackson, "Plan Colombia Supply and Troop Flights to Operate from Panama," *Panama News*, April 11, 2001; Betty Brannan Jaén and Rafael Pérez, "EU insiste en operaciones desde Panamá," LP, April 18, 2001; Richard L. Stern, "'We're Opportunists,'" *Forbes*, December 10, 1990, 56; Synopsis for Solicitation F11626-01-R0015, on Web site, ⟨http://www.eps.gov⟩ (subsequently withdrawn).

60 "Arreglo complementario entre Panamá y Estados Unidos," *El Panamá América*, February 15, 2002; Jorge E. Illueca, "Los arreglos de Arias Calderón y Salas," *El Panamá América*, February 25, 2002.

61 Associated Press, "US Coast Guard Fires at Drug Boats," September 13, 1999.

62 Julio César Aizprúa, "Empeoran desigualdades económicas en Panamá," LP, December 9, 1997. In 1991, the top tenth of the population in income made eighty-three times more than the bottom tenth of the population.

Chapter 7

1 Gil Blas Tejeira, *Pueblos perdidos* (Panama: Impresora Panamá, 1962), 206, translation by the author.

2 Major, *Prize Possession*, 185.

3 Harry A. Francke, Zone Policeman 88 (New York: The Century Co., 1913), 123.

4 Major, *Prize Possession*, 186; Jean Bailey, "Mapping in Latin America," *Army Information Digest* 20 (February 1965): 20–25.

5 Captain Charles E. McBrayer, "The Civic Aspect of the Sanitary Measures That Have Been Taken at the Atlantic Terminal of the Canal," *Proceedings of the Isthmian Medical Association* 10 (1917): 82.

6 Major, *Prize Possession*, 261.

7 Conn, Engelman, and Fairchild, *Western Hemisphere*, 339–40.

8 General David Stone to General Craig, as quoted in "Acquisition of Land in Panama Canal Zone," *History of the Panama Canal Department* (Canal Zone: 1945), 1:111.

9 Lieutenant-Colonel John E. Goldoni, "The Jungle: Neutral Adversary," *Army Information Digest* 16 (May 1961), 3.

10 Ibid., 5; U.S. Army South, "Installation Condition Report, Fort Sherman," draft, July 28, 1998, 5.

11 *Materiel Testing in the Tropics* (Canal Zone: U.S. Army Tropic Test Center, 1976), 5th ed., 12.

12 Ibid., 13–14.

13 See Institute of Medicine Committee to Review the Health Effects in Vietnam Veterans of Exposure to Herbicides, *Veterans and Agent Orange: Health Effects of Herbicides Used in Vietnam* (Washington, D.C.: National Academy Press, 1994).

14 Tropic Test Center, Web site (1997, subsequently withdrawn).

15 *Material Testing*, 9, 11.

16 Hanson W. Baldwin, "Caribbean Chiefs Work in Harmony," *New York Times*, March 6, 1949.

17 Gionela Jordán V., "Se Van los 'ojos y oídos' del Comando Sur," *La Prensa* (Panama), February 28, 1999.

18 Stephen Fox, *The American Conservation Movement: John Muir and His Legacy* (Madison: University of Wisconsin Press, 1981), 125–28.

19 Samuel P. Hays, *Conservation and the Gospel of Efficiency: The Progressive Conservation Movement, 1890–1920* (New York: Atheneum, 1980), 123.

20 Army officers sometimes defended this imperative by using racist images. Colonel Goethals tied the economic inefficiency of tropical people to canal security. "I did not care to see a population of Panamanians or West Indian negroes occupying the land," he wrote, "for these are non-productive, thriftless and indolent": George W. Goethals, *Government of the Canal Zone* (Princeton, N.J.: Princeton University Press, 1915), 64.

21 Bernadette Bundy, telephone interview by the author, February 28, 2001.

22 The idea of the military as a force that would protect wildlife was not new. From 1891 to 1913, Army cavalry troops patrolled Yosemite National Park, leading some advocates to propose an Army force to guard all of the nation's forest reserves: John W. Bingaman, *Guardians of the Yosemite* (Palm Desert, Calif.: Desert Printers, 1961), 83.

23 Associated Press, "U.S. Troops to Guard Rain Forest," June 5, 1997; U.S. Southern Command, "Western Hemisphere Defense Environmental Conference," n.p., June 2–4, 1997.

24 Office of the Secretary of the Army, "Information for Members of Congress," November 5, 1998, 1, n.p.

25 N. C. Thompson to author, letter, December 3, 1997.

26 Rivkah Peller to author, letter, October 10, 1997.

27 Guillermo Castro Herrera, "Vacas y buques: Cultura, historia y desarollo sustentable en Panamá," in Comité organizador del encuentro académico internacional sobre el Canal de Panamá, *El Canal de Panamá en el siglo XXI* (Panama: UNESCO, 1997), 382.

28 Ibid., 382–83.

29 Major, *Prize Possession*, 125.

30 H. R. Parfitt, Responses to Public Information Survey, February 1, 1967, and by U.S. military, undated, in "Public Information Questionnaires and Responses," APICSC.

31 Lewis Amselem, "Siete muertos, sólo son siete," *Este País* 44 (November 1998): 18.

32 Walter Pincus, "From Tiny Aircraft to Robots and Radars, Pentagon Pursues New Tools," *Washington Post*, March 29, 1998.

33 Ibid.

34 Office of the Secretary of Defense, press release, April 2, 1998.

35 Raúl Leis to author, communication, January 1998.

INDEX

Wray, William, 90, 91
Wright, Hamilton, 105

Yabiliquiña (Kuna Indian), 95–96
Yarborough, William, 106, 234
  n.11

Yellow fever, 7, 14, 30, 31, 33, 194
Yuma Proving Ground (Ariz.),
  157, 163

Zumwalt, Elmo R., Jr., 73

John Lindsay-Poland coordinates the Latin American
and Caribbean program of the Fellowship of Reconciliation, an interfaith pacifist organization, in San
Francisco.

Library of Congress Cataloging-in-Publication Data

Lindsay-Poland, John.
Emperors in the jungle : the hidden history of the U.S. in
Panama / by John Lindsay-Poland.
p. cm. — (American encounters/global interactions)
Includes index.
ISBN 0-8223-3100-4 (cloth : alk. paper)
ISBN 0-8223-3098-9 (pbk. : alk. paper)
1. United States — Foreign relations — Panama.
2. Panama — Foreign relations — United States.
3. Panama Canal (Panama) I. Title. II. Series.
E183.8.P2 L475 2003
327.7307287′09 — dc21   2002013820